HEROES IN THE SHADOWS

HUMANITARIAN ACTION AND COURAGE IN THE SECOND WORLD WAR

HEROES
IN THE
SHADOWS

HUMANITARIAN ACTION AND COURAGE
IN THE SECOND WORLD WAR

BRIAN FLEMING

AMBERLEY

ACKNOWLEDGEMENTS

I am grateful to Siobhán McCrystal and Emma Broughton of my local library for their assistance in accessing books from various parts of the country through the excellent inter-library loans service. Walter Doolin's help in researching a book written in Spanish was very helpful. In completing this project Ciara and Conor made up for their father's many deficiencies in the area of information technology and that was crucial.

First published 2019

Amberley Publishing
The Hill, Stroud
Gloucestershire, GL5 4EP

www.amberley-books.com

Copyright © Brian Fleming, 2019

The right of Brian Fleming to be identified as the Author of this work has been asserted in accordance with the Copyrights, Designs and Patents Act 1988.

ISBN 978 1 4456 8732 2 (hardback)
ISBN 978 1 4456 8733 9 (ebook)

British Library Cataloguing in Publication Data.
A catalogue record for this book is available from the British Library.

Typesetting and Origination by Amberley Publishing
Printed in the UK.

CONTENTS

LIST OF ILLUSTRATIONS

INTRODUCTION

It is a strange irony that war, while it has a devastating impact on many people and families, brings out wonderful examples of individuals going to extensive efforts to care for others. The Second World War was no exception in this regard and there are literally thousands of cases of outstanding humanitarian actions during that period. Many people had reason to fear the growth of the Nazis in the 1930s and during the conflict itself. These included those whose political views were 'unacceptable' and, as the war progressed, Allied servicemen who ended up in territories occupied by the Third Reich or the other Axis powers. Of course, those most at risk from the rise of the Nazis were Jews and people who came to their assistance.

When Hitler attained total control over Germany in 1933 some were quick to recognise the implications. Indeed many advised their Jewish friends to leave. Of the half million or so Jews living in the country at that time about 60,000 emigrated within two years. Others followed in the next few years. The events of early November 1938, *Kristallnacht*, removed any remaining doubts as to Hitler's intentions. Jewish-owned properties, including synagogues, were subjected to widespread destruction. About 30,000 Jewish men were arrested and interned in Dachau and elsewhere. Within months many thousands more Jews fled but the Nazi invasions of other countries meant they had to move more than once in the search for refuge. Various countries began to resist visa applications from Jewish families, to a greater or lesser extent. At the same time, individuals began to take a more humanitarian approach and stretch out the hand of friendship. Many are not recorded and have been forgotten over time. Individuals involved in such cases, as well as whole nations, were inclined to avoid dwelling on wartime events in the years immediately afterwards.

In 1953 Yad Vashem, the World Holocaust Remembrance Centre, was established to acknowledge the humanitarian assistance afforded to Jewish people by Gentiles, which resulted in many lives being saved. It took some years before active steps taken to identify and honour these people, and their actions, began to bear fruit. This is a measure of the reluctance to revisit wartime horrors notwithstanding the extraordinary heroic stories which were uncovered. So far, in excess of 20,000 individuals have been recognised as Righteous Gentiles. At the other extreme, in the case of countries such as Germany and Austria, any post-war celebration of humanitarian activities in rescuing refugees from the Third Reich would merely serve to highlight the worst excesses of the period and so were not welcome in the decades afterwards.

As well as countries, individuals displayed a reluctance to publicise events. The natural post-war instinct for many people was to treat the appalling events of the period as a closed chapter, even if this meant concealing admirable activities on one's own part. Some felt guilty at the danger they had placed their family members in and took some time to come to terms with that. For example, a Dutch couple, Aart and Johntje Vos, decided, at a very early stage, to come to the assistance of Jews who found it necessary to go into hiding. The Vos family lived outside Laren, a town which is about 30 km from Amsterdam. From the house they built a secret passageway to a nearby nature reserve as an escape route for those they were hiding. The entrance to the passage was concealed beneath a false bottom in a coal chute. When a member of their support group was arrested they realised that a raid on their house was likely and decided to move the refugees to another location. Just as they were preparing to do that the Gestapo arrived. Of course, in Holland and elsewhere, the German authorities had a range of organisations that might generally be described as Secret Police. People did not tend to distinguish between them, referring to all as Gestapo, and that's the practice generally followed in this book. The Jews all managed to enter the tunnel and Aart Vos went with them to act as guide. However, they left behind identity documents which would have confirmed who they were and the fact that the family had concealed them. In panic, Johntje, as the raid commenced, hid the papers in the sweater her son was wearing and told him to leave the house as soon as he could and dispose of the documents. He managed this successfully but, for the rest of her life, she looked back in horror at the risk she took with his safety.

Others had more idiosyncratic reasons for secrecy. A Polish businessman bought an apartment and used it to hide Jews who were on the run. In his wife's best interests he considered it appropriate to conceal his activities from her during the conflict. Afterwards he deemed it prudent not to tell her, as she would have been annoyed to learn that he had put both their lives at risk.

For some, their wartime actions had the potential to cause them problems even after the conflict was over. Over a period of time Jean Kowalyk hid more than a dozen Jews in the attic of her farmhouse, where she and her mother lived in a rural part of Poland. Many living in the area held anti-Semitic views so Jean had to be very careful. This applied even to simple things. So, for basic necessities such as soap, she travelled to neighbouring towns in order not to alert shopkeepers that she was purchasing more than might be expected. Another example was washing and drying clothes. An excessive number of items on the clothes line where only two people were believed to be living could arouse suspicion. She solved this by drying the clothes of her 'guests' indoors at night. Despite the care she took, the house was raided by the Gestapo on a number of occasions, probably as a result of local tip-offs. Her brother had adapted the attic by constructing a double wall and this provided a very small hiding space with the result that the raids proved fruitless. The conclusion of the war did not mean she was out of danger. Indeed she received an anonymous letter threatening to expose the role she had played in assisting the Jews. Eventually she and her husband, Samek Berger, one of those whom she had saved, and subsequently married, moved to live in the United States of America.

Of course for many others emigration after the war was not an option. So, rescuers of Jews in areas of Russia and Ukraine, as well as Poland, found it necessary to conceal their roles for years afterwards or indeed, in many cases, forever. By contrast, other communities took a completely different approach. Anti-Semitism was not as strong in Italy as it was in Germany. Wolf and Esther Fullenbaum, Jews originally from Poland, were living in Milan with their baby daughter Charlotte when war broke out. In due course they were rounded up and incarcerated. However, they managed to escape in September 1943 and, like many refugees at the time, began to move south in the hope that the Allied advance would eventually liberate them. The progress of the Allied armies through Italy was much slower than some had anticipated so the Fullenbaums decided to go into hiding pending the Liberation. In the village of Secchiano, near Rimini, they were taken in by local shopkeeper Virgilio Virgili and his wife Daria. For safety they were moved at a later stage to an attic room in the local school where they lived for almost a year. Locals supported them with food and the necessities of life. It is believed that the entire population of the village of approximately 600 people were aware of their existence but they were never betrayed. So, the different responses to the conflict and the moral issues it raised affected whether stories of humanitarian actions were, likely to emerge in the post-war years.

Even though the dangers for Jews living in Germany became all too clear with the rise of Nazism, fleeing the country was not always an option. The poor, the elderly or those needing to care for an aged relative, were more likely to stay notwithstanding their fears. Sigmund and Grete Weltlinger, a Jewish couple, survived in Berlin throughout the war. During the period from 1942 onwards they were hidden in turn by six different families. Each of these was risking certain execution for assisting Jews. There were also practical difficulties, most particularly sharing the limited food that was available on the ration books of those hiding them. When the danger of discovery increased they were passed on to the next couple. Sigmund was in a position to return the favour when the Red Army invaded. As he was able to speak a little Russian he managed to ensure that none of those who had helped him came to any harm.

In other cases the onward march of the forces of the Third Reich meant that Jews had to either flee again, or take evasive action. Some found themselves having to separate from their children to do so. Arthur and Rosetta Cohen were living in Rotterdam together with their baby daughter Miriam when, in 1942, it became necessary for them to go into hiding. Miriam was handed into the care of Jelle and Elizabeth van Dyck, a Protestant couple who had no children of their own. Miriam was not quite a year and a half old when this happened. Jelle van Dyck was involved in the underground movement in the locality, as was his father-in-law. The fact that the child had not yet learned to speak was reassuring as she would not be able to say anything which might betray her new 'parents'. They called her Anke. Having explained to the authorities that she had been left abandoned on their doorstep they secured permission to adopt the child. Whether the local officials were persuaded as to the truth of this claim is not clear. Sometimes people in authority took a humanitarian approach to their duties by turning a blind eye. The van Dycks operated a bakery in which they employed a number of locals. As a consequence, quite a few people in the general locality must have known the true story. In caring for the child, the couple were taking a considerable and serious risk. As it happened Jelle's underground activities led to his arrest in 1944 and he was imprisoned until the end of the war. At that stage Miriam was returned to her natural parents.

Rescue efforts varied in their nature. An individual or a couple of people organised some, whereas other cases involved larger groups. All were risky for those offering the hand of friendship and were certain to have severe implications, including possibly death, if uncovered. Most of these cases involved just a couple of people saved by the actions of an equally small group of individuals. Occasionally a single individual was in a position where it was possible for him or her to save hundreds. A number of these cases involved diplomats of neutral countries. The best-known case is that of Raoul Wallenberg and his extraordinary bravery and achievements in rescuing Jews from the Nazis and local anti-Semitic gangs in Budapest. While in no way underestimating Wallenberg's achievements, he had the advantage that he was fulfilling the policies of his government in his actions. There were other diplomats at that time who took similar initiatives partially or totally in defiance of directives issued by their superiors. In Chapter One the actions of various diplomats are described, including some who were acting without the official approval of their governments. In addition, the activities of one individual who posed as a diplomat without any authorisation whatsoever are recounted.

Of course most rescue efforts involved a number of people working in concert, invariably at risk to their own lives, and over a protracted period during the war years. In this book four such cases are outlined in which groups of people worked together in a very courageous way to save others. They were distinctive both in their mode of operation and general focus. The refugees fell into various categories, broadly speaking, and consisted of both servicemen and civilians. The numbers were so great that, inevitably, different humanitarian groups specialised in the category of refugee they were helping and this became known to those seeking help.

One of the groups whose story is outlined was centred in the area around Marseille and was targeted, in the main, at offering assistance to Allied servicemen on the run. As the major port in the south of France, it was an obvious place for fugitives to head towards in the hope securing safe passage out of the country. A group there under the leadership of an extraordinary Belgian responded to the needs of those arriving seeking help. The second group has an even stronger Belgian connection. To a large degree those who organised and ran it were all natives of that country and they were insistent that it remain throughout as a Belgian operation. The founder and leader was a charismatic and determined young woman who, with friends and colleagues, helped airmen who had been downed in the Low Countries to return to their units via the Iberian Peninsula. A third group whose activities are outlined was different in the sense that it was community-based and located around Assisi in Italy. The community there, under the leadership of a local Franciscan priest, managed to house and hide those fleeing from the authorities. In the vast majority of cases the reason they were hounded is because they were Jews. An internationally renowned cyclist who had won both the Tour de France and the Giro d'Italia performed a key role in the effort to ensure their safety. Perhaps the most interesting aspect of this case relates to the local German commander. It seems highly likely that he knew what was going on but decided to turn a blind eye to it. The final case examined features a Capuchin priest who worked initially in Marseille and Nice with a multi-denominational group of people to save Jewish fugitives. Following transfer to Rome, he linked up with a Jewish organisation there to continue this work. Thousands were saved as a result.

CHAPTER 1

Aristides de Sousa Mendes

Aristides de Sousa Mendes was born in July 1885 in Cabanas de Viriato, Portugal. His family were well-to-do and had aristocratic links. He and his twin brother studied law at the University of Coimbra, after which he joined the diplomatic service. Having served in various parts of the world, he took up duty as Portuguese Consul General in Bordeaux in 1938. Assignment to the consulate in Bordeaux carried with it authority over all Portuguese diplomatic personnel working in south-west France. Portugal, like its neighbour Spain, had adopted a neutral stance as war broke out. The Portuguese dictator Antonio Salazar, who came to power in 1932, was careful as war approached to tread a fine line between the Axis powers and Spain on the one hand, and the UK and her allies on the other. He was aware that his Spanish counterpart General Francisco Franco, while nominally neutral, was favourably disposed towards Hitler. He also appreciated that his country's fate was closely bound up with that of Spain so he was anxious to maintain good working relations with the Spanish authorities. In his view both Spain and Germany were important forces in that they were significant obstacles to the spread of Communism. On its own, this consideration would have prompted him to follow Franco's approach which was, to a large degree, a policy of closed borders when it came to dealing with those fleeing the Nazis. On the other hand, very long-standing cordial relations with the UK meant that while remaining neutral, he was anxious to be seen as willing to offer assistance to any of its citizens who were in difficulty.

In November 1939 Salazar issued a directive to his government officials, including diplomats stationed abroad, prohibiting the issuing of visas to various categories of people seeking access to Portugal. These included those who could not return to their country of origin and stateless persons. Essentially all refugees were encompassed by this regulation. Also included among those to whom visas could not be issued were Jews and Russians. Anti-Semitism was not a major feature of Portuguese society relative to some other jurisdictions, so this provision was more a reflection of anxiety to stay out of the conflict and a fear of foreign infiltration than any other consideration. The directive specified that in all these cases a visa could only be granted if prior sanction to do so was provided by the Foreign Ministry in Lisbon. Two weeks after receiving the directive, Sousa Mendes ignored instructions and issued a visa without prior clearance to a Jewish refugee, Professor Arnold Wiznitzer, who had fled Vienna. When he was asked by his superiors to justify this, Sousa Mendes outlined that the applicant had explained that if he could not leave France immediately that day he would be placed in a detention camp and his wife and young son would be left stranded. On 1 March 1940, he issued a visa to Eduardo Neira Laporte, a Spanish republican, who was a critic of the regime of the Spanish dictator. For the

Portuguese authorities this was an even more politically sensitive case and the diplomat's actions provoked a strong response. Sousa Mendes was advised in writing that any further transgression of this nature would result in disciplinary action. Despite this, in the next few months he broke the regulations in a number of other cases.

Refugees

During May and early June 1940 more refugees were fleeing the forces of the Third Reich as French resistance to the invasion collapsed and the numbers approaching consulates in Bordeaux and elsewhere seeking assistance increased dramatically. Traditionally France had an open-door policy to refugees. It is estimated that even prior to the outbreak of hostilities there were about 180,000 in the country. Being careful to avoid further conflict with his superiors, Sousa Mendes sent many telegrams to the Ministry in Lisbon outlining individual circumstances in each case and seeking permission to issue visas. These elicited little or no positive response. Meanwhile many of the refugees who were seeking visas had no place to stay and were accommodated in the consulate, sleeping on chairs or the floors, awaiting a decision. They were looked after by the consul's wife Angelina, assisted by her sons. By this time, Sousa Mendes had repatriated the younger members of his family and placed them in the care of relatives for their own safety. On occasion he sent telegrams to his superiors in Lisbon detailing the emergency situation he was dealing with and seeking authority to act. The response was to refer him to the directive already in force and instruct him to comply. At this time his private life was in some turmoil as it became known that he was involved with another lady, Andrée Cibial, who was pregnant with his child. The increasing pressure in relation to his personal and professional lives impacted on his health and for three days in mid-June 1940 he was indisposed. He described this afterwards as a mental breakdown. Subsequently he emerged reinvigorated, with a clear mind as to what he must do. His son Pedro Nuno described the scene:

> My father got up, apparently recovering his serenity. He was full of punch. He washed, shaved and got dressed. Then he strode out of his bedroom, flung open the door to the chancellery, and announced in a loud voice: 'From now on I'm giving everyone visas. There will be no more nationalities, races or religions.' Then our father told us that he had heard a voice, that of his conscience or God, which dictated to him what course of action he should take, and that everything was clear in his mind.[1]

Defiance

Some of his family advised against this but he went ahead. His sons, Pedro Nuno and José Antonio, and the consular secretary, José Seabra, set up what was in essence an assembly-line operation to implement this policy. Also helping were some of the refugees including Chaim Kruger, a rabbi who had left his post in Brussels ahead of the German invasion. He was one of those seeking a visa from Sousa Mendes to gain access to Portugal for himself and his family. He had explained to the diplomat the likely fate of many Jews at the hands of the Third Reich. Although he was given the necessary documentation, Kruger resolved to stay and help until all the applications had been processed. This was the day of Pétain's broadcast to the French people advising that he was seeking an armistice and so speedy action was necessary.

Sousa Mendes and his colleagues worked all through the day, to past midnight, and again on the following days. The record that was kept of those to whom visas had been issued may not be complete and the usual fee was not collected. To speed things up, the diplomat just signed 'Mendes' in some cases. On 19 June German aircraft bombed the city causing the many refugees still awaiting visas to flee, many moving to the city of Bayonne about 200 km further south. By now Sousa Mendes was fully engaged in meeting the needs of the refugees so he followed them. The Portuguese vice-consul in Bayonne was complying with official instructions and refusing requests for assistance from the many refugees, both those who had fled from Bordeaux and others. Aristides de Sousa Mendes promptly 'pulled rank' as a more senior diplomat and began issuing visas to those gathered at the consulate, while at the same time assuring the vice-consul, Faria Machado, that he would take full responsibility for his actions. Machado declined to take part in the endeavour but reported what was happening to the ministry in Lisbon. Around this time, Sousa Mendes contacted Portugal's honorary vice-consul in Toulouse, Emile Gissot, and directed him to also issue visas. Gissot complied. The issuing of visas in Bayonne continued until 22 June when Sousa Mendes moved on to the town of Hendaye in the south-west corner of France, located at the border with Spain. There, operating in the public street, he issued more visas, many on scraps of paper. All the documents provided by Aristides de Sousa Mendes to refugees were accepted by the Spanish authorities at the border post at Irun, just across the River Bidasoa from Hendaye. Many of the refugees reached the Portuguese border, usually by train, quite quickly, so it became obvious that Consul Machado's account of events was accurate. In response telegrams were sent to

Sousa Mendes in Bordeaux and Bayonne instructing him to cease issuing visas and to return to Lisbon. He received neither as, by this time, he was in Hendaye.

The senior Portuguese diplomat in Spain, Ambassador Pedro Teotónio Pereira, a close associate of Salazar, was instructed to go to Irun, a town in northern Spain just across the border from Hendaye, to deal with the situation. Teotónio Pereira was already aware that the Spanish officials were expressing misgivings about the numbers of refugees crossing their borders. On arrival in the area, he advised the Spanish authorities that recognition of the visas provided by Sousa Mendes should cease and they complied. Many thousands were still waiting to cross the border but his actions seemed to obviate the possibility for doing so at that time. Pereira met with Sousa Mendes and reported back to Lisbon that the consul had 'lost the use of his faculties'. Sousa Mendes returned to Bordeaux where the telegram recalling him to Lisbon awaited. He complied but not in any great hurry. On his journey home he stopped in the border area for some days. There are suggestions that Sousa Mendes, during that period, continued to issue visas though possibly in smaller numbers than previously and directed them and refugees whose documents he had authorised previously to another Spanish border post where the guards were not aware that his authority had been withdrawn. It is believed that the vast majority of the refugees to whom he had issued visas succeeded in crossing the border.

Called to Account

On return home he was called before a disciplinary council that was appointed to deal with the case. The main charges were fairly straightforward: disobeying orders regarding issuing visas and instructing others to do likewise. His claim that it was an emergency situation that he faced in June was weakened by the fact that he issued visas contrary to regulations prior to that date. His previous transgressions and the fact that he had been cautioned as to his future behaviour were also taken into account. The overall charge was one of dishonourable conduct. His response issued on 12 August 1940 was forthright:

> It was indeed my aim to save all those people whose suffering was indescribable; some had lost their spouses, others had no news of missing children, others had seen their loved ones succumb to the German bombings which occurred every day and did not spare the terrified refugees.[2]

He outlined his view as to what was likely to happen to many of those whom he helped if they fell into German hands. These included statesmen, officials and senior army officers of occupied countries. These were from countries with whom Portugal had always been on friendly terms. He also mentioned that many of those to whom he had issued visas were Jews 'who were already persecuted and sought to escape the horrors of further persecution'. He summarised his position:

> I could not differentiate between nationalities as I was obeying the dictates of humanity that distinguish between neither race nor nationality; as for the charge of dishonourable conduct, when I left Bayonne I was applauded by hundreds of people, and through me it was Portugal that was being honoured.[3]

In mid-October the disciplinary council issued its verdict. He was found guilty of 'disobeying higher orders' and a demotion was recommended. At the end of October, Salazar implemented a decision of his own. Sousa Mendes was sentenced to complete inactivity for one year on half-pay and retirement thereafter. The files on the case were to be sealed. His pension entitlements were reduced. In a society where the objective of many was to be seen to please the dictator it is not surprising that the diplomat and his family were, to a great extent, ostracised.

As time passed the situation in Portugal changed somewhat. Many of the refugees travelled onwards to places such as the United States. Others made their home in the country and had been well received. The citizens generally were proud of their country's part in this humanitarian endeavour. Of more significance to the dictator Salazar, international opinion was favourable. An issue of *Life* magazine carried a major article lauding the humanitarian actions of the Portuguese government in assisting so many refugees. Clearly the nuances of the situation were not fully understood by the author as Salazar was described as the 'greatest Portuguese since Henry the Navigator'. From the point of view of the authorities, it was important to ensure that this narrative was preserved. So, Aristides de Sousa Mendes and his story were airbrushed from Portuguese public life for decades.

After the war Salazar revelled in the image of one who had done so much to assist Allied citizens during the war years. Aristides de Sousa Mendes suffered a stroke so this ended any possibility of returning to his profession as a lawyer. The extent of his 'disgrace' probably meant that this was limited anyway. His wife Angelina died in 1948, after which he married Andrée Cibial and they lived at the family mansion, Casa do Passal, in the small town of Cabanas de Viriato about 70 km from the university city of Coimbra. Throughout his later years he sought opportunities to restore his reputation, with the help of his twin brother César, also a lawyer, but Salazar ensured that these requests were denied. Compared to the lifestyle he had enjoyed as a child and in the pre-war era, he was living in relative poverty. Aristides de Sousa Mendes died in April 1954. Two days later a card from Salazar was delivered to the family home. It contained just a two-word comment: 'My condolences.' Portuguese newspapers, all subject to censorship at the time, carried no obituary notice or even reference to his death. The narrative began to change when his achievements were recognised. Yad Vashem, the Holocaust Remembrance organisation in Israel, issued a commemorative medal recognising his contribution to ensuring the safety of thousands of Jews.

Belated Vindication

Meanwhile some members of the family began to mount a long campaign for an appropriate state response. As long as Salazar survived, there was no chance of this happening. He was replaced in 1968 by Marcelo Caetano but, despite early promises to the contrary, the new regime retained Salazar's repressive approach. It was overthrown in a remarkably peaceful revolution in 1974, prompted by the armed forces. The move towards a more democratic form of government commenced, although fairly slowly. A Portuguese government official, Dr Nuno de Bessa Lopes, opened the sealed files and began to assess the case of Sousa Mendes. He concluded in his 1976 report that the diplomat had been victimised by the Salazar regime for its own political purposes and that he had been punished unjustly. However, the remnants of the dictatorship were still in powerful positions in the Portuguese government and society so the Bessa Lopes report remained secret for more than a decade. But the increasing openness in Portuguese society prompted those interested in the case to renew their appeals for justice. In particular Sousa Mendes's youngest son, John Paul, who was living in Dublin, California, was working with others, and began to lobby politicians there for their support. In 1986, seventy members of the US Congress wrote to the then Prime Minister of Portugal, Mario Soares, asking that the good name of Aristides de Sousa Mendes be restored. Eventually campaigns within Portugal and in the US paid off when, in 1988, the Portuguese parliament unanimously dismissed all charges against him, a decision which they marked with a standing ovation. His achievements have been honoured in various ways since then in different countries. Fittingly, a bust of the diplomat now stands in Bordeaux, where he began to come to the assistance of Jews in distress. A campaign by the Sousa Mendes Foundation to have his family home refurbished as a museum has also been successful and the project is well underway.

Estimating the numbers whose safety was ensured by the actions of Sousa Mendes is a matter of some debate. While records exist of the early visas he issued, as the emergency grew there is at least a possibility that this arrangement began to fall by the wayside. A speedy response, rather than keeping the usual ledger of names and details, was what was required in Bordeaux and Bayonne. By the time he got to Hendaye, he was operating on the street. Some historians suggest that between him and Emile Gissot in Toulouse, who followed his lead, something of the order of 20,000 visas were issued during

June and early July 1940. A more particular difficulty in all these cases is that one visa was often issued to cover a group of people. So visas issued to parents routinely also covered their children. In such circumstances even a perfect record of the visas issued does not give us a figure for the number of beneficiaries. A conclusion that his actions assisted 10,000 is probably a reasonably safe and conservative assertion.

Ensuring the safety of so many people in the matter of a couple of weeks by his own direct action was a singular humanitarian achievement. There is little doubt that the noted Holocaust scholar Professor Yehuda Bauer is correct in describing it as 'perhaps the largest rescue action by a single individual' during that time. However, it seems certain that indirectly Sousa Mendes saved far greater numbers of individuals. Furthermore, his actions prompted a changed approach by Salazar once he appreciated the goodwill that could be generated by a humanitarian approach to refugees. Welfare organisations were established to support those reaching the country and the Portuguese citizens proved very welcoming. It is estimated that one million refugees arrived in the country over a five-year period. Some stayed and others used it as a base from which to travel further, many to the US. This is an extraordinary figure, even if an overstatement, for a country whose population at the time was about six million. It is likely that, as the balance of advantage in the conflict swung towards the Allies, Salazar would have adopted that approach anyway but it would have come much later. Sousa Mendes' actions were the major factor in promoting that policy development. As the Director of the Foreign Ministry archives pointed out some years ago, 'The image of Portugal as a safe haven was born in Bordeaux.'

Chiune Sugihara

Chiune Sugihara was born on the first day of January 1900 in Yaotsu, which is located in the Gifi Prefecture of Japan, about 350 km from Tokyo. His family background was relatively modest, although his mother could trace her family line back to the feudal lords of the area. His father, Kosui, worked for the state as a tax collector with the result that the family moved to live in various locations during Chiune's early years. Chiune, together with his brothers and sister, attended a number of different schools during this period. He graduated from high school in Aichi district in 1917. All the indications are that he was a very bright and committed student. His attendance record was exemplary and he secured very satisfactory results as he moved through the education system.

This was a quite turbulent era in the history of the country. Victory in the Sino-Japanese war of 1894–5 had established Japan as a formidable power and resulted in it attaining control over some Chinese and Korean regions. This in turn led to increased tensions between Russia and Japan which, in due course, resulted in a war between the two countries in 1904–5. Japan was victorious. This was the first victory for any Asian country over a European power, and clearly underlined Japan's new status as a colonial state.

Kosui Sugihara transferred to work in the colonial service in 1910 and took up a position in Manchuria, which had come under Japanese control. As a result of his father's occupation, Chiune spent most of his time away from home during his teenage years. Even after he left the colonial service in 1916 Kosui remained in Seoul running an inn, which he had purchased there.

Father and son became estranged in the following years. The reasons are not fully clear but we know that they had a severe disagreement over Chiune's career choice. He wanted to study English with a view to becoming a teacher, whereas his father was determined that his son should become a doctor. Chiune moved to live in Tokyo and, in early 1919, enrolled in Waseda University to study English. Trying to support himself financially and pursue his studies at the same time proved too much, and he quickly dropped out of college. As luck would have it, the Foreign Ministry announced a scholarship scheme around that time. Presumably arising from the country's new role in the world, it had decided to make funding available for fourteen students to engage in international studies. Chiune Sugihara sat the examination on 16 July 1919 and was successful, no mean achievement and another indication of his talents. His choice of subject was Spain but that was awarded to another candidate so he opted to study the Russian language and culture. Traditionally a rival, Russia was at the same time always an object of curiosity to the Japanese. The Russian Revolution would have added to this and there was a widespread interest in the country's culture and the arts. So in some ways it was a straightforward choice on Chiune's part and certainly proved a fateful one.

He was sent to study Russian language, history and culture at the academy in the city of Harbin. Located in Manchuria in the north-eastern region of China, Harbin was originally a fishing port. The area was under the control of the Russian empire. Indeed in the late nineteenth century, Tsar Nicholas II encouraged Russians to settle there to solidify control of the region. Jews were incentivised to do so also with promises of freedom of religious practice, and the provision of schools under their own control.

The arrival of the Chinese Eastern Railway (CER) at the start of the twentieth century transformed the area. The railway was built by the Russians to consolidate their dominance of the region. Harbin was chosen as the administrative centre for the enterprise and the focal point of Russian control of Manchuria. The result was that Harbin quickly became quite a cosmopolitan urban area. Political dominance in the region passed to Japan after its victory over Russia in 1905 but Harbin retained a strong Russian tradition. As a consequence of the revolution in 1917 many White Russians fled their native country, including about 100,000 who moved to live in Harbin.

Although the native Chinese formed the largest ethnic group in the population, Harbin was a very Russian city by the time Sugihara arrived in October 1919. Russian-language newspapers were in circulation, and schools and churches had been provided for the local Russian community. The Harbin Academy, while it had yet to attain the status of a university, contained a strong Russian faculty. There was also a sizeable and growing Jewish community of about 10,000 people and a similar number of Japanese residing in the area.

Harbin was an ideal place for Chiune Sugihara to study the Russian language and culture and to get to know the attitudes of various ethnic groupings. His studies were interrupted in October 1920 when he had to undertake a year of compulsory military training. After that he was enrolled in the army reserve but returned to Harbin, where he completed his service. On graduating in Harbin he achieved his ambition when he was employed to teach Russian in the faculty there. However, his expertise in Russian matters, including fluency in the language, inevitably led his career in another direction. From time to time he was consulted on matters by staff at the Japanese consulate in Harbin. The growing power of the Soviet Union and the increasing strength of its armed forces prompted concern in Japanese government circles. As such, someone with his expertise and knowledge made him an obvious recruit for the diplomatic service. He also had good sources in the Russian community and had married a White Russian, Klaudia Apollonov, in 1924. It is not exactly clear when he left his teaching post and embarked on his career as a full-time diplomat, but it was probably in late 1924.

Sugihara spent the next eleven years working in the Japanese consulate in Harbin. He was never destined for the highest-ranking jobs in the diplomatic service. These were reserved for graduates of the prestigious Tokyo University but he secured promotion on a regular basis. What exactly he was doing is somewhat shrouded in mystery. Harbin was the centre of a region that had been contested between China, Russia and Japan for centuries. Indeed, the Japanese army occupied it and established a puppet regime, which took control of the region in 1931. After protracted negotiations, Japan bought out the Russian interest in CER in 1935 to secure their control in the area. This was not a complete negation of Soviet ambitions in the region. Rather, the increased belligerence of Germany had prompted a re-think in Moscow in order to avoid a possibility of fighting wars in two theatres simultaneously. It was a tactical rather than complete change of direction. The long-term Japanese plan, at the time, was to extend control further into China.

Throughout Sugihara's time there, Harbin was home to a disparate collection of ethnic groups, including two sets of Russians with differing loyalties. Inevitably it was a centre of intrigue. While not a spy in the narrow sense of the word, it seems certain that he was gathering information from sources in the various groups and providing analysis to the government in Tokyo. It is noticeable that at some stages he was described as reporting to the Ministry of Foreign Affairs whereas at other times it was to the Ministry of Interior Affairs. In either case he was engaged in intelligence work, though assignment to the Interior Affairs Ministry may signify a more direct involvement with the agencies involved in that type of activity. In the summer of 1935 he returned to Tokyo where he remained for the rest of the year, assigned to the Foreign Ministry. In December he was selected to take up a role at the embassy in Moscow. There are contradictory accounts of what happened in that regard. While he certainly travelled to Russia, whether he actually took up that position is unclear. What is certain is that he moved to Finland in 1938 to fill the position of deputy to the minister (ambassador) there. He was accompanied by his second wife, Yukiko Kikuchi, whom he married in 1936 after an amicable separation from Klaudia Apollonov.

A feature of the 1930s was the number of pacts agreed between various countries as relationships became more fractious. In 1936 Germany and Japan agreed the Anti-Comintern Pact. Ostensibly directed towards the international communist movement, in reality it was a response to the growing might of the Soviet Union. In order to safeguard their common interests, the countries agreed that, in the event of an attack, they would consult each other. They also exchanged undertakings that neither party would agree a pact with the Soviets. Italy and Spain signed up to the agreement the following year. Hitler and Mussolini had also signed a treaty in 1936.

In March 1938 the forces of the Third Reich took over Austria and invaded Czechoslovakia. In these circumstances sending Sugihara, an expert on Russian affairs, to Finland in order to assess developments in Europe was an obvious step for the Japanese authorities to take. The particular event that caused most concern to the Japanese government at that time was the agreement between Germany and USSR, a non-aggression pact, which was announced in August 1939. Obviously it was a clear breach of the existing German–Japanese pact. More particularly, the Soviets were already threatening Japan's dominance in Manchuria and border skirmishes were very frequent. This new pact opened up the possibility that the Russians would be free to devote greatly increased attention and resources to that effort.

It is against this background that Sugihara's move to Finland, and then to Lithuania, is best understood. It reflected an anxiety on the part of the Japanese authorities to be informed about the shifting alliances and military intentions in Europe. While Finland was a useful listening post, a presence in Lithuania was likely to prove an even more fruitful source of information. There was an affinity between those who looked with apprehension at the growing strength of the USSR, such as the Baltic States. There was also an existing good relationship between Poland and Japan. After some months the Lithuanian government agreed, in August 1939, to a Japanese request to open a consulate in Kaunas. Vilnius, the traditional capital of Lithuania, had been under foreign control since the First World War, initially Soviet and then Polish, so Kaunas, sometimes known in an anglicised version as Kovno, was the seat of government. Traditionally it was a centre of academic and cultural life and there was a significant Jewish population living in the city.

Lithuania

In autumn Sugihara took up his post as consul in Kaunas, having rented accommodation in which to live. (The actual title assigned to the position was vice-consul but, for our purposes, the difference is not significant.) The purpose of his presence there is clear from the fact that there was no record of any Japanese citizen living in Lithuania at the time. The senior diplomatic Japanese presence in the region was the embassy in Riga, but he had no reporting obligations to it. He was the Foreign Ministry's eyes in the region reporting directly back to Tokyo. They already had intelligence that Hitler intended to attack Japan's traditional enemy Russia, notwithstanding the non-aggression treaty between the countries. Sugihara recalled the circumstances some years later. 'My consulate's main task was to rapidly and accurately determine the time of the German attack. It became clear to me that this was the reason why the Japanese General Staff had urged the Foreign Ministry to open a consulate in Kovno.'[4] A neighbour in Kaunas recalled many years later that the consul often went for drives into the countryside, sometimes with his family, but often on his own. It can be assumed that at least some of these journeys were for the purpose of intelligence gathering, particularly with the help of the Polish underground movement with whom he had quickly established good relations. Certainly there is no evidence of the consulate being involved in ordinary day-to-day diplomatic work, such as issuing visas, during 1939 and early 1940.

Of course Sugihara would have been conscious of the concerns of various groups within Lithuania regarding the developing situation. Aside from official sources of information, he had become acquainted with some local families. In 1994 Solly

Ganor recalled the consul, his wife and his sister-in-law being in his family home at a Hanukkah celebration in 1939 following a chance meeting in a local shop. Some of the guests, refugees from Poland, took the opportunity to tell Sugihara of the events in Warsaw. One, a Jacob Rosenblatt, broke down when outlining his experiences and the Japanese consul became visibly upset. Also, as events unfolded during 1940, visa requests to the consul began to arise. These he dealt with on a case-by-case basis. The evidence from his actions at the time suggested a willingness to bend, if not actually break, official procedures. An early case was that of Alfred Katz, a Pole, who had sought refuge in Lithuania and applied for a visa to go and live with his brother-in-law in Japan. The role of the consul was to verify that the applicant had a destination visa, which specified the country he intended to live in. If so, Sugihara could then issue a transit visa, which allowed the applicant to travel through Japan en route to his destination. Alternatively, the applicant was required to provide evidence of a guarantor in Japan who would support him or her while there. Sugihara secured confirmation that the brother-in-law was in a position to support Katz. As Poland was occupied, strictly speaking Katz was stateless. He possessed only a Nansen passport, named after the League of Nations official who devised these for people who found themselves in such difficulties. The document provided proof of identity but did not confer a right to citizenship. Also, countries required holders to apply for a visa when wishing to either to enter their jurisdiction or to travel through it. If he were afraid to act Sugihara could have used this as an excuse and referred the case to the Foreign Ministry, but he took more direct approach which he outlined to his superiors in a cable.

I issued the entrance visa to Alfred Katz ... on March 21st and
I will send the report about this visa and others. I gave this visa
for the following reasons so please acknowledge. He has asked for
the visa from us after finishing the departing procedure by 'Nansen
Passport' and if we refuse to issue a visa on this passport, it will
actually be impossible for him to leave the country.[5]

This was a clever tactic in that he acknowledged the limitations
applying to a Nansen passport holder but gave humanitarian reasons
for proceeding. In a sense he created a precedent for future cases,
which the reference to 'others' would imply were already on his
desk or anticipated. It seems his approach when dealing with a case
was to ask the applicant a lot of seemingly trivial questions about
their family circumstances and background before identifying the
approach that would allow him deal with the case most positively.

Stella and Stanislaw Kaspcik, together with Stella's parents,
were refugees from Poland where Stanislaw had served as a
lieutenant in the intelligence service. As such the outlook for him
was very grim and the family were determined to get away to
safety, though they had no idea how this was to be achieved.
Stella's mother, a Belgian national, mentioned one day that she
had been friendly with a Japanese man called Kavagoe many
years previously when they had been university students together
in Brussels. Sugihara gave his account of this case in 1967 to Dr
Roman Korab-Zebryk, a Japanese scholar engaged in research on
these matters:

I made some enquiries in Japan and after some time I told the
couple Kaspcik that I was prepared to help them get a visa to
Japan ... Stella was born in Belgium as the daughter of Kavagoe,

who at that time was a student, and a Belgian girl ... however, obeying his parents, [he] returned to his fatherland breaking all ties with Stella's mother ... I found that Kavagoe had become the manager of a fashionable hotel and golf club in Kavana, Japan, and he immediately answered that Stella was indeed his daughter and he wanted her to come to Japan.[6]

The question then arose as to the safest way for the couple to travel to Japan, either through Germany and Italy and onward by ship, or across the Soviet Union. Both were equally dangerous for the lieutenant, and Sugihara concluded 'three days to the Mediterranean was better than seventeen across the Soviet Union'. The evening before they left in May 1940, he gave Stella a package. He explained that it contained a pair of gloves, 'a present for my Foreign Minister which you will deliver in Tokyo. Show this envelope at all border crossings. You will be like diplomatic couriers.' This ruse worked on the numerous occasions when they were questioned by Nazi and Italian Fascist police. Kavagoe was no more than a friend from decades previously, who generously agreed to play his part. In his account, Sugihara makes no mention of knowing that Kavagoe was not Stella's father but that is almost certainly a case of a careful man covering his tracks – hardly surprising as he was, by the time he gave details of this case, working in Moscow. It is also obvious that Sugihara made exceptional efforts to assist this couple, which suggests that perhaps Lieutenant Kaspcik may have rendered useful service in providing intelligence.

The Curacao Visas

Jan Zwartendijk arrived in Lithuania in 1939 as a representative of Philips, the famous Dutch electronics group. The Germans invaded Holland in early May 1940 and quickly assumed control. The Dutch leadership fled to London, where it established itself as a government in exile. The senior Dutch diplomat in the Baltic, L. P. J. de Decker, the country's ambassador in Latvia, remained loyal to the government and immediately took steps to dismiss the consul in Kaunas, who was known to have Nazi sympathies. At the same time, he was anxious to ensure a continued diplomatic presence in Lithuania as, unlike the Japanese case, there were a sizeable number of Dutch citizens living in the country. He overcame Zwartendijk's initial reluctance and finally persuaded him to accept the post of Honorary Dutch Consul in Lithuania in late May 1940.

The following month two people approached Zwartendijk for help. One was Pessia Lewin who was Dutch-born but had surrendered that status on her marriage to Isaac Lewin in 1935, when she was granted Polish citizenship. Her fear was that the Soviet authorities would repatriate both of them to Poland where the couple, both Jews, would probably fall into the hands of the Nazis with predictable consequences. So emphasising her Dutch birth she began to explore the possibility of a journey to Curacao, one of the Dutch-controlled islands in the Caribbean, which was a relic of Holland's colonial past and still under the control of the government in exile. If she could secure visas then she could claim that destination to be the end point of their journey. Zwartendijk consulted his superior, de Decker, but the initial response was not encouraging. Curacao was unusual in that it did not require a visa for entry. However, de Decker advised that permission to enter the island had to be sought from the governor and such requests were usually refused. Pessia Lewin persisted, asking if de Decker would agree to a partial statement of the position making no reference to the issue of the governor's permission to enter being required. His response on this occasion held out more promise as he asked her to send on her passport. On 11 July he responded by providing a hand-written document, which proved invaluable. 'The Dutch Royal Legation in Riga hereby declares that no visa is required for entry by foreigners to Surinam, Curacao, and the other Dutch possessions in America.'[7] Zwartendijk, and other Dutch diplomats in the region, were authorised to enter that text on the papers of anyone who applied for assistance. On 22 July 1940 Zwartendijk entered this statement on Isaac Lewin's passport. It was the first of many he was to issue.

These destination visas gave Sugihara the opening he required to issue transit documents to the Lewins. In the meantime, he had established that the Soviet authorities would allow holders of Japanese transit visas to travel on the Trans-Siberian railway across to Vladivostok. This was an arduous and difficult journey. Often travellers were not allowed disembark when the train was stationary and found it necessary to use bribery to obtain essentials. Yet for those in desperate situations, it was an escape route. From Vladivostok a sea journey took them to Japan and from there by boat to Curacao via the Panama Canal.

The second case Zwartendijk dealt with was that of a fellow Dutch national, Nathan Gutwirth. There were at that time a number of Yeshivas in Lithuania, where the pupils engaged in Jewish studies. Gutwirth was a student at the Telshe Yeshiva who recognised the approaching danger for someone like himself and was anxious to leave Lithuania. Returning home was out of the question as, by now, it was under Nazi control. He was also conscious of the possibility of travelling to the colonies in the Caribbean. As a Dutch citizen he was quite entitled to enter an island such as Curacao but was anxious lest bureaucracy interfere with his plans along the way. Zwartendijk authorised his passport on 23 July in the same manner as those of the Lewins. News of this development spread quickly among his fellow students and, very soon, the Honorary Dutch Consul was inundated with requests. In an eight-day period, working with two assistants, he certified 2,400 Curacao visas. This included processing hundreds for students and staff of the Mir Yeshiva, which were brought to him by one of their number, Moshe Zupnik. As the Soviets assumed full control of Lithuania, Zwartendijk was ordered to close the consulate service and did so on 3 August 1940.

Crucially, the news of the Curacao visas reached the ears of Dr Zorach Warhaftig. He was one of many Polish refugees who had sought safety in Lithuania and was more realistic than some leaders in the Jewish community in feeling that a further move would be necessary as a matter of urgency. He realised that to move eastwards was the only option. Most of Western Europe was Nazi-occupied and entry to Palestine, then a matter for the British authorities, was extremely restricted. Reaching America would have been the ambition of many but it was not welcoming refugees at that time. The emergence of the so-called Curacao visas offered some hope. Warhaftig led a delegation, in early August 1940, to meet with Sugihara to seek his assistance by issuing ten-day transit visas for Japan. The consul promised an answer within a few days. In the meantime he had been issuing visas on a case-by-case basis and, noticeably, applying increasing flexibility. Ludvik Salomon received his on 26 July. He recalls the consul looking at his American visa, commenting 'no problem' and writing a Japanese visa longhand. Sugihara made no reference to the fact that the American visa had lapsed. It is ironic that during that summer he found himself more engrossed in the traditional work of a consul, having been sent to Kaunas for an entirely different purpose.

He was expressing increasing concern, in cables to the Foreign Ministry, about the deteriorating situation in Lithuania. On 28 July he referred to widespread arrests in Vilnius and elsewhere in the country and expressed fears for Jews and former members of the Polish army and administration. While this was going on, the consul made the pretence to the authorities in Tokyo that all was routine, sending the occasional query about particular cases. Inevitably the reality soon became obvious as refugees began to arrive in Japan including some who had no Curacao visa. On 14 August he was reminded of the need for all holders of Japanese transit visas to have documents proving an entitlement to enter their destination country. Two days later the authorities took a more pointed line:

> Recently we discovered Lithuanians who possess our transit visas which you issued ... Among them are many who do not possess enough money and who have not finished their procedure to receive entry visas to their terminal country ... you must make sure that they have finished their procedures for their entry visa and also they must possess the travel money or the money they need during their stay in Japan. Otherwise, you should not give them the transit visa.[8]

The consul's response was a classic diversionary tactic. He raised the case of a Leon Polak, a Polish businessman, whose wife and child had fully authentic visas to move to the USA. While the husband's papers were being processed the American consulate closed and so he was never issued with a passport. Sugihara ends his cable with a very gently phrased line. 'I would like to know whether it would be permissible to grant him a visa.'

Responses were not always received, possibly because there were differing factions within the government at the time and a cabinet reshuffle on 22 July had created some uncertainty. For some years there had been a group within Japanese government circles who favoured an open and welcoming attitude to Jews. The hope was that the wealth and influence they would bring would prove very beneficial to Japan, not least in improving relations with the United States. Others held a view which was anti-Semitic though not to the same extent as the Nazis. Of course, by the time Sugihara was contemplating what he should do, Japan was in alliance with Germany. Any overt assistance to Jewish people from then on became more difficult for the Japanese authorities. Advice was routinely issued to Japanese diplomats re-iterating the need to check documents thoroughly and, ensure that applicants had a destination visa and the resources to support themselves while in Japan. Sugihara had received one such instruction by cable: 'Concerning transit visas … advise absolutely not to be issued to any traveller not holding firm visa with guaranteed departure date ex Japan … no exceptions … no further inquiries expected.'[9] In other words the regulations had to be implemented precisely and he was not to refer any cases to the Foreign Ministry pleading special circumstances.

A Decisive Response

The plight of applicants, the increasing numbers arriving at his office, and his awareness that the consulate was destined for closure within weeks as a result of the loss of an independent Lithuania brought things to a head for Sugihara on 10 August 1940.[10] Rising very early that morning, muffled sounds outside prompted him to look out his window. A large crowd of seemingly destitute people had gathered overnight and were clearly waiting for the consulate to open. Very few, if any, satisfied the requirement that they possess the resources to support themselves while in Japan or to cover the cost of the onward journey, whether a notional one to Curacao or elsewhere. It was then that he decided that, rather than bending the rules and relying on incomplete or dubious information from applicants, he would begin to issue transit visas to all who sought them.

In the next few weeks hundreds of visas were issued, some to applicants with little or no documentation other than the Curacao destination visas, others relying on false information or forged papers. It became an assembly-line service with the consul and his secretary working day and night to process cases. Moshe Zupnik arrived with the papers of approximately 300 staff and students of the Mir Yeshiva, which had been authorised by Jan Zwartendijk. These were processed but Moshe also found himself recruited to help with the ongoing work, stamping papers day after day. Interviewed many years later in Manhattan where he eventually settled, he described the experience as 'the best days of my life sitting there in the Japanese consulate with Sugihara'.[11] Clearly, by this time, Sugihara knew that at the very least his career with the government would be terminated. Having decided on his course of action, he was making sure, by these tactics, that he would be able to continue his humanitarian approach until the closure of the consulate at the end of August.

Calculating how many were saved by his actions is difficult. When in 1941 the Japanese authorities called him to account he reported that he had issued 2,132 visas, more than half of which were to Jews. It is likely that the figure was an understatement, which is hardly surprising in the circumstances. Official Japanese records indicate that 5,580 visas were issued during the period. Among those were slightly in excess of 2,000 Curacao visas issued by Zwartendijk. As it became known that Sugihara was issuing visas it became impossible to continue handwriting the documents so two stamps were made. It is probable that in the panic of those final days many were issued that never made it onto a list, if in fact he was keeping one. Moreover as in other cases these would have covered not just the holder but also children. The probability is that something of the order of 10,000 people, the vast majority of whom were Jews, were saved by Sugihara's actions while in Lithuania. Indeed it is possible that his actions had some impact even after he left. Mystery surrounds the fate of the two official stamps and consular headed notepaper. Evidence has emerged that at least some of these items came into the possession of the local Jesuit community who issued 'Sugihara visas' after his departure.

Feng Shan Ho

Dr Feng Shan Ho was born in 1901 in Yiyang, a city in Hunan province about 1,500 km from Beijing, to a family of modest means. He was a bright student in his local school, which was under the patronage of the Lutheran church, and he proceeded to university at the College of Yale-in-China, which had been established by the noted American institution. He subsequently attained a doctorate in Political Economy at university in Germany, after which he joined the Chinese diplomatic service. During his time in Munich he had learned German and so he was well equipped to fill the post of consul-general at the Chinese consulate in Vienna, which he took up in 1938. His facility in the language meant that he soon established a wide range of contacts in the city.

Dr Ho, a gregarious and friendly man, soon became well known in the Austrian capital. He immediately recognised that Austrian Jews, who numbered almost 200,000, were in danger following the *Anschluss*. Indeed, they were in more immediate danger of violent oppression in Austria than almost anywhere else. It seems that many Austrians were determined to prove their loyalty to the Nazis, in particular by taking action against the Jews.

In the early stages after they took control of Austria in 1938, Nazi policy towards the Jews was that they could leave. A regulation was introduced that any Jew wishing to emigrate had to have proof of arrangements to travel to a particular country. Many wanted to go to the United States but applications from Austria were not being accepted as the quota set by the American authorities had been reached. The British had applied similar restrictions to those wishing to travel to Palestine.

Dr Ho quickly became involved in trying to help, initially by supporting various church and charitable organisations and subsequently in a more official capacity. He began to issue visas for Shanghai, which was then under Chinese control. This would enable the holders to leave Austria, although he knew only too well that the vast majority of the recipients had no intention of ever going there. Word soon spread and by the autumn of 1938 queues were commonplace outside the consulate. Often those waiting were subject to harassment by the Gestapo. Some came up with ingenious plans to 'jump' the queue. Norbert Lagstein copied Chinese characters from his family encyclopaedia onto an envelope. Arriving at the embassy, he explained that he had a personal letter for the consul. Once he was admitted he presented the passports for his family of five, and visas were granted immediately. All departed Vienna successfully. Hans Kraus, a young man of nineteen, was in the queue one day when he saw the consul's car arriving. The window was open and he passed in the five passports of his family. Shortly afterwards visas were issued and, in this case, the family actually went to Shanghai.

Some of those who were saved were already in concentration camps. Morris Grossfeld was one of those rounded up by the Gestapo on Kristallnacht, 9/10 November 1938, and sent to Dachau. His son Bernard obtained Chinese visas for both his parents and himself from Dr Ho. This secured Morris's release from Dachau in July 1939 and they travelled to Shanghai. As was often the case even when visas were available, older people chose not to take advantage of them and family members stayed behind to care for them. Bernard's grandmother and his two uncles remained in Vienna and were subsequently interned. They did not survive the Holocaust.

The official Chinese position on the issuing of visas was inconsistent. Chinese diplomats had been advised by the Ministry of Foreign Affairs that they should accept such applications and process them. By contrast the Chinese Ambassador in Berlin, Chen Chich, who was Ho's immediate superior, believed that in order to maintain friendly relations with the Third Reich a different approach should be taken. He rang Dr Ho and ordered him to suspend issuing visas while the ambassador took up the issue with the Foreign Ministry. Ho ignored this instruction, which prompted Ambassador Chich to send an assistant to Vienna claiming that rumours were circulating of visas being sold by staff there. No evidence of any such practice existed so Feng Shan Ho ensured that visas continued to be issued.

He had one direct experience with plain-clothes policemen at this time which gives us some idea of his strength of character. He had called to see friends of his, a Jewish couple named Rosenberg, who were due to leave the next day on visas he had issued. When he arrived, Mr Rosenberg had already been arrested and taken away for questioning. While Dr Ho was in the house, the two officers called again to search the premises. On seeing him they asked for his papers, in response to which he asked for their identification first, in accordance with procedure. A confrontation ensued but despite one of them producing a pistol, the diplomat never identified himself. The officers withdrew and, learning on the way out who he was, berated Mrs Rosenberg. Her husband was released some hours later and the family departed for Shanghai the next day.

In May 1940 Dr Ho was removed from his post as consul in Vienna but continued in his country's diplomatic service. His replacement, Yao Ding Chen, complied enthusiastically with the wishes of Ambassador Chich. At the same time the Chinese authorities in Shanghai began to close the door to immigrants. So the chance for Jews to access Shanghai visas disappeared. Dr Ho was reprimanded for his actions but not to any serious extent and he continued in the diplomatic service before retiring to San Francisco where he died, aged ninety-six, in 1997. An essentially modest man, Ho devotes little attention in his biography to his humanitarian activities in Vienna. 'I did whatever I could to help them [Jews] but I do not know how many we saved.'[12]

Not all to whom he issued visas went to Shanghai. We do know, however, that approximately 18,000 Austrian Jews made their way to Shanghai during the period. It is likely that the vast majority of these were enabled to do so by the actions of Feng Shan Ho.

Budapest

As distinct from the cases already described, the situation in the Hungarian capital was quite different. In Budapest there was a group representing various countries working in concert. In March 1944 the Nazis occupied Hungary. The Hungarian regent, Admiral Miklos Horthy, was an ally of Germany but not always willing to rigorously implement Nazi policy. From 1938 onwards Germany had supported Hungary in securing control over territories that it had lost as a result of the First World War. So, by 1941, parts of Czechoslovakia, Yugoslavia and Romania had come under Hungarian control. The total population was just over 14.5 million of whom approximately 725,000 were Jewish. There were also about 100,000 Jews who had become Christians. The Hungarian government had adopted various anti-Semitic pieces of legislation but resisted the more extreme suggestions of their Nazi allies. On two occasions, Horthy had refused requests from Hitler to deport Jews to Germany. On the other hand, in August 1941, he agreed to send 20,000 Jews, mostly from regions of Czechoslovakia which Hungary had annexed the previous year, as slave labourers to German-occupied Russia. Most were killed, 11,000 on one day, by the SS. However, by comparison with events in other countries, Jews in Hungary were relatively left alone during the early war years.

The Hungarians had established contact with the Allied authorities in 1943 with a view to withdrawing from their alliance with the Axis countries. To avoid such a possibility, Hitler ordered the invasion of the country in March 1944. A few days later Adolf Eichmann arrived in Budapest with a team of SS members whose objective was to deport all Jews without delay. Initially they concentrated on the rural areas, villages and small towns. Within two months close on half a million Jews had been deported to Auschwitz. In carrying out this work Eichmann's team had considerable assistance from many in the Hungarian security services, although small numbers escaped deportation as a result of individual humanitarian actions by neighbours and the intervention of some Hungarian army officers. For example, Kalman Horvath was the officer in charge of a Labour Battalion. These were groups of men, aged between eighteen and forty-eight, who were employed on public works and so free from deportation. Horvath automatically admitted to his battalion all Jews who applied irrespective of age and health, ignoring whether their backgrounds equipped them for the role.

Throughout this period Horthy remained as head of state but power was in the hands of Döme Sztójay. Serving as Prime Minister and Minister for Foreign Affairs, he was happy to co-operate with the Nazis. His government, which included many anti-Semitic ministers, approved of the roundup of the Jews on the pretext that the deportees were to be used for the provision of labour in public works. Meanwhile escapees from Auschwitz let it be known what was actually happening there. They compiled a detailed report, which was smuggled to Switzerland and published in June 1944. It received widespread coverage. As a result international pressure came on Horthy from various sources, including President Roosevelt, Pope Pius XII and the King of Sweden, to halt the deportations.

Swiss Diplomats Give a Lead

At local level, when the Nazis in Hungary turned their attention on Budapest, help had been sought from the various diplomats in the city representing neutral countries. Carl Lutz was a member of staff at the Swiss embassy. As well as their routine duties the Swiss authorities were acting on behalf of countries which had no diplomatic representation in the city and Lutz had been assigned responsibility for such cases. For many of the Jews emigration to Palestine, then under British control, was the primary objective, though America or similar destinations were also seen as possible avenues of escape. Lutz ended up dealing with them and in June he secured approval from the Hungarian authorities for the emigration of 7,000 Jews. He interpreted this as 7,000 heads of families, so issued papers to all their dependants, probably numbering in the region of 40,000. No permission was forthcoming for the departure of such a large group because of objections from the German authorities but at least they now had papers which afforded some protection. A protest from the Germans to the Swiss Ambassador, Maximilian Jaeger, regarding the actions of Carl Lutz was dismissed. Indeed, the ambassador ordered Lutz to continue.

Others in the diplomatic service followed the example of the Swiss. The Spanish Ambassador, Ángel Sanz Briz, responded immediately. Under Spanish law, Jews of Spanish ancestry could claim nationality. He received permission from his government, and the Hungarian authorities, to offer citizenship to 200 such cases. Like Lutz he interpreted this as 200 families and issued protective documents to in excess of 2,000 individuals although, as he recalled later, he was careful to ensure that no individual document was numbered above 200. Many of these people were given accommodation in houses flying the Spanish flag. He was well aware that in many cases the claim to Spanish ancestry was very dubious.

Monsignor Rotta, the Papal Nuncio in Budapest, had received authorisation to issue Vatican papers to those Jews who had been baptised. It was estimated that at time there were about 2,500 such people living in Budapest. He instructed his officials not to look too closely at such applications. It has been estimated that the number who were issued with Vatican papers over the period was approximately 15,000.

Raoul Wallenberg

The Swedish embassy also became involved, issuing hundreds of documents. More than 700 provisional documents were issued to people who had a family or business connection with Sweden. The workload became so great that the minister at the legation, Carl Ivar Danielsson, sought additional help from his government. In January 1944 President Roosevelt had founded the War Refugee Board. The objective of the group was to rescue victims of enemy oppression and provide them with temporary safe havens. As the war developed, in 1944 Hungary was the most urgent case. The board appointed Wallenberg, a Swedish businessman, in June 1944 and, in response to Danielsson's request, sent him to Budapest with instructions to come to the assistance of Hungarian Jews. Before agreeing to the appointment Wallenberg sought and received a range of guarantees. He was assured that he would have a free hand to do whatever he deemed necessary. So, bribery, permission to avail himself of the services of UK and US secret agents to make links with well-disposed officials in the Hungarian services, and authority to use Swedish-owned buildings to provide asylum on his own initiative were all measures at his disposal. His mission was financially backed by the US government. He acquired diplomatic status when his own government designated him as a First Secretary at the Swedish Embassy in Budapest.

When Wallenberg arrived in the city, Carl Lutz tutored him on how best to use protective documents and gave him the names of Hungarian officials who were well-disposed to appeals for assistance. With assistance from Per Anger, first secretary in the embassy, Wallenberg played a leading role in the humanitarian effort. As well as normal passports, and the temporary ones issued to those with business connections in Sweden, they began to make a third type designed by Wallenberg, carrying the Swedish coat of arms and, under the name of the holder, including a statement written in both Hungarian and German: 'The Royal Swedish Legation in Budapest confirms that the aforementioned will travel to Sweden in accordance with the scheme of repatriation as authorised by the Royal Swedish Foreign Office. The aforementioned is also included in a collective passport. Until his repatriation the holder and his domicile are under the protection of the Royal Swedish Legation. Validity: Expires 14 days after entry to Sweden.' In many ways these were meaningless documents and had no legal diplomatic standing. Yet they looked important and significant, and served a very useful purpose in protecting people. Within the first couple of months in the role, Wallenberg had issued in excess of 4,000 documents and more than thirty buildings were flying the Swedish flag.

Meanwhile the mounting diplomatic pressure resulted in Horthy issuing orders on 7 July 1944 that all deportations were to cease. Eichmann and his colleagues were instructed to leave Budapest. By this time various restrictions had been applied to the city's Jewish population. They were required to live in accommodation marked with a yellow star and their movements were restricted to a limited number of daylight hours. Even with Eichmann and his group gone, Jews were still at risk from members of the Arrow Cross political party, an anti-Semitic group, many of whose members were willing to take violent action. So in late July Lutz took over a commercial building, known as the glass house, and opened it as a virtual branch office of the Swiss legation. Many Jews were able to register there and secure diplomatic protection.

Rumours began to circulate in August that deportations were to be resumed. Again diplomatic pressure was applied. Monsignor Rotta and Carl Danielsson presented a joint protest to the government on 21 August. As well as the Vatican and Sweden, the document was signed by the representatives of Switzerland, Portugal and Spain. They cited the recent report on Auschwitz, the document that made clear that deportations, while described as being for labour services, actually meant extermination. This proved effective and no deportations followed. Also, some days later, Horthy replaced Sztójay as Prime Minister with General Geza Lakatos and many anti-Semitic ministers were demoted. The diplomats in the city under Monsignor Rotta's leadership established an 'International Ghetto' in a group of several dozen apartment blocks. All were designated as being diplomatic buildings, flying the flags of various countries. In due course about 25,000 Jews sought sanctuary in the area.

Valdemar Langlet arrived from Sweden in 1931 to take up a post as lecturer in Swedish at the University of Budapest. In August 1944 he was appointed as representative of the Swedish Red Cross in Budapest. Nominally operating under the authority of Danielsson, he tended to act more informally and tensions ensued. Langlet used the fact that his position was an unpaid one to justify his independent approach. Using notepaper with the Swedish Red Cross emblem on it, he issued approximately 2,000 protective letters. While of no legal standing they were formal enough to influence the average official. Langlet used resources placed at his disposal by local people, many of them Jews. He placed refugees in safe houses or in hospitals and supported them there. In May 1945 Langlet and his wife Nina returned to live in Sweden.

Chaos

All this time Horthy had been trying to extricate the country from the conflict, fearing not just the Germans but also the Russians who were gaining ground and seemed to be about to invade the country. On 15 October he declared Hungary's exit from the war but this move had been anticipated. The pro-Nazi party, the Arrow Cross, staged a coup d'état and he was deposed and replaced by the leader of that group, Ferenc Szálasi. A reign of terror followed as gangs of Arrow Cross youths began looting property and killing members of the Jewish community. Within days of the coup, Eichmann returned to the city with plans for huge numbers of Jews to be arrested and deported. In excess of 25,000 men and 12,000 women were rounded up by the

Hungarian police within a week in October 1944. Meanwhile, the diplomats of various countries tried to extend their protection to as many people as possible.

Under the leadership of Rotta, the diplomats opened negotiations with the new Arrow Cross government. By holding out the possibility that their superiors would agree to afford diplomatic recognition to the new regime, they secured acceptance that the protective papers already issued would be recognised as valid. By that time they amounted to about 15,000. Of these about half the people holding them had Swiss papers, more than 4,000 were under Swedish protection, 2,500 were holders of Vatican papers and the remainder had Spanish or Portuguese documents. Rotta and his colleagues also persuaded the government to agree to recognise the diplomatic status of various extra-territorial buildings. These were properties the various diplomatic missions already owned or had quickly acquired to house members of the Jewish community. The Spanish representative Ángel Sanz-Briz rented several buildings and provided accommodation and protective documentation to those who moved in. A sign in both Hungarian and German was hung on the outside of each building identifying them as extra-territorial buildings belonging to the Spanish embassy.

The Portuguese chargé d'affaires, Carlos de Liz-Texeira Branquinho, had been granted permission by his government to issue 500 protective documents to Jews who had relatives in Portugal. In fact, by the time the government in Lisbon decided to withdraw him from Budapest in October 1944, he had provided papers to slightly fewer than 1,000 individuals. The International Red Cross took a similar approach. Their representative, Frederich Born, took charge of Jewish institutions in the city including hospitals and homes for the elderly and designated them as Red Cross institutions.

Approximately 3,000 individuals benefitted from this move. He also issued documentation to another 4,000 Jewish men and women which identified them as employees of the Red Cross and acquired properties as 'safe houses' in the city where they could live. Many of those who had Vatican papers were housed in various religious institutions throughout the city. Of course there were other Jews in the city who were still at risk and many were rounded up.

Of those Jews who had been rounded up on Eichmann's orders, the first group were force-marched out of the city on 9 November. The arrangement was that they were to be escorted on foot to the Austrian border almost 200 km away, walking about 30 km per day in freezing conditions. Monsignor Rotta immediately appointed a Father Baranszky to approach Jews who were being marched to Austria and supplied him with blank Vatican papers to issue to as many as possible so that they would be allowed to leave and return home. Raoul Wallenberg, with help from the International Red Cross, arranged for diplomatic checkpoints to be set up and manned on the roads outside Budapest and at the border with Austria to ensure that nobody possessing diplomatic papers was being forced to continue on the march. The extent of Wallenberg's efforts at this time is clear from the fact that he was now employing more than 400 individuals, forty of whom were doctors working in two hospitals he was running. He was also operating a soup kitchen to feed the poor. Many of those working for him were Jews to whom he had provided protective papers.

On 10 November an additional 10,000 Jews were arrested and imprisoned in a former factory outside the city without food, water or any form of heating. The Swiss Ambassador, Jaeger, had been recalled by the Swiss government as a protest against the coup d'état and his place as senior representative in the city fell to Harald Feller. He continued to offer protection and diplomatic support to Lutz. Indeed he became directly involved in some of the cases himself and was seized by the Arrow Cross in December 1944, and tortured, but subsequently released. So Carl Lutz, and his wife Trudy (Gertrude), began daily visits to this factory to interview the internees. Many had diplomatic papers and Carl and Trudy, by force of personality as much as anything else, exerted enough pressure on the guards to ensure that these papers were respected and the holders were released. Other diplomats followed suit and indeed some Hungarian Army officers delivered papers to people who were entitled to them. In this way significant numbers of people were allowed to leave.

The Hungarian government, under pressure from the diplomats of the Vatican, Sweden, Spain, Portugal and Switzerland agreed, on 19 November, to forbid further deportations but to little avail as the city was almost in a state of anarchy. Groups of Arrow Cross members were happy to implement Eichmann's plans without any reference to the authorities. Deportations resumed on 21 November with captives being sent by train to concentration camps at Ravensbrück and Mauthausen. The railway station became a scene of diplomatic activity as efforts were made to rescue Jews. On 23 November Wallenberg managed to save a large group of Jews at the station by supplying them with Swedish papers. He repeated the process some days later and again on 10 December.

On 29 November the Hungarian government issued a decree that all Jews were required to live in what became known as the Big or Sealed Ghetto. It was centred on the old Jewish quarter and non-Jews living there were given little over a week to relocate.

It was sealed off from the rest of the city, and normal services such as rubbish collection and food delivery were no longer supplied. Overcrowding resulting from so many people living in a confined area, and lack of basic essentials, facilitated the spread of disease and many died. This added to the burden of the diplomats and other humanitarians in the city as provision of food and medical assistance became necessary to a greater extent than previously. Similar to other cities under Nazi rule, as all people of Jewish faith were required to live in the ghetto (other than those protected in diplomatic buildings or in hiding), it made their arrest and deportation far easier.

Giorgio Perlasca

In some respects the most extraordinary of those involved in diplomatic efforts was Giorgio Perlasca. An Italian by birth, he was living in Budapest and operating an import-export business. As a young man he had served in an Italian battalion that had participated in the Spanish Civil War on the side of Franco. Totally opposed to Mussolini's regime in Italy, he applied for and was granted a Spanish passport by Ángel Sanz-Briz. The two became friends and Giorgio Perlasca, now calling himself the more Spanish-sounding Jorge, helped with the running of the Spanish safe houses.

On 30 November the Spanish government recalled Ángel Sanz-Briz for his own safety. Before leaving he was anxious to provide practical recognition of the role Perlasca had played in the humanitarian work of the legation. As he was not entitled to the protection of an accredited diplomat there was an obvious risk that he would pay a severe price for his activities. So Sanz-Briz assured his friend that when he got to Spain, he would make arrangements for Perlasca's safe passage to Madrid. The offer was declined and Perlasca chose to remain in Budapest. He 'assumed' the role of Spanish representative in the city although he was not a diplomat and there is no evidence that he was authorised by the Spanish government to act on their behalf. He filled the position with aplomb. On 3 December he met with the Deputy Foreign Minister to express concerns regarding the safety of those living in Spanish protected property:

I reminded him that there are thousands of Hungarians living peacefully in Spain but if, for any reason whatsoever, the Spanish Embassy and the Hungarian government were to fail to reach a satisfactory solution concerning conditions for the Jews under Spanish protection, the Spanish government, albeit with great regret, would have to put its relations with Hungary under review.[13]

Asked whether this should be considered a threat, he replied in the affirmative. A few days, later instructions were issued to the Hungarian military to respect all letters of protection issued by the Spanish legation. In the space of a little over a month he issued 3,000 protective letters on the headed notepaper of the Spanish legation. In the situation of virtual anarchy prevailing in the city at the time, he was also obliged to take more direct action.

Avraham Ronai was a young Hungarian Jewish boy living in a Spanish-protected house. It was raided by an Arrow Cross gang and all the adults, including his mother and sister, were arrested to be taken away and shot. 'Suddenly, out of nowhere Perlasca arrived and began berating the Arrow Cross commander,' was how Ronai described the scene years later.

How dare you behave like this on the property of a friendly country? I insist that you release these people, otherwise you will have problems with your superiors. If I have to cable Madrid about this violation of Spanish interests there will be grave consequences.[14]

The Arrow Cross men left in a hurry. Edith Weiss, a resident in another Spanish-protected property, recalls a similar episode. 'He was mesmerizing. In this forceful, powerful way of his he told them to go away and leave us alone. The leader of the Nazi group ... was so stunned he couldn't even talk. Perlasca had such authority, he was so strong, that there was no way anyone could defy him. They simply went away.'[15] Perlasca also attended meetings with the diplomats of the other neutral countries as they shared experiences and planned their moves to bring pressure to bear on the authorities in the interests of the Jews in the city. On one occasion he explained his unofficial status to the Papal Nuncio. Monsignor Rotta advised that if he was found out, sanctuary would be made available to him in the nunciature.

Meanwhile the Soviet forces were gaining ground in their approach to the city. By 23 December most diplomats had left. Only Rotta, Wallenberg, Lutz, and his Swiss colleague Peter Zürcher remained, together with Perlasca. What was due to be the final deportation train was filled and scheduled to leave the railway station on Christmas Eve, 1944. Wallenberg intervened and it never left. The Soviets laid siege to the city on the following day. However, this didn't stop the Arrow Cross gangs from continuing their murderous activities. Fifty Jews who were resident in the International Ghetto were removed from there and killed. On 8 January almost 300 Jews in a Swedish-protected building were taken out and shot. A further 150 or so were also removed from another building but Wallenberg successfully intervened and saved them. He also learned of a plan to massacre the entire population of the Big Ghetto. He immediately called to see the senior German officer in the region, General Schmidhuber, and advised that if it occurred he would ensure that the general was held accountable after the war and prosecuted as a war criminal. Perlasca had also heard of the rumour and protested vigorously to the Hungarian Minister of the Interior. As a result of their actions, the planed massacre never took place. Soviet troops entered parts of the city including the International Ghetto and freed the residents there. A couple of days later the Big Ghetto was also liberated.

The humanitarian activities in the Hungarian capital during the period were by no means limited to those in the diplomatic world. Many individuals, lay and religious of various persuasions, risked their lives to save their Jewish neighbours. For example the Sisters of Mercy of Szatmár gave sanctuary to twenty Jews. Their convent was located in a large tenement building. Despite the fact that the other the inhabitants were aware of what was going on, they were never betrayed. About 200 Jewish women and children were successfully hidden in the Convent of Sacré Coeur. More than 100 girls were sheltered in the Convent of the Good Shepherd. It was raided twice by the Arrow Cross but the nuns had anticipated this and relocated their charges in neighbouring houses and all survived. On the other hand, a raid on the Convent of the Sisters of the Order of Divine Love resulted in the murder of nearly all of the 150 children hiding there. Five survived by escaping through the attic.

Pastor Gábor Sztehlo was leader of the Good Shepherd organisation. He organised sanctuary for about 1,500 Jewish children and adults. With help from two other Lutheran pastors, and working closely with Frederich Born and the Red Cross, he ensured that they had food, clothing and accommodation in various institutions throughout the city that were under his control. Soviet bombardment of the city destroyed some of the property belonging to the Good Shepherd organisation so the pastor and his wife, Ilona, looked after thirty-three children in their own home until the danger had passed. In his memoirs the pastor recalled that quite a few German army officers were well aware of his activities and chose to turn a blind eye. Indeed, one major warned him to be on the look-out for a particular SS lieutenant whose total focus was on finding and killing Jews.

Captain Laszlo, a captain in the Hungarian army, was in charge of a labour company outside the city. He enrolled in excess of 1,000 Jews in the group, the majority of whom were women and children, and in this way ensured their safety. In addition he used the manpower at his disposal to assist the work of the Red Cross, delivering food to Jews in hiding in various locations. There were of course individual humanitarian gestures also, made on the spur of the moment. Twenty-year-old Rose Rosner was one of those being marched towards the Austrian border. A Hungarian soldier gave her his cross and Bible and allowed her to slip away unnoticed. He gave her directions to his parents' house where she secured sanctuary.

There were about 150,000 Jews in Budapest when the Nazis took control in March 1944. A total of approximately 120,000 survived, 95,000 in the Big and International Ghettos and the balance in hiding. While the murder of 30,000 individuals is an appalling record, the heroic efforts of the diplomats and local individuals and groups ensured that an even more obscene calamity was avoided.

When they took control of the city the Soviets arrested Wallenberg, Anger and Perlasca. While the latter was released a few days later Anger was detained for three months. Wallenberg remained a captive of the Soviets for the remainder of his life. No satisfactory explanation has ever been offered for their actions. Per Anger remained in the Swedish diplomatic service and spent much of his time trying to find out what happened to his colleague and friend Raoul Wallenberg. Monsignor Rotta, Ángel Sanz-Briz and Carlos de Liz-Texeira Branquinho continued their diplomatic careers. It is noticeable that the latter did not experience the same treatment at the hands of Portuguese officialdom as Aristides de Sousa Mendes after the war but, of course, he was not acting contrary to instructions. By that time the outcome of the conflict was becoming clearer and his government had softened its line. In addition he was acting in concert with a group of diplomats, including the Vatican representative, rather than on his own. Frederich Born of the International Red Cross was expelled from Hungary by the Soviets and resumed his career as a businessman in his native Switzerland. In the immediate aftermath of the war Carl Lutz was criticised by the Swiss government for exceeding his authority and compromising the country's long-standing position of neutrality. However, in the late 1950s the position was reviewed and his outstanding achievements were officially recognised in his homeland and elsewhere. A group who owed their survival to Giorgio Perlasca tried for many years to find him. Not surprisingly, their search was focused on Spain. It wasn't until 1987 that they located him in his native Italy and his remarkable exploits became known.

CHAPTER 2

In September 1939 the armies of the Third Reich invaded Poland. In solidarity with their ally, the British and French governments responded by declaring war on Germany. However, they did little that would be of practical assistance to the Poles in their difficulties. It was hoped that a quick settlement would emerge after this period, which was described as the 'phoney war'. At the same time, the French particularly had been aware for quite a period of time that a German invasion of their country was a possibility. Indeed, senior figures in the French military establishment believed, correctly as it transpired, that German anger over the provisions of the Treaty of Versailles, which was imposed after the First World War, could contribute to an outbreak of hostilities.

The official policy in France for many years was that as a precaution the country should prepare an appropriate defensive system. The French Minister for War for a period after the First World War was André Maginot. He secured government funding for the creation of what was to become known as the Maginot Line. Essentially, it was a series of outposts along the German French border. This left France open to attack through Belgium and Luxembourg. Part of the border there was covered by the forests in the Ardennes. These consisted of dense forestry, trees and marshy ground, to such an extent that the area was considered impenetrable and so provided a defence against attack. Each of the main outposts on the Maginot Line contained accommodation for approximately 1,000 soldiers with supporting artillery. These were approximately 9 to 15 km apart. In between these were smaller outposts, which could house a couple of hundred soldiers in each. The various outposts were linked by tunnels so that men could move from one to the other in order to assist, depending on the point of attack. This was deemed a satisfactory arrangement by the vast majority of the French military leadership although a junior officer, Charles de Gaulle, in 1934, published a book which criticised the over-reliance on a static defensive system. He foresaw that, unlike during the First World War, mobility, speed, as well as mechanised vehicles and aircraft, were likely to play a more significant role.

In the First World War the approach had been to bombard an area with heavy artillery and follow up with infantry, supported by mechanised tanks spread sparsely over a wide front. De Gaulle's different approach to warfare was reflected in the higher ranks of the German military command, most notably in the case of Heinz Guderian. His idea was that the bombardment should be followed by an attack on a narrow front, with the infantry supporting a concentration of tanks and, of course, accompanied by aircraft. This was to be done at speed, giving rise to the term *blitzkrieg*, lightning war. With memories of the First World War war still fresh, the German High Command was determined not to repeat the mistakes made then. Static warfare and the huge loss of life was to be avoided.

The attack was launched on 10 May 1940. Three German armies were deployed. In the south the Germans took a position opposite the Maginot Line, which seemed to confirm French expectations. However, this was the weakest of the three German armies and served, in the main, as a distraction. A more powerful group moved into Belgium and Holland and this had a dramatic impact on Allied thinking as they, in response, moved their best forces to defend that position. In the meantime, Field Marshal von Rundstedt, supported by Guderian and Erwin Rommel, led the third group around the top of the Maginot Line through the Ardennes. The penetration of the Ardennes, and at such great speed, was a turning point. The French Army Command had discounted such a possibility and was caught totally unawares. Very quickly the German forces headed west for the Channel coast, reaching Abbeville on 20 May. This threatened to cut off the Allied forces serving in the north and they began to fall back. Hesitation by Hitler, and a courageous defensive action by Allied forces, made possible the evacuation at Dunkirk when almost 250,000 British troops and more than 100,000 French colleagues were rescued. Notwithstanding that, the German tactics had been hugely successful. Belgium and Holland had fallen and the British had been pushed back across the Channel, leaving a lot of their armaments behind.

Exodus

The French authorities, in anticipation of a German attack, had already adopted evacuation plans which involved moving large sections of the population to the south and west away from the anticipated conflict zones. A long war of attrition is what they expected and their plans were formulated on that basis. The invasion of France, and more particularly the speed at which it occurred, brought about a great air of defeatism and panic among the population generally, and undermined these plans. In fact what became known as the *exode* began outside France as citizens of Holland, Luxembourg and Belgium began to flee towards the south. This was a repeat of the experience in the First World War when thousands of Belgians and French fled before the advancing German troops preceding French victory on the Marne quelled the panic.

The exodus spread through Northern France quite quickly. Rheims on 20 May 1940 was followed by Compiegne the following week. Private Gustave Folcher, who was a member of a French unit retreating through Northern France, observed the scene:

> What is most pitiful is to see entire families on the road, with their livestock that they force to follow them ... The wagon is driven by a woman, often in tears, but most of the time it's a kid of eight, ten or perhaps twelve years old who leads the horses. On the wagon, on which furniture, trunks, linen, the most precious things, or rather the most indispensable things, have been hastily piled up, the grandparents have also taken their place, holding in their arms a very young child, even a new-born baby.[1]

The writer Antoine de Saint-Exupéry, then flying over the area as a pilot in the French Air Force, used a striking metaphor to describe the scene below. 'Somewhere in the north of France a boot had scattered an anthill, and the ants were on the march.

Laboriously. Without panic. Without hope. Without despair. On the march as if duty bound.'[2]

In Paris rumours abounded as to what was likely to happen next. The sight of so many from other countries travelling through France away from the advancing Third Reich armies added to the uncertainty and panic. Many people in Paris and the surrounding areas began to evacuate in the second week of June. For those without cars, travel by train was the obvious option. Approximately, 20,000 individuals crowded the Gare Montparnasse and chaos ensued. The system was soon overcome so other arrangements became necessary. Rupert Downing, an Englishman living in Paris, recorded the scene as he joined the exodus on 12 June:

> There were lorries, cars, bicycles, horses, perambulators, and wheelbarrows all mixed up with pedestrians of every age, type, size and description. Some of the cars were straight from the showroom; others looked as if they had been rescued from refuse dumps. And every vehicle was laden to its capacity with anything you can think of, from an empty parrot cage to a grandfather clock. [3]

Two days later the scene in the capital had changed dramatically. 'The *grands boulevards* … as far as the eye could carry, absolutely deserted, all shops closed … and the silence!'[4] In the city itself, the population dropped from about 3 million to 700,000 in the course of early June. All in all, about 8 million people were on the move. Most were women and children as husbands were enlisted in the French forces. About three-quarters of those on the move were French. Some had no specific reason for doing so except for fear of the unknown. Others were more keenly aware of the fate which was likely to befall them if they fell into the hands of the German authorities. Many were Jews, members of families which had previously fled from persecution in the late nineteenth century in Russia, Romania and Poland or after the collapse of the Russian and Austro-Hungarian empires in 1917. Others had left Germany when the Nazi party assumed power in 1933. Tens of thousands arrived in France, though many moved on subsequently. By 1939 there were probably 25,000 German Jews in the country and these were most at risk. In addition, the vast majority of the French Jewish community – in excess of 300,000 – lived in the Paris region. Aside from Jewish people, another group seeking sanctuary were those who had reason to fear reprisals for political views they had expressed in the years leading up to the invasion.

One of these was a Scottish pastor, Donald Caskie. He was born in 1902 on the Isle of Islay and followed his father into the ministry. In 1935, while serving in the rural parish of Gretna in Scotland, he was transferred to take up the position of minister at the Scots Kirk on the Rue Bayard in Paris, a well-known place of worship. For example, during the peace negotiations after the First World War both President Wilson of the US and British Prime Minister Lloyd George had attended services there. It was also there that Eric Liddell chose to deliver a sermon one Sunday during the 1924 Olympic Games rather than compete in an event on the same day. With the German advance it was necessary for Caskie to leave. While as a clergyman he might have escaped any harassment, his sermons in recent months had been fairly explicit in condemning Nazi aggression. Furthermore, he had reason to believe that Nazi spies had taken note of his forthright views. So on Sunday 9 June he prepared to depart.

Having celebrated his last morning service, he said goodbye to his congregation, locked the kirk, and gave the keys to his friend Monsieur Gaston, the owner of the café next door. On the following morning, like thousands of others, he left Paris on foot. Some were just fleeing the conflict. Others, with more reason to be fearful, were trying to leave the country. They headed for the Atlantic ports, to the west of the country, or the Mediterranean coast to the south. In Caskie's case he hoped to reach Bordeaux, a distance of about 240 km from Paris.

It was a hazardous and difficult journey. Aside from the heat, there was very little food available other than that which could be gathered from roadside orchards and vineyards. By day there was the additional hazard of attack from above as the German air force dropped bombs and used their machine guns on the refugees below. The only possible escape was to dive into ditches once the sound of aircraft was heard. By night it was a question of sleeping wherever accommodation could be found, whether on the village green or in a barn. In the city of Tours, Caskie was lucky enough to purchase a second-hand bike, which made the travelling somewhat easier.

When he reached Bordeaux he found it to be, like Paris, rife with rumour and fear. Any available vessels had already left for the UK and indeed the first one to depart was torpedoed, with few survivors. He was advised to travel further on to Bayonne, a port on the Atlantic coast near the border with Spain. En route he was lucky enough to get a lift for part of the journey in a car driven by a Jewish man also trying to escape the country. In Bayonne, Caskie made contact with the British Consulate who secured for him a place on board the last ship destined to leave the port. By then, however, his experiences on the journey from Paris, when he met so many in need of help, and his own commitment to humanitarian work, had persuaded him that remaining in France was the right course of action for a Christian minister. He watched the last boat leave without him and then began to journey further south. A few days later he was spotted in a small village by an acquaintance from Paris, who was driving by on the way to Marseille. He was happy to accept the offer of a lift.

Vichy

By now there had been significant changes at political level. The government of France had left Paris the same day as Caskie, 10 June, and eventually settled in the spa town of Vichy, in early July. Not surprisingly there was considerable disarray regarding what course of action to follow. Eventually it became clear that majority opinion was in favour of reaching a settlement with the invading forces. Marshal Henri Phillipe Pétain, a First World War hero, became Prime Minister of France on 17 June, at the age of eighty-four. He clearly was not one given to false modesty, stating in a broadcast to the French nation, 'I am making a gift of my person to France to attenuate its misfortune,' before advising them that he had sought an armistice with the forces of the Third Reich. This was in marked contrast to the stance taken by the Belgian and Dutch authorities. Their armies surrendered to the invading forces but their governments went into exile rather than follow that with an agreed political settlement. In their negotiations the French leaders were in a very weak position and essentially had to agree with whatever was offered. In one sense the German approach was quite stringent even to the extent of the choice of meeting place, which was precisely the same location at which they had surrendered in November 1918. Many of the main features of the Treaty of Versailles reappeared on this occasion. For example, France was obliged to pay the cost of the occupation, which over the next few years amounted to more than half its national income. The size of its army was greatly reduced with a specific limit being placed on the number of officers involved, thereby depriving it of leadership. Any of its citizens who offered assistance to Germany's opponents would not enjoy the protection of the Geneva Convention.

French negotiators had been briefed by the government to seek three concessions. They were to minimise the area of France which would be occupied by the Germans, resist any attempt to take over control of the country's overseas territories, and preserve the naval fleet. In theory they were successful in all of these objectives, which may seem surprising given the weakness of their position. However, to a large extent, granting these concessions suited German interests. Hitler was anxious not to create the possibility of a French government in exile being formed and so it suited him to be seen to preserve at least a semblance of sovereignty. So, allowing the continued existence of a French government, which would encourage its citizens to co-operate with his forces and reduce the possibility of resistance, suited his purposes.

The German–French agreement was signed on 22 June. The French National Assembly met in a local casino in Vichy on 10 July and voted itself out of existence. The following day Pétain assumed full powers as Head of State. The French and German leaders met some months later in the town of Montoire in central

France. The photograph of their handshake was circulated widely throughout the country. Pétain justified his stance to the French people:

> It is with honour, and in order to maintain French unity, a unity which has lasted ten centuries, and in the framework of the constructive activity of the new European order, that today I am embarking on the path of collaboration.[5]

The perception of what was meant by the term collaboration changed over the next few years.

Once its ally France reached agreement with the German authorities, the most immediate worry for the British government was to ensure that the Third Reich was not able to use the extensive French fleet to full effect. The position arrived at in the armistice negotiations in relation to the continuance of the French Navy was not entirely clear at the time, although it seemed that the fleet was to be rendered inactive by remaining in port. Given the likelihood that Hitler would have to invade an island to complete his control over Western Europe, quite why he declined to take over the French Navy is not obvious. Some have suggested that he was of the belief that, with the collapse of France and the other Western European countries, Britain might have sought an agreement with the Third Reich, and this may have been a factor.

Churchill was keenly aware of the strategic importance of the French fleet. Under *Operation Catapult*, Admiral James Somerville sailed with a fleet of British ships to Mers-el-Kébir where a major portion of the French navy was at anchor. He offered his French counterpart the option of sailing the French ships to Britain or moving to neutral waters such as those of the US. When this was rejected Somerville, acting on Churchill's direct orders, attacked and destroyed many of the ships there. A small number managed to escape and made for Toulon. There were about 1,500 French casualties, most of them fatal. In other locations such as the port of Alexandria, French captains agreed to demobilise. Almost 200 French vessels in English ports came under the control of the British navy. Their captains had made for British ports in response to a call from de Gaulle that they do so in order to continue the conflict.

The actions at Mers-el-Kébir by a recent ally caused widespread revulsion in France and certainly made the lives of Britons on the run there, and their helpers, more difficult and risky especially in the immediate aftermath. On the other hand, it did not prompt many of the anti-Vichy population to change their stance. At the very least it displayed a resolution and ruthlessness on the part of the British to resist the Third Reich, and for many this would have been an overriding consideration.

In relation to the continued existence of a French government, the concession by Germany was not a major one and had advantages for the Nazis. The Third Reich immediately annexed Alsace and the department of Moselle in Lorraine which at various times in the past had been under German control. Italy was granted occupation of an area in the south-east including Nice, Toulon and Grenoble, as a gesture by Hitler towards the expansionist policies of his ally Mussolini. The remainder of the country was divided into two parts by a border running roughly east to west from a point on the Swiss border near Geneva to south of the city of Tours. Thence the dividing line ran due south to the Spanish border. North and west of this line was known as the occupied zone. By constructing this division the Third Reich retained direct control over the major portion of France in industrial terms, plus access to the entire Atlantic coastline and part of the border with Spain.

In a formal sense, the French government, which relocated to the town of Vichy, remained sovereign over the whole country. This created the impression that France was in control of its own affairs. If not, French resistance to the occupation would almost certainly have been greater and more forceful in the early years. In practice, the French administrative apparatus in the occupied zone took its orders from the German authorities. The southern area was controlled by the government headed by Pétain based at Vichy and, as time passed it became more responsive to the wishes and policies of the Third Reich and gradually became a 'puppet' administration. This device of retaining a French government proved to be successful in diplomatic terms. Pétain's government was recognised internationally by more than forty states. It was viewed as the legitimate government of a neutral state and a number of other countries, including the US, opened diplomatic relations with it and established embassies there.

The Public Mood

In the early years at least, the majority of French people, deeply shocked by their speedy humiliation, supported Pétain and the new arrangement. The deaths of almost 100,000 French army personnel, with almost twice as many wounded, exercised a profound influence on public opinion. These losses were similar in magnitude to those suffered by France at Verdun in the First

World War. Aside from the obvious impact of such tragic loss of life, the sense of shock was deepened by how quickly these events occurred. The battle at Verdun had lasted almost a year, whereas the German army overcame the French forces in less than two months on this occasion.

Pétain was a popular figure, revered by many for his role in the previous war. Some even believed that he was engaged in a tactical manoeuvre, reaching agreement with the Germans but at the same time planning with the British to launch a counter-offensive. In those early days Pétain was greeted very warmly by the people wherever he went. His reception on a visit to Marseille in December 1940 was described as almost religious in fervour. He and his associates cultivated an image of him as the leader of the nation, rather than a politician in charge of government.

Inevitably the vast majority of those who had left as the German army advanced on Paris returned home. The chaos in the towns and cities where they ended up was such that a return to normality seemed an attractive option. In addition, the invading forces went out of their way to behave appropriately and engender goodwill in those early months. This was supported by an extensive propaganda campaign portraying them in good light and presenting them as a force for order amidst the chaos. Aside from that, many believed Britain would have to surrender and the war would not last very long.

At the same time there were others who were sceptical of the new arrangement and were quicker to recognise the long-term reality. One of these was Jean Guéhenno, a teacher and writer living in Paris. He was a well-known left-wing commentator on social, political and cultural affairs during the inter-war years in France. Although he contributed to the underground press occasionally, he withdrew from his public role as an intellectual observer during the German occupation as a form of protest. In his view, to do otherwise would imply an acceptance of the propaganda and censorship that were features of the German occupation. His response to the experience was to record his feelings in a private diary, *Journal des années noires* (Diary of the Dark Years). In his own words 'I am going to bury myself in silence' (23 June 1940).[6] Quoting his compatriot, the poet and philosopher Charles Péguy, this was his method of resisting 'the most dangerous of invasions, the invasion that enters inside us, the invasion of the inner life, infinitely more dangerous for a people than a territorial invasion or occupation' (5 July 1940).[7]

His journal records daily life in Paris including the curfews, arrests, and executions, the shortage of food and in adequate means of heating homes during a couple of harsh winters. He also stridently comments on the activities of some of the artistic and literary community, including acquaintances and friends, who collaborated with the occupying forces by writing for publications which were by now under German editorial control. 'The man of letters is unable to live out of public view for any length of time; he would sell his soul to see his name appear ... all he quibbles about now is the size of the font or the characters that will print his name, or his place in the table of contents' (30 November 1940).[8] In his view they are assisting the occupying forces in the pretence that everything is as it was before. The diary reflects his sense of despair as to what the future might bring, particularly in the early years of the war, but from time to time he draws comfort from the approach and attitudes of ordinary people. 'I am pleased with the Parisians.

They pass by the German the way they pass dogs and cats. It seems they neither see them nor hear them' (7 September 1940).[9]

Restricted Movements

The border between the occupied and free zones was about 1,500 km long and impossible to seal completely. Usually a force of about 2,500 German soldiers guarded the line on the occupied side. On the Vichy side patrolling was less than rigorous. The Germans usually patrolled in groups of four, with the result that there were gaps between each group of sentries. So, someone with local knowledge could guide people through. Even though it was a source of inconvenience to local people, it was possible, though dangerous, to go from one zone to the other without permission. To cross the border from the occupied zone to Vichy France, a person needed a special pass, *Ausweiss,* and these were not readily granted. This created great difficulties in the ordinary day-to-day lives of people, particularly those located near the border.

The *Ausweiss* was just one of a number of important documents that French people needed following the German invasion. Everyone was required to carry a basic identity card, which recorded details such as name, nationality, place of birth, address and occupation. It also included a photograph and it was a requirement that it was stamped by the local police. So, those wishing to help fugitives needed a supply of blank documents together with the services of a discreet photographer. The stamping was achieved with the help of an understanding police officer or by obtaining a copy of the stamp. Another vital document at that time was the *carte d'alimentation*, the ration card, with its various stamps detailing entitlements. The allowances varied depending on circumstances and location. In general, the diet of the average person declined in both substance and quality to a level far below the norm. The result was that a black market flourished in all the major areas.

In the summer of 1940, while many who had joined the exodus returned, restrictions were introduced in the case of Jews, who were prohibited from going back to the occupied zone by an edict in late September. Many would have been reluctant to do so in any event. Also unlikely to return home were those who had fled from the Low Countries. So there were a considerable number of foreigners in Vichy France, usually without legal status. Many of these were living in accommodation registered with the local civilian authorities. Some were placed in internment camps, though many escaped in the confusion during the collapse of the French government and in the early days of the Vichy regime.

Early indications of the attitude Pétain and his colleagues were going to adopt to foreigners in general, and Jews in particular, came shortly after the government was formed. The measures taken against the Jews varied from those designed to make ordinary life difficult to the more sinister. An example of the former was a regulation which restricted the time of day when they could do their shopping. It also had another implication in that, as the war progressed, supplies became scarcer and limitations on when one could shop could have a practical impact. A diarist of the time,

Janet Teissier du Cros, recalls an episode when local people managed to subvert this limitation. From the early days of the conflict goods were in scarce supply so queuing outside shops became the norm. By the time an elderly Jewish woman could leave home a queue of people, including Janet, had formed. She hovered nearby but hesitated to join it:

> The moment people in the queue saw her they signed to her to join us. Secretly and rapidly, as in the game of hunt-the-slipper, she was passed up until she stood at the head of the queue. I am glad to say that not one voice was raised in protest, the policeman standing near turned his head away, and that she got her cabbage before any of us.[10]

On 17 July the Vichy government introduced regulations prohibiting individuals whose fathers were not French, from employment in the public service. This regulation was extended to various professions some months later. By early September of that year, local authorities were authorised to intern foreign-born individuals who were considered to be a danger to national security. Also, a long-standing scheme of government welfare payments to recent immigrants was in the process of being discontinued. Later that month, at their own discretion, local authorities were empowered to intern anyone aged between eighteen and fifty-five who was deemed superfluous to the economy. Alternatively, those threatened with this provision could be enrolled in forced labour groups of foreigners. These groups were assigned tasks on the construction of roads and other public works for subsistence wages.

Anti-Semitism

Specific measures targeted at Jewish people were also promulgated. In August a law prohibiting attacks on individuals in the media based on their race or religion was revoked and this resulted in a rise in anti-Semitism. Many of the 350,000 or so Jews living in France were foreign-born, having arrived there to escape persecution elsewhere. Not surprisingly a large proportion of these joined the exodus south after the invasion of France. The following month, the taking of a census of all Jews living in the occupied zone commenced. A regulation introduced in October specifically banned Jews from employment in areas of public service such as teaching and in the media generally. It is significant that this provision, which was allowed to apply throughout France, was introduced on the initiative of the Vichy government rather than at the behest of the German authorities in Paris. Guéhenno was watching these changes in his native France with sadness and was alert to the significance: 'The victor is inoculating us with his diseases' (19 October 1940).[11]

This approach was developed further in June 1941 when the range of prohibited occupations was extended and a census of Jews living in Vichy France was carried out similar to one introduced in the occupied zone during the previous year. In Vichy France about 140,000 registered themselves as Jews. When the signs were becoming ominous, it is reasonable to wonder why they did so in such numbers, probably five-sixths of the total at the time. The likelihood is that a number of factors came into play as families reached decisions as to what to do. Naive faith in the Pétain regime, fear of the consequences of disobedience and pride in their own race and religion were considerations at the time. The situation for foreigners who were also Jewish was even more perilous as local authorities were empowered from October 1940 to intern them, place them in a forced labour group, or require them to live in assigned accommodation. This was followed in 1941 with a provision that all Jews aged between eighteen and fifty-five who had moved to France after 1936 were obliged to join forced labour schemes. In Vichy a law authorising the confiscation of Jewish-owned property was introduced in July 1941.

However, it is important to bear in mind that the Vichy policy was never as extreme in its anti-Semitism as that of the Third Reich. The approach was different to some degree between the two zones. From June 1942, Jews in the occupied zone over the age of six were required to attach to their clothes a piece of yellow cloth in the shape of a star with the word *Juif* or *Juive* on it in black letters. This was one Nazi requirement that the Vichy regime declined to implement. The objective of the Vichy government was to remove Jews from positions of influence rather than kill them. Of course, there is clear evidence that the Vichy regime facilitated the Nazis in actions that led to thousands of deaths. In the early years of the war most of the initial actions against Jews in both parts of the country, such as roundups and arrests for example, were carried out by French officials. On the other hand, while the Vichy government could introduce regulations it was reliant on thousands of public servants to implement them. At local level many took a humanitarian approach to fulfilling their duties.

The Iberian Peninsula

Watching these developments with great concern were the two dictators who ruled Spain and Portugal. They differed in their attitudes to the combatants. In Spain, Francisco Franco was pro-Nazi. In the bitter Spanish Civil War, Hitler had provided practical assistance to him. Most notably German planes and pilots participated in the bombing of Guernica in April 1937 when many non-combatants were killed. Stalin, the Soviet leader, had sided with the Republican forces, providing military advisors. In Portugal, Antonio Salazar was pro-British, not least because of the longstanding alliance between Portugal and the UK. However the two men were of one view on a couple of issues. Both feared the spread of Communism. More significantly they were agreed that a neutral stance on the conflict was absolutely in the best interest of both their countries.

Because of the devastation caused by the civil war, Franco was not in a position to add greatly to the Axis forces even if he were of a mind to join the conflict. However, the Allies feared that he would permit Hitler to send his forces through Spain to attack Gibraltar. If successful there, he would have secured control of the Mediterranean. So, the primary objective of UK policy in the region was to ensure that both Spain and Portugal remained absolutely neutral.

For most of the war the British Ambassador in Madrid was Sir Samuel Hoare. He had enjoyed a varied career. Having served in the forces during the First World War he undertook some intelligence missions before embarking on a political career. Indeed, during the 1930s, he held senior cabinet positions including in both the Foreign Office and as Home Secretary for two years until 1939. An absolute loyalty to Neville Chamberlin led to his political demise and prompted some cynics to conclude that sending him to Madrid in 1940 was Churchill's way of getting rid of him. It's an unlikely scenario in view of Spain's strategic importance. In the event it proved to be a successful appointment though tensions between him and those engaged in less formal activities were inevitable. As ambassador he could not be seen to have any involvement in covert activities.

Such restrictions did not apply to Alan Hillgarth, naval attaché at the Madrid embassy. Under his original name of Hugh Evans, he joined the navy in 1914, aged fifteen, and was wounded at Gallipoli two years later. Leaving the navy in 1922 he travelled widely and concentrated on writing novels under the nom-de-plume Alan Hillgarth, which he eventually adopted as his name by deed poll in 1926. There is some evidence that during his travels he engaged in informal intelligence gathering for the authorities in London. In 1929 he married and the couple settled in Majorca the following year. In 1932 he was appointed to the honorary position of British Vice-Consul there. The outbreak of the Spanish Civil War in July 1936 moved his role onto a more formal level as he began to send secret reports on the situation to the Foreign Office in London.

When the island became a battleground between Franco's forces (aided by the Italian Air Force and Navy sent by Mussolini) and the Republicans, Hillgarth played a humanitarian role and made a favourable impression on both the Spanish authorities and the UK government. As such he was an obvious choice for the position in Madrid when the Second World War broke out and so he was recalled to active service in the navy. The part he played for the next few years was greatly strengthened by his friendship with

Churchill and they regularly communicated with each other as the situation developed. The Prime Minister considered him to be a 'very good man' with 'a profound knowledge of Spanish affairs'. Hillgarth's role during the next few years was two-fold. He used considerable sums of money supplied by the UK government to bribe senior Spanish military figures whom he relied upon to use their influence in ensuring that Franco remained neutral in the conflict. The conduit for these payments was Juan March, a millionaire Spanish businessman with good links to Franco's regime. Hillgarth's other function was to establish a series of informants and agents throughout the region. On his arrival he found that British Secret Service capacity in the region was weak and so he addressed that issue immediately with the help of his assistant Salvador Gomez-Beare, a native of Gibraltar.

Hitler and Franco met during October 1940 at Hendaye in France near its border with Spain. Hitler's objective was to get Franco to join the Axis Powers but day-long negotiations proved fruitless as the Spanish dictator was determined that Spain should remain neutral. Presumably the bribery campaign by Hillgarth and March played a part in this, though how great is not clear. Another influence on Franco at the time was Salazar. His Portuguese counterpart had supported him during the civil war and Franco greatly valued his expertise. During the 1920s Salazar had served as professor of law at Coimbra University. In 1928 he was appointed Minister for Finance and set about reforming the country's economy. Famous for his work ethic, and intellectually gifted, he achieved a lot of success in the economic area and was eventually appointed Prime Minister in 1932. As head of a right-wing government, he introduced a new constitution and gradually assumed a dominant position in the business of government. Unlike Spain, the country was not of any great strategic importance so maintaining a neutral position resulted in less pressure from the combatant governments.

The Pastor

On arrival in Marseille, Caskie found the city was in even more disarray than Paris and the other areas he visited. It had become a destination for those seeking to leave the country. There were many civilians, foreigners in general and Jews irrespective of nationality, who were becoming increasingly aware of their precarious position because of the repressive legislation being enacted by the Vichy regime. There were others who because of their known political orientation had reasons to be fearful of the advance of the Third Reich. In addition there were many ordinary British civilians who were stranded in the city. Another big group seeking to leave the city were servicemen. These included British soldiers and airmen who had not managed to participate in the evacuation at Dunkirk. There were also large numbers of merchant seamen whose ships had been torpedoed. As well as members of the British Armed Forces there were also French, Belgian, Dutch and Polish troops seeking to escape to safety, many with the intention of rejoining the conflict. Large numbers of them were in very poor condition, suffering from hunger and tired after trekking south from Dunkirk. Some had been wounded and were in need of medical treatment.

A clergyman colleague had found lodgings for Caskie and when he became established he began to assess how he might come to the assistance of those in need. A visit to the local police station provided an answer for him. They suggested he should take over the British Seamen's Mission, which had fallen into disrepair, but cautioned him that if any assistance were offered to British soldiers he would be interned immediately. So, when the building reopened a notice was pinned on the door: 'Now open to British civilians and seamen only.' The numbers arriving at the mission seeking assistance grew very quickly and they included many in the categories he was prohibited from helping.

It was some time before Caskie realised why the influx of army and navy personnel was so great. It seems that British Secret Service members, operating in the north of France, when they came upon members of the British Armed Forces seeking to get out of the country, recommended that they make for Marseille and the seamen's mission run by Reverend Caskie. Hiding places were needed and a few imaginative solutions were found within the building. These included under the roof, in between the joists supporting the floorboards, and in spaces behind cupboards. Clothes were also an issue as many of those arriving were still wearing some parts of their uniforms. Feeding those who arrived was an additional problem as many had no ration books. Securing papers that would identify the holder as a civilian was yet another major concern.

In the course of the first few weeks there, Caskie met a fellow clergyman, Reverend Heuzy, who was anxious to help. He began to organise a collection of second-hand clothes and indeed some of his congregation were willing to offer accommodation in their own homes. Clothes were also supplied by Sister Brigid, a member of a locally based congregation of Irish nuns. This caused Caskie to wonder: 'Just how this healthily happy lady and colleagues interpret the neutrality of the Irish Republic is a mystery that I would not care to try to elucidate.'[12] On the other hand disposing of the uniforms many were wearing when they arrived at the mission also proved a challenge. Parcelling them up into small packages, some of those living in the mission would go for a walk after dark and, as they strolled along the old harbour, drop them into the sea.

Crucial assistance was also forthcoming from the staff of the American consulate. At this time the US had not entered the war so they, as representatives of a neutral country, were empowered to act on behalf of British citizens. They took a very flexible approach to this role in their dealings with Caskie, and were willing to supply resources and papers that identified the holders as American citizens. They supplied false documents to significant numbers of individuals. Financial resources also began to reach Caskie from British ex-pats living along the Riviera. A sum of 100,000 francs was made available in early January 1941 by the British government to the US consulate in Marseille for the use of Reverend Caskie. He was also in contact with British secret service agents in the region and, through them, as armed forces personnel arrived, he was able to send word via Lisbon to families awaiting news at home.

It seems fairly clear that the local Vichy police had strong suspicions of Caskie's operation. Regular early-morning raids were carried out and, while there were some narrow escapes, nothing incriminating was found. Their suspicions would have been obvious to Caskie and this, together with the increasing numbers, meant that his overriding concern was to find some way to move those in danger of arrest out of the country. Aside from that, having established control in the north, the Gestapo were able to send more plain-clothes personnel into Vichy-controlled France. So, the risks were becoming greater.

Becoming Organised

Already in existence in late 1940 were the beginnings of an escape line operated by British Army officers Charles Murchie, Harry Clayton and Ian Garrow. Murchie and Clayton had found it necessary to leave for Spain early in April 1941 as the authorities were becoming aware of their activities. Captain Ian Garrow, a South African of Scottish descent, and a member of the Seaforth Highlanders, had led his men towards Dunkirk but did not get there in time to participate in the evacuation. From there, under his leadership and with help from locals along the way, the group arrived at the Spanish border near Perpignan. His men crossed to relative safety but he decided to stay to see what he could do to help others.

On arrival in Marseille he made himself known to Caskie and then proceeded to recruit local guides who were willing, for a fee, to guide refugees across the Pyrenees into Spain. This was a difficult process and raised the question of who to trust. Most likely to help, and with detailed knowledge of the terrain, were the Basque nationalists. Another possible group that might offer support without hesitation were those, Basques and others, who had fought against Franco in the civil war. However the instruction from London was not to do anything that would compromise Spanish neutrality and so working with these groups, who traditionally opposed Franco, was not recommended. In such circumstances Garrow was obliged, initially at least, to rely on mercenaries who might not be the most trustworthy. His fear was that they were available to the highest bidder. Passing on information was a far less risky occupation than guiding people across the Pyrenees. The danger was that they would sell information to the security authorities if sufficient inducement was offered in return.

Soon after Garrow started he was joined in the organisation by Jimmy Langley, a member of the Coldstream Guards who had defended Dunkirk in order to facilitate the evacuation. His location was bombed, which resulted in him being severely wounded and, in due course, captured. A British Army surgeon, Philip Newman, also in captivity, assessed his case and offered a grim choice: 'Dead in two days from gangrene, or life without an arm.' The arm was amputated. He was then moved to a hospital in Lille where he met, for the first time, Airey Neave, with whom he was destined to work closely later in the conflict.

When sufficiently recovered, Langley escaped from the hospital, which was only lightly guarded. A member of the cleaning staff, Madame Caron, had supplied him with the details of a house near the hospital where he could safely stay overnight before being directed onwards by the family living there. He subsequently stayed with the local priest in the village of Ascq about 10 km from Lille for ten days before a guide came to help him on his onward journey. Like so many others, his destination was Marseille, where he gave himself up to the authorities as a prisoner of war, on arrival there in November 1940, and was interned in Fort St Jean. Many arriving in the city were advised that this was a safe place to go.

While the Vichy government had agreed, as part of the armistice arrangement, to prevent British Army personnel from returning home they otherwise treated them reasonably well. Officers like Langley, interned in Fort St Jean, were allowed out into the city of Marseille on a promise not to try to escape. They were obliged to attend for roll-call on Monday mornings only, when rations for the week were handed out. Otherwise they were free to move around the locality and indeed stay in local hotels. Many availed themselves of this arrangement to seek a way of escaping from the area but, by then, getting out of the locality was very difficult. On one day trip out of the camp, Langley decided not to return and volunteered to help Garrow. His assistance in the initial stages was crucial, but in March 1941 he was allowed return home on medical grounds. By that time local civilians were becoming active in helping Garrow and Caskie.

Elisabeth Wolpert was born in Konigsberg, then part of Germany, in 1910, and raised in Berlin. Her father, a Latvian Jew, was a successful businessman. Her mother, also of the Jewish faith, was wealthy in her own right. In her twenties Elisabeth became a Communist Party activist, which resulted in her coming to the attention of the Gestapo. In the mid-1930s, she left the movement and moved to France where she began a relationship with Peter Haden-Guest, the son of a British MP. Their son Anthony was born in 1937 but the relationship was of short duration. When France was invaded she and her son moved to live with friends in Brittany. For a period Elisabeth Haden-Guest passed herself off as an American citizen but eventually her real identity became known and she was interned. However she managed to escape and headed towards the south of France with her three-year-old son and eventually arrived in Marseille.

On reaching the city she quickly identified those who were helping British soldiers on the run and she joined in the work. She filled the role of bringing those who were on the run to safe houses. In particular, she established good contacts with brothel owners who provided safe accommodation for those whom Garrow was helping to journey on to Spain.

The journey to Marseille, in very trying circumstances, had affected her son Anthony's health and she took him to a

Dr Rodocanachi. Over the course of a few visits she sensed that the doctor's sympathies were with the Allies. Taking a chance, she explained that she was working with an escape line, recruited him and introduced him to Ian Garrow.

Dr Georges Rodocanachi was born in Liverpool in 1876 to Greek parents. They moved to Marseille and he received his education there, qualifying as a doctor in 1903. When the First World War started, he took out French citizenship in order to enlist. He participated in several campaigns, winning seven citations in all. These included the Legion d'Honneur which was pinned on him by Marshal Pétain. His wife Fanny was also of Greek parentage and spent her childhood in London. Both had strong British sympathies and Georges became so disgusted at the actions of the Vichy regime that he ended his practice of always wearing the Legion d'Honneur ribbon.

The family lived in a large first-floor apartment on the Rue Roux de Brignoles. While as a prominent Jewish family they would have been monitored by the Vichy police, and even more acutely by the Gestapo when they reached Marseille, their accommodation had certain advantages as a location for clandestine activities. A common design of apartments in those days was to include internal shafts down through the building. These were open at the top to allow fresh air and daylight in, and the windows of some rooms in the Rodocanachis' apartment opened into these shafts rather than out onto the street. This was useful in the sense that a nosy neighbour might discern from the usage of toilets that there were additional people staying in the accommodation. Other windows opened into an internal courtyard but could be observed by occupants of neighbouring apartments. As a result of this design, and the fact that the ground-floor flat was occupied by their niece Helen, they were assured of large amount of privacy. The doctor's waiting room and surgery was also in the building, which meant that people coming and going in numbers and at unusual hours of the day or night was the norm. There were only three people living in the apartment: the doctor and his wife and their faithful and discreet servant, Seraphine. Despite many warnings as to the risks that would arise from her involvement with the escape line, she decided to stay. She soon became very adept at sussing out visitors and sensing danger. In addition, their only son Kostia was an adult living abroad and so was not at risk.

Initially the apartment offered a haven to those living at the seamen's mission, and internees on day release, where they could come, talk freely in English without arousing suspicion and garner information by listening to the BBC radio service. In due course, they began to house some of those on the run including Ian Garrow. Dr Rodocanachi played another more formal and public role that was helpful to allied personnel. When the Vichy regime was formed, a repatriation board was set up to consider the cases of POWs. While Vichy France undertook to ensure that those captured and interned would not be allowed to return home, an exception was made in the case of medical necessity. Such cases were considered by the repatriation board, and the American consul in Marseille had appointed Dr Rodocanachi as the US representative. With the help of some medical colleagues he stretched the interpretation of medical necessity to the limit and some who should have remained in captivity were thus allowed to return home.

Another important recruit was Louis Nouveau who lived, with his wife Reneé, in some luxury in a fifth-floor apartment at the Quai Rive Neuve, opposite the Fort St Jean. Their only son,

Jean-Pierre, had gone to England to join De Gaulle's Free French forces. In March 1941, assisted by Garrow, he had crossed into Spain and thence to London. The Nouveaus were acutely aware of the distress of Britons whom they saw entering and leaving the prison. Louis was a stockbroker and merchant banker who was well connected with wealthy people in the area. He had extensive business contacts in Britain and made no secret of where his sympathies lay. Indeed, even in his mode of dress he could be mistaken for a typical financier of the City of London.

Bruce Dowding was born in Australia in 1914. He was in France working as a teacher in 1939 when he decided to enlist in the British Army. In May 1940 he was captured by the German forces near Dunkirk and placed in a POW camp. Subsequently he managed to escape and, having made his way south, he reached Marseille in December 1940 and quickly joined those who were working with Garrow and Caskie.

Born in Istanbul in 1916, Mario Prassinos and his family moved to France in the early 1920s. He enlisted in the French army in 1940 and gave distinguished service for which he was awarded the Croix de Guerre. He joined the Marseille escape line soon after the fall of France.

Nancy Wake was a beautiful young woman, born in New Zealand and raised in Australia, who began a world tour in her early twenties, supporting herself by taking on jobs as a freelance journalist. At the age of twenty-three she met Henri Fiocca, a very wealthy Marseille industrialist, at a party in Cannes. They became engaged in 1939 and married later that year, settling down in a huge luxury apartment overlooking Marseille. On a trip to England she decided that, with the conflict coming, she should offer her services to the British war effort; however, she was rebuffed. Later in 1939 her husband Henri was called up to the French army where he gave active service. Following the fall of France he returned home to Marseille. He resumed his business life while she used some of his wealth to provide food and other necessities to neighbours and friends. Other than that, life seemed destined to proceed as normal. In October 1940 she had arranged to meet Henri for drinks at the Hotel du Louvre but he was delayed. Sitting unaccompanied at the other end of the bar was a young man and she became a bit curious. It turned out that he was a British Army officer, interned in Fort St Jean who was out on parole for the day. She and her husband, who had arrived by this time, invited him and some of his colleagues to dinner the next day. This led to a pattern developing whereby every day four or five British officers would arrive at the flat to be fed and provided with cigarettes and necessities of life.

One day the group included Ian Garrow and, shortly afterwards, Nancy and her husband became involved in supporting the escape line with large financial contributions and in other ways. Nancy's first role was to carry messages from place to place and this subsequently developed into leading groups of refugees to safe accommodation and towards the border with Spain. In addition, in order to avoid attracting attention, they bought an apartment in Marseille so that she could accommodate refugees there. When they got married her husband had bought her a chalet in the Alpine resort of Névache and this was also used for the same purposes.

Communications were difficult at that time. Telephone calls and letters were often intercepted so escape lines and Resistance groups needed to transmit messages directly by word of mouth. Women were less likely to be challenged and searched. Also, a young woman escorting a male fugitive could pass as a couple of lovers whereas two men were more likely to attract attention.

Easily the most unusual of the activists in the group at this time was a woman of about sixty years of age named Marie Louise Dissart, who was known in the group as Françoise. She lived in Toulouse near the police headquarters. Originally an employee of the city council, by the time the war broke she had opened a ladies' clothes shop, The Modern Mannequin, in Toulouse. She was unmarried and her main interests in life were her nephew, who was in a prisoner of war camp in Germany, and a formidable pet cat. Invariably she dressed in old-fashioned clothes, paid little attention to her appearance, smoked incessantly and consumed endless cups of black coffee. Her hatred of Germans was deep-seated and regularly expressed. After the fall of France she operated an escape line independently until, becoming aware of the group in Marseille, she joined in their efforts. Like Nancy Wake she provided accommodation to those on the run and helped lead them on their journeys to safety. Her clearly expressed opposition to the Third Reich and the Vichy regime led to her coming to the attention of the security forces. A Vichy police report dismissed the possibility that she was involved in any unauthorised activity. They mistook her eccentricity for simple-mindedness, describing her as not being in full possession of her mental faculties. This proved to be a grave error of judgement as she was a clever, committed and indomitable woman who outwitted them, and subsequently the Gestapo, until the Liberation.

So, with the help of these and other local sympathisers, Caskie and Garrow now had an efficient escape line in operation.

Aside from the seamen's mission, safe accommodation had to be found in the general locality where fugitives could say until arrangements had been made to evacuate them to Spain. The accommodation available ranged from the very humble to the luxurious. Included in the latter category was the Nouveaus' apartment. Aside from the nature of the accommodation, there was the added advantage there of an extensive library. Among his collection Nouveau had seventy volumes of the works of Voltaire. In volume forty-four, writing in the margins of separate pages, he began to record details of those who were hidden in the apartment by himself and his wife. In the period between May 1941 and November 1942 the total number of guests exceeded 150. The first guest was a Sergeant Philip Herbert, who came to stay with them in May 1941. He and some colleagues had crash-landed in a Wellington aeroplane, having run out of fuel over the Mediterranean. They drifted for a more than a week on an inflated dinghy before being picked up by a French vessel. They were brought to Marseille and arrested. Herbert managed to escape and reached the seamen's mission where Caskie put him in touch with Louis Nouveau. He moved in, and stayed for almost two weeks before he was evacuated.

Among the men awaiting evacuation and accommodated in the mission or elsewhere, raising expectations could lead to problems. Caskie quickly learned that giving advance notice as to who was to join the next escape run caused complications among the men, both those due to go and the disappointed. So he adopted a fairly straightforward approach. All were advised to be ready to leave at short notice. Having decided who was listed for the next escape, Caskie woke the men involved at midnight. They gathered all they needed for the journey and he ensured that none of them was carrying anything that would compromise the mission or the escape route. A prayer was offered by the group and they then departed with a guide around 2 a.m. About two dozen men were sent each week on the start of their journey to freedom. The duration of the journey varied depending on the fitness of those being escorted. Even among the army personnel this could be an issue, as a lack of adequate food in their journeys through France had led to many of them being somewhat debilitated. Generally speaking the journey took five to seven hours with a ten-minute break for a rest allowed by the guide every two hours.

The Belgian

In April 1941 a ship was sent out from England destined for the French port of Collioure, which is on the Mediterranean coast of France just south of Perpignan and close to the Spanish border. On board were six members of the British Secret Service and the objective was to land them on French soil. In addition, twelve Polish airmen, who had been hidden by the French Resistance, were to be picked up and returned to Britain. All did not go according to plan as the Polish airmen were not at the designated point in time. While awaiting their arrival the group who had gone ashore to try to locate them were arrested by the French authorities. One of these was using the name Pat O'Leary.

In reality O'Leary was a Belgian army doctor whose real name was Albert Marie Guérisse. When his own country was invaded, he made his way to Britain and enlisted in the armed services. Following the arrest on the French coast he was questioned by

French and Italian naval officers. In his fluent French he claimed that he and his colleagues were just fishermen attempting to reach Spain as a way of joining de Gaulle's Free French forces. While they didn't accept his story they failed to uncover his true identity. He was placed in the naval prison at Toulon. On further questioning he adopted the tactic of claiming to be French Canadian and sought rights as a prisoner of war.

In due course he, with two of his colleagues from the original six, was moved to St Hippolyte du Fort in Nîmes. This building was more in the nature of a barracks than a prison and crucially it bordered on a busy main street. Guards paraded all night both inside and outside the building. Soon after his arrival O'Leary became involved in the escape committee. It successfully organised a few individual escapes before it was O'Leary's turn to make an attempt to leave.

Contact already been made with a well-disposed prison guard by the name of Maurice Dufour. Members of the escape committee had identified a possibility in that there was a locked and disused storeroom with a barred window overlooking the street. Outside there was a path, which was routinely patrolled by a sentry. One of the prisoners forged a key that made access to the room possible. Every evening, for a week, two men slipped into the room and locked themselves inside, with colleagues outside keeping watch. They picked out what seemed to be the weakest bar in the window and began to work at it with a hacksaw, which had been smuggled in by Dufour. They stopped when the sentry's patrol came nearby, and in order to mask the sawing sound they smeared the hacksaw with margarine. Eventually the bar was virtually cut through.

The plan was for Pat to make an exit the next day at noon so he accessed the room shortly beforehand. At precisely 11.55 a.m.

the approximately 200 men, who were forming a queue in the courtyard for lunch, set about making a mass escape in order to distract the guards. Hearing the commotion, the guard patrolling outside the room where Pat was hiding ran towards the main entrance of the prison. Pat broke the window bar and dropped to the ground outside, but the guard heard him and started shouting. He alerted some of his colleagues and the chase began. As the day was very hot many front doors were open and O'Leary chose to run into one house. It turned out to be an old people's home run by an order of nuns. Once they Knew who he was the Mother Superior was called and she took him up into a storeroom in the attic, where he hid in a large trunk full of old clothes.

The guards arrived quickly afterwards and she explained that somebody had run in the front door but also ran through the building and out the back. 'In the sight of God, there is no Englishman here.' Strictly speaking this was of course true but perhaps she didn't know that. In any event, having left some guards around the building the search party moved on. After about half-an-hour she brought him down from the attic through to the kitchen and down into the cellar. There was a vineyard at the back of the house and this was connected to the cellar by way of a tunnel to facilitate work at harvest time. She led him through there, out into the vineyard, and soon he was in open country and free. The advice given to him in prison was that, if the escape proved successful, he should make for Marseille and seek out a man called Ian Garrow. From there he would be helped to return to England so as to resume his duties.

By this time Garrow was living with the Rodocanachi family in their apartment on the Roux de Brignoles. For him the arrival of O'Leary was an important development. He brought new skills to the organisation in his ability to speak the language fluently and his training in undercover work. Before long it became clear that he also possessed exceptional leadership skills. His arrival was timely as the organisation was facing increasing challenges. The number of Gestapo personnel operating undercover in the Vichy area of France had increased greatly. Also the Spanish authorities had taken steps to improve security on their border with a view to refusing entry to those seeking to use the country as a means of escape. To make use of O'Leary's skills, Garrow had to persuade him to stay in Marseille rather than return to Britain. O'Leary agreed to do so but only if this was cleared by the British Secret Service in London. Through a Frenchman who operated a clandestine radio transmitter, he sent a message for the consideration of Claude Dansey, Deputy Director of MI6, who had responsibility for espionage. A coded message was included by means of which a response could be issued. By this time Pat O'Leary was living with Garrow in the Rodocanachis' apartment.

Every night at 9 p.m. the BBC broadcast thirty minutes of news under the title '*Les Francais parlent aux Francais*' ('The French speak to the French'). Listening to the BBC was a risk as it was declared an offence that could lead to six months in prison. Yet for many in France doing so was a daily event. It became something of a community activity as not every household possessed a radio and people gathered to hear the broadcast. It usually included a five-minute insertion by the Free French of de Gaulle, which contributed greatly to his emergence as a rallying figure for opposition to the German occupation and the Vichy regime. The programme was also used to transmit coded messages of particular significance to British agents and Allied supporters in France. So each night Garrow and O'Leary listened to the BBC broadcast. After some weeks, the seemingly innocent announcement 'Adolphe must stay' came through, which in fact meant O'Leary's instructions were to remain in Marseille and work with Caskie, Garrow and their colleagues.

O'Leary immediately set about expanding the escape line and increasing the number of safe houses that could be used. His greater facility in French allowed him to move into the surrounding countryside with ease, which was not a possibility that was open to Garrow. He also brought to the group a keen awareness of the need for security. There was always a danger that the organisation would be penetrated. In terms of security the mission itself was an obvious concern, particularly as, there were now Gestapo plain-clothes agents in the area. A Vichy detective, going by the name 'Frankie' and claiming to be sympathetic to the cause, began to visit the mission. Given his background Caskie was slow to completely trust him although he seemed genuine enough. However his denunciations of the Nazis were so vehement as to arouse suspicions. When a recent arrival, perhaps being unaware of the need for security, introduced himself to the detective as a member of the Cameron Highlanders, the attitude changed. 'Frankie' arrested the soldier immediately and he was interned. Three weeks later, 'Frankie's' body was found in a backstreet riddled with bullets. In Caskie's mind the obvious suspects for the murder were either British Secret Service personnel or members of the French Resistance, which was growing in strength locally. It is a sign of the conflicting loyalties pertaining at the time that he also allowed for the possibility that Vichy colleagues of 'Frankie', who were in sympathy with what the escape line was doing, carried out the assassination.

Initially the main focus of the escape line organisers was on helping those British Army personnel who had not managed to escape at Dunkirk. There were about 50,000 individuals in that category. The majority were captured by the Germans in mid-1940. Of course significant numbers of these subsequently escaped. Others were never captured at all. There is a distinction between these different categories. Evaders were those who were never captured by the authorities. Escapees, on the other hand, had at some stage been under arrest or incarcerated. Under the Geneva Convention escapees, if subsequently arrested in a neutral country such as Spain, were entitled to repatriation whereas evaders were likely to be interned for the duration of the war. In practice, with the passage of time, this distinction became somewhat blurred. As part of their training aircraft crew, for example, were told to always claim to be escapees and to have a cover story ready to back that up.

The speed of the German invasion of France meant that the Germans were not as organised as they might otherwise have been. This allowed many members of the British forces still there after Dunkirk to evade them and the fine summer weather that year facilitated movement south through France. Of course, they did not have money to buy food, pay for lodging or travel. In addition, they needed to get rid of their uniforms and acquire civilian clothes. Some had been wounded but seeking medical assistance might expose them. An additional handicap was very few had any knowledge of the language. In the course of late 1941 the numbers of evaders and escapees altered somewhat as RAF raids over Germany and occupied France increased and the need then was to come to the assistance of aircrews that had been shot down.

Developing the Line

There were two significant challenges facing the escape line in Marseille as time passed. One was to extend its operation northwards into occupied France and the other was to ensure that the route through Spain to safety was relatively secure. The Franco government, although neutral, was anxious to present a supportive image towards the Axis authorities. Their security personnel were making serious efforts to stop the flow of refugees. In addition, German agents were facilitated by the authorities in undercover operations in Spain. If captured in Spain, a detainee faced either deportation back to France or internment in a concentration camp at Miranda del Ebro where conditions were appalling.

In London, Claude Dansey of MI6 and the security authorities generally were becoming aware of these difficulties and the need to respond. They also, for their own purposes, had identified a requirement to establish an effective way of finding out what was happening in France. While Dansey and MI6 retained overall control, a new branch of Military Intelligence, MI9, had been set up in December 1939 under the leadership of Major Norman Crockett. Its main function was to facilitate the return of service personnel to England so as to enable them to rejoin the forces. As part of that effort, in mid-July 1940, Donald Darling was assigned responsibility for developing a system of safe passage through Spain for escapees and evaders and a channel of communication with sources in France. He was an astute choice given his familiarity with the area; in the mid-1930s he worked as a travel courier in both France and Spain and had subsequently maintained friendships there. In the pre-war period he had occasionally undertaken some work for the intelligence services and so, following recruitment and briefing, he undertook the task. Initially he had hoped to base himself in Madrid but Ambassador Hoare's nervousness that anything might emerge to upset relations with Spain rendered that impossible. So he settled in the less sensitive location of Lisbon, where he took up the position of vice consul in the embassy there. Using that as a pretext he began to work with the help of some pre-war acquaintances and Michael Creswell, a diplomat stationed at Madrid, who didn't share the ambassador's extreme caution. Darling worked with various escape lines for the next few years, from his Lisbon office until 1942, and subsequently from Gibraltar, where he was assigned the nominal post of assistant to the governor.

On appointment Darling was briefed to expect that something between sixty and a hundred airmen would need his assistance. This proved to be a gross underestimate. Many escapees were assisted to return to Britain via Lisbon or Gibraltar by means of various subterfuges. Darling's early channel of communication between the Iberian Peninsula and the South of France was people who had legitimate reasons for travelling to and fro, most particularly Marge Holts, the wife of a Norwegian businessman, and the millionaire Nubar Gulbenkian. In this way he was able to garner a lot of information that was very valuable to the Secret Service in London in their ongoing operations.

In the case of those incarcerated at Miranda del Ebro, efforts were made by the various diplomatic services and the International Red Cross to come to their assistance. Food and the other necessities of life were delivered to supplement the meagre rations supplied by the authorities. In the case of UK citizens, their diplomats brought pressure to bear to secure their early release, particularly in the case of members of the services. A doctor who had been recruited to the staff of the British Embassy by Alan Hillgarth also played a part for a period. Eduardo Martinez Alonso had grown up in Liverpool where his father was in the Uruguayan diplomatic service. He called regularly to the concentration camp with his assistant, Nurse Carmen Zafra, to attend to the medical needs of the inmates. The merest hint that a prisoner had a serious illness, especially if it was a contagious one or could be described loosely as such, ensured permission was granted quickly for him to be removed to a hospital or nursing home. Dr Francisco Luque, director of the Red Cross hospital in Madrid, authorised the provision of ambulances to move the 'patients'. Subsequently Dr Martinez Alonso certified that they had died while in reality they had been supplied with alternative papers prepared in the Madrid embassy and smuggled home to rejoin the war effort. There were plenty of German agents and informers in Spain, and indeed Portugal, during the war years. Eventually word reached Hillgarth that the doctor's role was attracting suspicion so he arranged for him to leave. In January 1942 he was driven to Lisbon and some days later flown to Bristol where he secured employment in a local hospital. After the war he returned to Madrid.

As regards those released from the camp, and others who crossed into Spain without being arrested by the authorities, the task of securing their safe return home fell, in the main, to Michael Creswell. Some were transferred onto ships on the north-western coast of Spain. The family home of Dr Martinez Alonso was at Redondela on the Bay of Vigo in Galicia. His brother lived there and he looked after refugees until the opportunity arose to link up with British ships. They were rowed out to ships in the bay by local fishermen, most frequently members of the Otero family. Others made their way home via Lisbon but delays in securing clearance were frequent. So, the most direct and speedy way to get service personnel home was across Spain and into Gibraltar. Creswell, with assistance from Britons living in the area and some locals, established a number of safe houses in Madrid where he could lodge refugees until the time was opportune to move them on. This usually involved providing them with false papers, clothing and, in some cases, medical treatment.

Given the number of German agents in Spain, many of them located in Madrid, the operation was fraught with danger. An important role in the process was played by Margaret Kearney Taylor. She was born in England but of Irish descent. Margaret, who lived in Madrid most of her adult life, always emphasised her Irish background. In 1931 she opened the Embassy Tea Rooms on Paseo de la Castellana in Madrid. It was a classic English-style venue, which quickly became a fashionable gathering place for members of the aristocratic families and other prominent citizens. Located in the embassy district of the city, it was patronised by diplomats of various nationalities. The author and journalist Jimmy Burns grew up in Madrid, where his father Tom was employed as press attaché, and he met her in the tearooms regularly:

I always remember this quite small delicately framed lady ... with very Celtic bluish eyes. You stepped into the Embassy on Castellana and you were in a completely different world. This eccentric woman presided over this almost theatrical scene. [13]

Margerita, as she was known, closed the premises during the civil war but reopened in 1939 and patrons returned. One of the political figures who regularly ate there was Ramón Serrano Suñer, Franco's brother-in law. He served as Foreign Minister and was the most pro-Nazi voice in the regime. With a distinguished clientele drawn from the upper echelons of Madrid society the Embassy Tea Rooms was an unlikely safe house but, precisely for that reason, an ideal one. People of all nationalities frequented the premises. British faces were no more unusual than others. So, Creswell was able to direct his charges in there and no one noticed that they managed to slip upstairs to Margareta's apartment, where they remained until it was time to head for Gibraltar. Her friendship with so many prominent citizens and her 'eccentricity' protected her from suspicion.

Another of Creswell's helpers there was an Irishman, Walter Starkie, a member of a quite distinguished family. His father served as Resident Commissioner of National Education in Ireland in the final years of British rule. From the turn of the century until 1920 he was one of the most influential educationalists in the country. Walter was appointed Professor of Spanish in Trinity College Dublin in 1926 and served there until the start of the war. An appointment as British Council representative in Madrid proved attractive to him as a lover of Spain. In addition, the warmer climate was helpful in dealing with his asthmatic condition. From the British government's point of view, appointing a Catholic to serve in Spain had clear advantages. Aside from his love of the country, his right-wing views were supportive of Franco and this ensured that he was popular with the regime and, as a result, able to operate freely. Crossing from Spain into Gibraltar was relatively easy. Large numbers of Spaniards did it on a daily basis on their way to work so checks were not very robust. In any event, the Spanish authorities were not disposed to make the practice of UK nationals accessing the area an issue, especially when the tide in the conflict began to turn in favour of the Allies.

While Darling was getting established in Lisbon, and Creswell was devising means of moving escapees through Spain, O'Leary was making progress in expanding the escape line. In many ways Marseille was an ideal base from which to operate. The exodus from the north to the city meant that it was full of strangers described by one writer as 'people without a country'. Paris had 'melted' into Marseille. So, a huge proportion of the residents were new and not known to the security services. Moreover, the local police force was noted for not being totally committed to implementing in full the instructions emanating from the Vichy government.

For O'Leary and his colleagues, securing sufficient financial resources was an ongoing problem. Financially supporting those who were hiding evaders was costly. While hiding in these houses they had to be fed and the majority of the families hosting them would not have had the resources to meet the extra expense. As those on the run did not have ration cards, food had to be bought on the black market, very often at hugely inflated prices. Travelling was also expensive as refugees were advised to occupy first-class carriages on trains where they were less likely to be questioned. On occasion hiring a car became necessary, even though it was expensive. Acquiring fuel on the black market was also costly. Guides in many cases had to be paid for the work. Bribing officials in order to secure their assistance was an additional cost. It was obvious to O'Leary that individual contributions would never generate sufficient resources to meet growing demands. He became aware of a Mr Gosling, living in the locality, who had been manager of a local enterprise, which was owned by British company M & P Coates. Louis Nouveau was dispatched to open negotiations with him. The plan was to secure funding from him, which would be replicated by payments from the British government to M & P Coates in London. It took six weeks of negotiation, involving sending a friendly businessman to the British Embassy in Madrid to explain the plan, before agreement was reached. Eventually this channel proved successful and the necessary money began to reach O'Leary. The initial amount paid through this mechanism was a million francs. Additional money from British government sources began to be channelled through Donald Darling in late 1940.

In deciding which guides to work with, O'Leary did not feel constrained by any fear of upsetting Spanish sensibilities. He tended to have more faith in the politically motivated than the pure mercenaries. One of those he co-operated with throughout was Francois Ponzan Vidal, a young teacher and anarchist. He had become involved in left-wing politics in the 1930s. In the Spanish Civil War he fought on the Republican side as a guerrilla behind enemy lines. Franco's victory prompted him to leave Spain and he moved to live over the border in France. He used this as a base to set up an antifascist group operating in the Pyrenees. His motivation for helping on escape lines was not a particular loyalty to the Allies but rather a means to gather resources to continue the fight against Franco. This stance meant that he had many well-placed people who were favourably disposed to his activities. Indeed, the fact that so many Spanish republicans had moved to live in the south of France after the

Spanish Civil War was of great assistance generally to those assisting fugitives and to the various Resistance groups.

Another aspect of O'Leary's work was recruiting additional helpers in various parts of France. As always this was a risky process as he could never be sure as to the motivation of those whom he was meeting. On occasion differences of opinion would arise between O'Leary and his colleagues as to whether a newly recruited volunteer should be trusted. The tactic adopted was to work with the recruit on a couple of operations before trusting him with details of the wider organisation. A case in point was that of Jean de la Olla who approached O'Leary and Garrow in a coffee shop in Nîmes one day. His ambition was to get to England to join the Free French forces of de Gaulle. He had heard of the Marseille escape line and was endeavouring to make contact to seek their assistance in reaching England. Naturally, O'Leary and Garrow treated this approach with caution. Without disclosing the nature of their organisation they asked de la Olla for his assistance in conveying three Englishmen to the Spanish border. When he completed this and a few similar tasks successfully they quickly realised he was a valuable recruit. Also recruited in Nîmes at this time was Gaston Negré, who owned a local grocery store and was particularly adept at accessing items on the black market. Recruiting additional help enabled O'Leary to extend the line into occupied France. De la Olla was assigned the role of building up the northern end of the line. Near the demarcation line between occupied France and the Vichy-controlled area, Marie-Claire Lindell, an English woman, who had lived there for years, helped many to leave the north and head for Marseille. North of Paris near the Belgian border Norbert and Marguerite Fillerin in the village of Renty near St Omer, Jacques Wattebled in

Pas-de-Calais, and the priest Pierre Carpentier in Abbeville were important recruits. In particular Carpentier had a gift for forgery, which was to prove invaluable. In Paris, Suzanne Warenghem and two former members of the French police, Guy Berthet and Albert Leycuras, were skilful in placing those on-the-run in safe accommodation before moving them south. The line had a strong presence around Lille with Paul (sometimes called Harold) Cole, Madeline Dammerment, Roland Lepers and Francois Dupré.

Treachery

Paul Cole was a member of the British Army left behind after the Dunkirk evacuation. A Londoner by birth, he had trained as an engineer but, in the 1930s, he became involved in petty crime and was something of a confidence trickster. He enlisted in the British Army in 1939. After Dunkirk was over-run by German forces he was captured but subsequently escaped and went into hiding in Lille and, in due course, began to assist those trying to escape to the south of France. Those involved in the Marseille escape line became aware of him initially in 1941 when he began to escort evaders and escapers down to Vichy France from the north. He seems to have provoked different reactions among those in the organisation whom he met. It seems O'Leary had doubts when he became involved but Garrow was more favourably disposed. Caskie was uneasy, sensing that Cole was not to be trusted. However, Cole was proving to be very successful at bringing refugees down from the north. All were impressed with these skills and perhaps this unduly influenced their assessments. Of course, their accounts were written with the benefit of hindsight and so this is a factor which must be taken into account. Undoubtedly the authorities in London should have advised O'Leary and his associates to be wary of Cole as soon as they became aware he was assisting the escape line. There was no such person as Captain Paul (or Harold) Cole in the British Army records so his claim to be an officer in the British Army was false. There was a Sgt Harold Cole, a member of the forces, who had a criminal record pre-war and had disappeared with the sergeants' mess funds in spring 1940. This and his criminal activities before the war should have prompted a warning to O'Leary and been followed by further investigation.

In September 1941 O'Leary became aware that Cole was due to attend a party in Marseille when he was supposed to be operating in northern France. He prompted Garrow to go and confront Cole, which he did. Cole explained he had a few things to attend to but would be leaving in the morning. This in itself was not a major concern as Cole was a regular partygoer but it did prompt O'Leary to proceed with caution and gather some information on Cole. In the meantime Garrow was arrested by the Vichy authorities, though there is no evidence that Cole had any part in this. Garrow was a very tall man, speaking schoolboy French in a Scottish accent, and quite conspicuous around Marseille. The German authorities would have been well aware at that time that an escape line was in operation and probably brought pressure to bear on the Vichy police to close it down. Identifying Garrow as the ringleader in October 1941 was hardly difficult.

Garrow was taken to Fort St Nicolas and held there until he faced trial in May 1942. Little conclusive evidence against him had been gathered so a sentence of ten years in a concentration camp at Mauzac et Saint Meyme de Rozens, some 150 km east of

Bordeaux, was handed down. Throughout the period in captivity he was supported by regular visits from Nancy Fiocca who provided food and other necessities. After Garrow was captured, O'Leary took over the leadership of the organisation. His role in its activities subsequently was so central that the organisation became known as the Pat Line.

In the same month as Garrow's arrest, Cole had a spectacular success in bringing fourteen airmen and soldiers down to Marseille. He, Roland Lepers and the latter's girlfriend Madeline Dammerment took them first to Abbeville where the local priest, Abbé Pierre Carpentier, printed passes for each of the men, which would enable them to cross into Vichy France. In Paris they linked up with Suzanne Warenghem, one of the escape line's most able guides. She arranged for them to be accommodated overnight in safe locations. The next day, they boarded the train in Paris, and splitting up into smaller groups, they travelled to Tours. From there a short walk across the demarcation line brought them to the village of Loches. Thence by bus and train, reaching Marseille was relatively straightforward. A few days later, by different routes, they journeyed into Spain and eventually home.

O'Leary was away when Garrow was arrested. He had gone north with Maurice Dufour, the guard who had originally assisted his escape from St Hippolyte du Fort. Dufour had subsequently become an active member of the group running the escape line. Aside from his ongoing concerns, O'Leary had become intrigued by the substantial amounts of money that Cole was seeking to pay for the escape line's operations in the north. He and Dufour first called to see François Dupré, a long-time supporter of their work, living in Lille. He and his wife had hidden many of the men who subsequently made their way south and had been mentioned by Cole as one to whom substantial payments had been made. It became clear fairly quickly, when O'Leary met him, that Dupré had neither sought nor received any payment whatsoever. It also became clear that both he and his wife had disliked Cole for some time. Annoyed by the accusation that he had been paid for his help, Dupré agreed to undertake the hazardous journey down to Marseille in order to help O'Leary resolve this issue.

Cole was invited to a meeting in Dr Rodocanachi's apartment in early November 1941. Also present were Bruce Dowding and Mario Prassinos. Cole presumed it was a routine meeting arising from the arrest of Garrow and was not aware of Dupré's presence in the next room. Also in the other room was André Postel-Vinay, who was based in Paris and had arrived by chance to have discussions with O'Leary. O'Leary questioned the payments to Dupré and Cole insisted they had been made. When Dupré walked into the room and denounced him, Cole made a bid to leave but was stopped by a blow from O'Leary. Cole was locked in a bathroom while they debated what they should do with him. Dowding favoured execution as soon as could be arranged. Prassinos, a gentle and more innocent soul, recoiled at this idea. He accepted that Cole had been guilty of misappropriation of funds, which was hardly surprising given his reputation as a womaniser with mistresses in various locations, but nothing more.

The bathroom in which Cole was locked had a window opening on to a shaft. Nearby was another similar bathroom. Cole jumped the narrow space between the rooms smashed the glass to gain access to the other room and thence into the corridor and from there downstairs to the street. O'Leary and the others heard the noise but chasing him through the streets was not really an option as it would draw attention to them. They recognised immediately that this was a crisis situation. Cole was in possession of a significant amount of information which, if disclosed to the Germans, could have fatal consequences. Together with Dowding and other helpers O'Leary went to the north to warn people who were potentially in danger. Before leaving he suggested to Dupré to leave Lille and move to Vichy France but he declined to take this advice. Some helpers began to take evasive action when they were contacted but others were slow to believe that Cole might be a traitor.

Shortly after his return to Lille, Cole was 'arrested' by the German counter-espionage service, the Abwehr. On 8 December Cole arrived at the Abbé Carpentier's house in Abbeville with members of the Gestapo and the priest was arrested. Dowding was actually in the house at the time but escaped by the back door on hearing Cole's voice. He proceeded to other houses to warn the occupants there but, on arrival at the third, the Germans were waiting for him and he was arrested. Francois Dupré was arrested some days later in Lille. Abbé Carpentier managed to smuggle a letter out of prison in March 1942, confirming Cole's treachery. During his interrogation he learned a good deal about the information Cole had handed over, which was quite extensive. All three, Carpentier, Dowding and Dupré, were tortured and later executed.

Cole betrayed many others at this time and, while estimates vary, the probability is that he cost more than fifty people their lives. It is not clear whether he was acting for the Germans right from his original capture in 1940. Did he escape after arrest at Dunkirk or was he released having agreed to help the Nazis? Certainly, the ease with which he led many refugees to the south would lend credence to the view that he was in league with the Gestapo. Alternatively he may have been 'turned' when arrested in late 1941 after the confrontation with O'Leary. Was he a person who worked sometimes with one side and sometimes with the other? Another possibility is that he was a double agent. The London authorities were slow to pass on details of Cole's army record. Was this merely incompetence or something more sinister? Another question arises in relation to those working with the escape line in the south. No action was taken against them at this time. Certainly he would have been able to supply a detailed description of Pat O'Leary and his activities. So concerned was Langley that he more or less instructed O'Leary to return to London but this was ignored. Was the failure to take action against O'Leary and those in the south because Cole did not betray them? Or, if he did, were the German authorities reluctant to move against them in a decisive manner because the area was under the control of Vichy authorities?

Cole's treachery cost many of the escape line's most effective helpers their lives and inflicted severe damage on the operation. It also prompted O'Leary to advise Caskie to begin the process of dispersing the men in the seamen's mission. Shortly after he started this process Caskie was arrested. Over the years he had built up good relations with the Vichy police. So, even though the charges against him were serious he received a two-year suspended sentence and an instruction to leave the area within ten days. In that time he managed to disperse his charges, about seventy in total, to people who would care for them. Caskie moved to Grenoble but was allowed by the authorities there to leave once a month to visit the prisoners in St Hippolyte du Fort. In this capacity it proved to be a useful channel of communications between the Pat Line and those planning escapes. For his early visits he was never searched and so began to bring in items that would help in such endeavours. However, a tip-off led to him stopping that practice. Inevitably he became involved with escapees in the Grenoble area and was arrested. Imprisoned in Paris, he was tried and found guilty of aiding escapees both in Marseille and Grenoble. Execution would have followed but for the intervention of a Lutheran chaplain, Hans Peters. He was freed when the Germans left Paris.

After the closure of the seamen's mission, Le Petit Poucet, a small and modest café on the Boulevard Dugommier, owned by the Dijon family, became the new meeting point in Marseille for those arriving in the area seeking assistance. Indeed airmen were given this information when being briefed before flights over France. In Toulouse its counterpart was the Hotel de Paris which was run by a member of the escape line, Mme Angeline Mongelard.

Re-building

In the meantime O'Leary and de la Olla went north and set about rebuilding the organisation there, by recruiting many new helpers. Early in the New Year, Darling made contact with a view to setting up a meeting in Gibraltar between himself, Langley and O'Leary. After he had been allowed to return home on medical grounds, Langley was recruited to work with MI9 in London. Through the good offices of Michael Creswell in the consulate in Barcelona, and contacts he had built up with the Spanish police, O'Leary was able to reach Gibraltar without any difficulty whereas previously some had hidden in the boots of diplomatic cars to cross the border. When they met in March 1942, O'Leary showed Langley the letter he had received from the Abbé Carpentier and expressed his extreme annoyance at how the Cole situation had been allowed to develop when it could easily have been avoided. He emphasised how the difficulties that had arisen in the Paul Cole situation could have been minimised by effective communications and more thorough checking of Cole's army record.

Inevitably, relaying messages to and from London by courier via Donald Darling took some time. Messages were brought by couriers who had business in both Spain and France and legitimate reason for travelling to places like Marseille. However, this inevitably meant that O'Leary's communication with Darling and London, and vice versa, was quite a slow process. Both O'Leary and Darling had been making the case for the installation of radio communications for some time. The debacle in relation to Cole forced the authorities to concede that a new, more efficient means of communication was necessary. At that meeting in Gibraltar it was agreed that a radio transmitter operator would be made available to O'Leary. Langley committed to ensuring that this initiative would be maintained and that in the event of an operator being arrested a replacement would be provided immediately. Also explored at that meeting was the possibility of evacvating people from France by sea. Langley formed a very favourable impression of O'Leary at the meeting, describing him as 'a born leader and a very great man'.

Evacuating by Sea

In April O'Leary returned to France but this time in a different manner presumably as a type of trial run. After dark he and the newly provided radio operator boarded the trawler *Tarana* in Gibraltar, and she proceeded to reach her destination off the

French coast. From there some members of her crew rowed O'Leary and the radio operator, ashore in a dinghy and onto the beach at Canet-Plage not far from Perpignan. The *Tarana* was a trawler that had taken part in the evacuation of Boulogne in 1940. Subsequently, the British Admiralty adapted it for a different use. Living quarters were installed as well as an amount of concealed weaponry. It was moved to Gibraltar as a small British naval vessel painted in the traditional colours and flying the White Ensign. The crew wore British naval uniforms.

Leaving Gibraltar at dusk they would proceed out to sea. There the crew would discard uniforms, dress as local fishermen, paint the upper parts of the boat in the colours traditionally used by local fishing vessels and alter the funnel outline. Flying the flag of one of the neighbouring countries, usually that of Portugal, with the result the vessel appeared to the casual observer to be a local trawler crewed by fishermen, meant that there was a good chance it would be disregarded by enemy aircraft.

The journey with O'Leary was the *Tarana*'s first venture and on return it brought back some Secret Service personnel. Again, under the cover of darkness, the crew reversed the process, changing back into uniform, repainting the boat navy grey and returning to port as it had left. Meanwhile, O'Leary and his colleague, having buried the transmitter, made their way to the Hotel du Tennis in Canet-Plage. The owner Mme Lebreton was a supporter of the escape line. Two days later they retrieved the transmitter and went by train from Perpignan to Marseille. At that time radio transmitters were all in suitcases made precisely to measure in order not to damage the delicate machinery. So travelling with them was always risky but no problem arose in this instance. At Marseille the escape organisation had long since devised a means of leaving the station unobserved by going into a toilet and then onto the main street. Operating the transmitters was also dangerous as the authorities had detector vans which could, over a period of time, identify the premises where any such machine was in use. The first operator supplied to O'Leary was not able to cope with the pressure involved so Langley, true to his word, supplied a replacement. This was Jean (sometimes known as Alex) Nitelet.

A Spitfire pilot, Nitelet had been shot down a few miles from Boulogne on 9 August 1941. Several of his colleagues in that sortie were also shot down. Three were killed and three others, including Douglas Bader, were captured. However, Nitelet was rescued by a local farmer, Louis Salmon, and taken to Vincent Ansel, one of Norbert Fillerin's team. However, he had suffered multiple injuries when he crash-landed and had lost the sight of one eye. The Fillerins, with the help of two local GPs, looked after him for the next two months while he recuperated. When he had fully recovered, the escape line organisation moved him down to Marseille and across the Pyrenees to Gibraltar. He reached home on Christmas Day 1941. Nouveau has described him as Jean le Nerveu, 'restless Johnny'. Unable to fly because of his damaged eye he volunteered to return to France to work with an underground movement. So he was trained as a radio operator and was flown back on a Lysander aircraft on 28 May 1942, where he linked up with the Pat Line again.

While O'Leary was in Gibraltar, Airey Neave and Hugh Woollatt arrived in Marseille in April 1942 seeking assistance from the Pat Line. Neave had been wounded and captured in Calais on 26 May 1940. He was hospitalised for a period before being moved to Germany where he was held in a series of POW camps. In May 1941 he was moved to the camp at Colditz. This was deemed to be the most secure of the prisoner of war camps and was where those guilty of persistent involvement in attempted escapes were held. His first effort at escape from there failed in August 1941. In January of the following year he and a Dutch prisoner managed to walk out disguised as German officers. Outside they buried their German officers' greatcoats and caps in the snow. They travelled through the country posing as Dutch electrical workers, which is what they were described as on their forged identity papers. They were dressed in what Neave has described as 'a curious mixture of converted uniform jackets and RAF trousers with ski caps made from blankets'.[14] With great skill, courage and luck they made it to Switzerland some days later.

Hugh Woollatt had been captured in May 1940 also and eventually ended up in the POW camp at Biberach in early June 1941. He was part of a mass escape from the camp by tunnel on 13 September 1941. Of the twenty-six who escaped only four remained at large and they, including Woollatt, reached Switzerland. Life there for Allied escapees was quite relaxed as the Swiss police were very favourably disposed towards them.

In April both Neave and Woollatt were summoned by the British military attaché in Berne and advised that a decision had been made to send them back to London. They travelled by train to Geneva where they were met by a British agent who supplied them with civilian clothing suitable for a journey through France and papers identifying them as Czech workers. The following day they were guided to the border by a Swiss policeman in civilian clothes who showed them where to cross without being observed.

The term used for refugees by those working on the escape line was 'parcel'. The case of Neave and Woollatt illustrates just how apt the term was. Once in France they were helped on the journey by six different French civilians at various stages, two of whom escorted them on the final leg of the journey to Marseille. As always in such cases, civilians acting in this way were risking almost certain death, as Neave notes, whereas he, if caught, would be entitled to the protection afforded by the terms of the Geneva Convention. On arrival in Marseille they were taken, by their guides, to the Petit Poucet. As they sat there, they noticed a policeman patrolling to and fro on the path outside. Eventually they were taken into a back room and were surprised that the policeman joined them by a rear door. Introduced to them as 'Jacques' he was, in reality, Police Inspector Boulard, a supporter of the Pat Line. Boulard went to fetch Louis Nouveau who arrived a short time later. Neave and Woollatt stayed with him and his wife for a week and are recorded as numbers 66 and 67 in his list of guests. A week later Francis Blanchain took them to the border and two guides from the Ponzan-Vidal group escorted them to Spain. By mid-May they reached home via Gibraltar. Woollatt was killed in action later in the conflict. Neave was recruited by MI9 and began to work there with an earlier Pat Line evacuee, Jimmy Langley, supporting evasion activities.

About this time O'Leary was approached by a young man giving his name as François Dulais. He claimed that he would be able to supply information on an ongoing basis regarding German security activities in the north of France. O'Leary suggested that they should meet again to discuss the possibility. In the meantime, he contacted Ponzan Vidal who was able to establish quite quickly that Dulais was a German agent who needed to be eliminated. So, the second meeting was arranged for Port-Vendres near the Spanish border. O'Leary explained that it wasn't safe to meet in the town so they went into the foothills of the mountains. There two of the Vidal's associates were waiting for them and Dulais immediately realised he was in some difficulty. O'Leary declined to save him, remembering all too clearly the tragic consequences that followed his reluctance to act on his suspicions in relation to Paul Cole. François Dulais was executed, all identity documentation removed from him and his body thrown into a ravine.

The *Tarana* was used to evacuate refugees in the summer and autumn of 1942. Also assisting with evacuations were two small fishing vessels, *feluccas*, which were manned by Poles. The availability of radio contact made scheduling such operations a practical proposition. This method of evacuation had obvious advantages compared to crossing the mountains on foot. Those seeking to return home could be taken straight to Gibraltar without having to deal with the Spanish authorities. In addition, the number who could be accommodated on any particular journey was far greater than escapes across the mountains. The only slight risk arising from carrying a big group was that the vessel would have to wait off the coast for a period while the escapees were ferried aboard. The possibility of using this means of transporting significant numbers of people to Gibraltar coincided with an increased presence of RAF pilots on the run in France. These were deemed as priorities for rescue by the authorities in London as there was a shortage of pilots and a considerable cost in time and money in replacing them. In addition, Secret Service personnel were evacuated and O'Leary also used the system to evacuate any of his helpers whose positions were becoming vulnerable. Dressed in a typical French fashion, evacuees began to make their way in twos and threes to Perpignan. Pat O'Leary had rented a villa on the beach at Canet-Plage to accommodate them while awaiting evacuation.

Prioritising some of those on the run ahead of others always caused controversy. So whatever those who were working on escape lines might think, they had to follow the instruction to prioritise pilots. Among these was Whitney Straight. American by birth, he was raised in London and had become an internationally well-known personality as a racing driver in the pre-war years. He proved to be an exceptional pilot with a very distinguished record, which explains why his safe return to London was deemed urgent. In late July 1941 he was shot down near Le Havre. After an adventurous trek through France, he reached the border with Spain before being picked up by the French police. He was incarcerated in St Hippolyte du Fort in Nîmes. His capture would have proved a propaganda coup for the authorities so when he was arrested he gave his name as Capt. Whitney.

The first effort to secure his release was made by Dr Rodocanachi. It was an easy one as Straight had a number of serious medical issues including damaged eardrums. He and eight others were passed for repatriation. However, in retaliation for an RAF bombing raid on a factory near Paris, the process of allowing sick prisoners to be repatriated was suspended. They were moved to Nice and hospitalised but Straight, and two others, with help from Francis Blanchain, one of O'Leary's team, managed to escape. All three were moved to various safe houses and ended up in the apartment of Louis and Renée Nouveau, where other escapees soon joined them. All were moved by train to Perpignan and then to the nearby beach. On 13 July 1942 they were picked up by the *Tarana* and taken to Gibraltar. In total thirty-four were evacuated on that occasion. Among them were two of O'Leary's most valuable helpers, Leoni Savinos and his wife.

Savinos had been arrested in April 1942 in Paris with another member of the organisation, Pierrot Lanvers. Savinos had in his possession a plan of a factory that was making accessories for German fighter planes. It was clear to his interrogators that he was involved in some underground activity. When confronted with cases like this, where the evidence against the arrested person was clear, one of the approaches taken by the Gestapo often was to try to 'turn' a captive into working for them. Luckily for him they saw potential in Savinos, a man who spoke French and German fluently and clearly was in touch with an underground movement. Eventually the proposition was put to him but he skilfully resisted, before agreeing to their strategy while displaying a contrived reluctance. Of course, they couldn't just take his word at face value and informed him that they would hold his wife as a hostage. Aside from the normal concerns this would cause, his wife Emi was German and a passionate anti-Nazi. He was certain that records somewhere would be unearthed, if she were arrested, with potentially fatal consequences. Displaying clear presence of mind he responded, 'Doesn't it make sense to you that I could never operate without suspicion in the south if you release me and hold my wife captive?' With some reluctance they accepted this point. He used the same argument to persuade them to release Pierrot Lanvers. Immediately on his return to Marseille, Leoni and Emi Savinos and Lanvers, were hidden by the Pat Line until the opportunity came to evacuate them on the *Tarana*.

The next priority prisoner identified for rescue by the Secret Service in London was Squadron Leader F. W. ('Taffy') Higginson. He was credited with thirteen 'kills' in aircraft duels before he was shot down near Abbeville in mid-June 1941. Again his capture had the potential to be used for propaganda purposes. Ironically he was taken south by Paul Cole. Arrested as he sought to reach Spain, he was imprisoned in St Hippolyte du Fort where he adopted the name of Captain Bennett. In March 1942 he was transferred to Fort de la Revere, located near Èze in the south-eastern part of France overlooking the Mediterranean. O'Leary had by this time two channels of communication with those in the prison: Vladimir Bouryschkine, a Russian coach to the Monaco basketball team, was providing physical training instruction to the prisoners, and Fr Myrda, a Polish priest, attended to their spiritual needs. Bouryschkine's appointment to the post in the prison arose from his friendship with the commandant's mistress.

O'Leary sent a message through him to Higginson to select four of his fellow pilots in the prison for a breakout. The plan was to reach the kitchens via a coal chute while a rather noisy prisoners' concert concealed what was happening. The entrance to the chute was protected by a locked grill but one of the prisoners had fashioned a key to open it. The kitchen windows were protected by steel bars but a hacksaw blade, brought in by either Bouryschkine, Myrda or Caskie, was used to remove them. A rope made of Red Cross parcel string assisted them in making a 25-foot drop into the moat surrounding the fort. From there access through a sewer brought them to freedom. They were to be met there by two of O'Leary's colleagues, Jean Nitelet, his radio operator, and Tony Friend, an Italian-born police officer of Australian descent based in Monaco. These two would escort them to Monte Carlo where O'Leary was waiting for them.

The escape took place on 6 August 1942 and all went reasonably according to plan, although they were almost overcome by the fumes in the sewer. In the meantime, Nitelet and Friend had been spotted by police and taken away for questioning. They were subsequently released but not in time to meet the escapees at the appointed location. Without their intended guides the group went astray in the darkness and found themselves in Cap d'Ail in France rather than in Monte Carlo. The next morning they were picked up by one of O'Leary's team and taken to Monte Carlo. There they were hidden in a safe house and looked after by some expats, May and June Arathoon, and Grace and Susie Trenchard. The Trenchard sisters ran a teahouse in the area, which was the first port of call for many of those on the run reaching Monte Carlo. Some days later, O'Leary arrived with a supply of clean clothes and forged papers for each of the men. Then they were returned to Marseille, with Higginson travelling in one of Fr Myrda's cassocks, and hidden in the Rodocanichis' apartment. On the night of 5/6 September a larger breakout from Fort de la Rivere took place. On this occasion inmates spent some weeks digging a tunnel with pieces of cutlery. In total fifty-eight prisoners escaped. All had been advised by the escape line as to various safe houses in which they would be provided with sanctuary. Inevitably given the size of the group extensive police action was initiated and more than half were picked up in the following days. They and those still in prison, over 200 in all, were relocated to another institution further inland.

Meanwhile those in the care of the escape line lay low for some days in response to the extensive police activity. Eventually equipped with false papers and French clothing, twenty-seven escapees began the journey to Perpignan. The scene at the railway station as each pretended to be a complete stranger was verging on the comical:

Most were wearing new suits. At the barrier every face that turned in our direction was familiar ... I tried to keep my features straight ... Hicky coughed into his handkerchief. I could see his shoulders shaking.[15]

They went to a villa at Canet-Plage, which the organisation had rented. There O'Leary briefed the group, thirty-one in total, just after midnight on 13 September. In the party were British, Free French, Poles, Belgians and one German lady. She was Paula Spriewald, the daughter of a German MP, who had filled a sort of personal assistant role to O'Leary for many months making sure the organisation ran smoothly. Another of his helpers who was at risk of arrest was Francis Blanchain and so a decision had been made to evacuate him.[16] Also there was André Postel-Vinay. He had also been betrayed by Cole and arrested in Paris some days before Christmas 1941. Held in captivity and tortured, he faked a suicide attempt and was in psychiatric care when he escaped on 3 September 1942. Although in poor physical condition after his treatment in captivity, a fellow member of the escape line, George Zafiri, a nephew of Fanny Rodocanachi, managed to bring him down through France to join the group waiting evacuation.

As well as the *Tarana* two other vessels, the *Seadog* and the *Seawolf* were used to ferry people to and from the French Mediterranean coast in clandestine operations. The *Seawolf* had left Gibraltar on 11 September with two Secret Service agents on board. At sea on 15 September the process of repainting the vessel in traditional fishing colours was barely complete when an Italian reconnaissance plane flew overhead. Having deposited the agents, the vessel picked up evacuees at a number of points along the coast including those supplied by the Pat Line. Spriewald was reluctant to leave until eventually O'Leary lifted her into the boat and instructed her to go. All were back in Gibraltar on 24 September and returned home in early October.

Not all evacuations went as smoothly. The *Seawolf* arrived at the French coast just after midnight on 6 October to pick up thirty-two evacuees. They were housed in a small villa consisting of three bedrooms, with one bed in each. Confusion as to the exact pick-up point meant that contact was not made with the *Seawolf*. After three days the vessel returned to Gibraltar. Meanwhile O'Leary had returned to Marseille and dispatched a radio message to London. '*Pas plus de bateau que beurre au cul*' reflected both his annoyance and his sense of humour. (It's difficult to translate the idiomatic expression but 'boat my arse' is getting there.) The *Seawolf* was dispatched again and the group picked up successfully on 12 October. The conditions in the house where they had to remain in hiding can only be imagined. By this time security in the area was tightening up and this was the last of the major evacuations by sea organised by the Pat Line.[17] However, the three vessels continued to work transporting secret service personnel to and from the coast.

While in Marseille O'Leary received word, from Mario Prassinos, that Jean Nitelet and Gaston Negré had been captured. All three had been collecting supplies dropped by an Allied aircraft in a field outside Nîmes in the early hours of the morning. The crew of the plane had found it difficult to locate the location of the 'drop' and flew over the area three times, which drew the attention of the local police. In the confusion and darkness Prassinos managed to escape but his colleagues were arrested.

A Changing Mood

Inevitably the attitude of the general population of France, both in the occupied and the free zones, to the German occupation and the Vichy regime did not remain static. Some were quick to realise the implications of the German invasion, whereas for others it was a more gradual process. As early as November 1940 there were signs of opposition. On Armistice Day, 11 November, the French usually celebrated the outcome of the First World War and remembered those who lost their lives in the conflict. Like all occupying forces, the Third Reich was wary of public commemorations of any sort lest they turn into demonstrations. An event called, as in this case, to commemorate their own defeat in 1918 was more than the Germans were willing to tolerate.

Anticipating that events on that day might be an opportunity for protest, the German commander in the Paris region banned any commemoration. This had the opposite effect to the one intended. Students planned a protest and citizens were encouraged in BBC broadcasts to join in. Initially the celebrations were fairly orderly although Guéhenno observed French police, under German instruction, removing flowers which citizens were leaving at the statue of Georges Clemenceau, the statesman and patriot, on the Champs-Élysées. However, the arrival of several hundred school students, led by two of their number carrying a floral Cross of Lorraine in red, white and blue, the symbol of De Gaulle's Free French, singing the *Marseillaise*, prompted a response. Strong reaction by German soldiers and French police eventually restored order and many of those involved were imprisoned. The episode illustrated growing resistance to the occupation among the citizens, particularly the younger ones.

The next clear example was when those associated with de Gaulle encouraged Parisians via a BBC broadcast to stay indoors between three and four o'clock on New Year's Day in 1941. Despite a German effort to sabotage the call with an offer of free potatoes to be collected during that hour, it received a widespread response both in the capital and other cities. In Quimper one citizen described the scene at four o'clock 'like a class being let out of school, people hurried into the streets again, laughing and bumping into each other in their happiness'.[18] With the passage of time demonstrations of opposition occurred in various parts of the country. May Day and St Joan of Arc's day, for example, were used to display growing disaffection by the French people as they asserted their patriotism. A somewhat despondent Guéhenno was encouraged when going for a walk on Bastille Day in 1941:

The unfortunate Parisians really did all they could to make their resistance known. What ingenuity to bring the three colours together, one way or another. It was easier for the women. Louisette in her red-and-white chequered dress and her blue scarf came down from Belleville like a republic. Men had fewer means of doing it. They let one of those match boxes decorated with the blue and white and red emblem stick out of their jacket pockets. Never had people looked at each other more carefully. Each one worked at recognising the others' intentions. The blue shoes, white stockings, and red dress of one woman. The red jacket, blue purse, and white gloves of another. What pathetic efforts. But, not wasted after all. That mutual attention ended up creating the joy of communion (17 July, 1941).[19]

Also, a campaign of daubing official buildings with a V for Victory and the Cross of Lorraine spread throughout the country. Occasionally arrests were made but these served to draw further attention to changing public opinion. Indeed Pétain was quick to sense the changing mood, commenting in a radio broadcast in August 1941, 'The authority of my government is being challenged, and its orders are often being carried out badly.'

In the free zone the picture as regards the shift in public opinion is complicated somewhat by the distinction many adopted between Pétain, who retained his hero status to some extent, and his government. There were those who were totally opposed from the outset. For some of those who originally favoured Pétain's stance, a gradual process of change was underway from quite early on. It was widely expected among this group that the fall of France would be quickly followed by a British surrender. Her survival during the Battle of Britain somewhat chipped away at their certainty. In June 1941 Germany and Italy declared war on the Soviet Union. To some French observers, with a keen knowledge of their own history as regards Russia, this would have seemed a foolhardy step.

While the Communist Party had been dissolved by the French government in 1939, this merely drove it underground and it remained a formidable political force. In the early war years it was in a compromised position due to the Hitler–Stalin non-aggression pact signed in 1939. The invasion of Russia removed this restraint from the movement throughout France. 'The Reich has declared war against the Soviets. As the enemies of our enemies are our friends, from now on we have 180 million more friends' (23 June 1941).[20] The release of the Communist movement to become actively involved in agitation provoked the adoption of a harder line by the German authorities in France as they sought to repress those in the country whom they perceived to be their enemies; this included Jews, political critics, suspected members of the Resistance as well as Communists. At the same time the requirements of the eastern front meant that their most able and disciplined army personnel were moved from the country. Another event contributing to a changed perception was the attack on Pearl Harbour in December 1941. The consequent change in American policy was widely seen as a turning point. For many French people, the decisive impact of the US's decision to join the First World War was also clear in the public memory.

Allied bombing of France began in March 1942. In the autumn of that year, Allied forces began to make moves into North Africa. The significance of this move was more than military in nature. Algeria, at that time, was part of France rather than a colony. More than a million French citizens lived there and were entitled to elect members of the French national parliament. Some of Pétain's early support was based on the belief that he had a clever strategy to outmanoeuvre the Germans but it quickly became clear that this was misplaced. The failure of the Vichy government to secure the release of French POWs in Germany also chipped away at the popularity of the government. These events were followed shortly afterwards by the German defeat at Stalingrad in early 1943, which was perceived by many as a further turning point.

Another factor influencing public opinion was the effort to recruit French people to work in German factories. The Third Reich needed a lot of labour to keep its factories operating to full capacity in order to sustain the war effort. With so many of its young people serving in the armed forces, recruitment of foreign workers was a strategic objective. This process began with the armistice signed by

Pétain in 1940 when attractive remuneration was offered to those willing to make their living in Germany. However it is noticeable that French people responded to the inducements in relatively small numbers. By late 1941, fewer than 50,000 had taken up the option even though there was an active advertising campaign extolling the advantages of going to work in Germany. Despite the difficulties French people were experiencing with shortages of food and supplies generally the response was poor, and was a lot less than the corresponding figure for neighbouring countries, including even smaller ones. A fresh publicity drive throughout France brought about some improvement in these numbers by mid-1942 but not enough to satisfy German needs.

Petain's second-in-command in the Vichy regime, Pierre Laval, saw this situation as an opportunity to address the long-standing issue of French POWs held in German camps. He also thought that agreeing to go to Germany to work might usefully be presented as a patriotic act as well as lucrative financially. After the short conflict of 1940 about 2 million French army personnel were taken prisoner. Some escaped subsequently and others, such as veterans of the First World War, were released. But by 1942 about 1.5 million were still in captivity. In negotiations with the German authorities, Laval sought an arrangement whereby for every two people volunteering to work in Germany, one POW would be released. Eventually he had to agree on a one-for-three deal. So, to secure the release of all POWs in excess of 4 million French people would have to agree to take up work in Germany. Quite apart from the principle involved, this was a completely unrealistic target. On 22 June 1942 Laval announced the outcome in triumphant terms during a radio broadcast as proof of his negotiation skills and the good relationship between the Vichy government and the Third Reich. The scheme was presented in patriotic terms as a means of securing the return of POWs. He also expressed his hopes for a German victory in that address.

Inevitably, with the passage of time, and reports coming back of very poor working conditions in German factories, the voluntary nature of the recruitment programme proved inadequate. As a result Laval introduced in February 1943 the *Service du Travail Obligatoire* (STO), which was a compulsory work scheme. Initially targeted at men between twenty and twenty-two it was subsequently extended to those between eighteen and sixty and women without children between eighteen and forty-five. This proved to be an extremely unpopular measure. Of course the roundup and mistreatment of Jews and actions taken by the authorities against their political opponents had generally elicited pity and anger amongst some. By contrast, the STO, as it had implications for a large section of the population, provoked active resistance and industrial action. It is noticeable that Vichy officials, at local level, were less committed to enforcing this than other German instructions. More than any other measure, the STO illustrated clearly to the French population the implications of collaboration. More than half those who should have complied with the STO regulation in the southern free zone of France did not do so. These were in addition to those who were already in breach of previous regulations, such as escapees from POW camps, people who had fled from the north following the 1940 defeat, and others who for political or religious reasons were 'undesirable' in the view of the authorities. The STO initiative and its failure was a major blow to the standing of the Vichy government, all the more so as it was largely self-inflicted.

As a means of avoiding the STO some joined the *Milice*, which had been established by Laval as a security service in January 1943. *Miliciens* were well paid at 2,500 francs per month, about double the average industrial wage. The force was 35,000 strong by the time of Liberation. Of course many of those targeted by the STO sought various ways to avoid it. Given the nature of the country with its vast rural areas, many of which were thinly populated, avoiding the authorities was relatively easy. Many a farmer was glad to accept the services of a labourer without asking too many questions. Significant numbers of those who were avoiding the STO, particularly young men, fled to the mountains and remote areas to join the *Maquis*. Literally they were bands of outlaws on the run from the authorities and the STO contributed greatly to their growth in numbers and extension throughout the country. The growth of the *Maquis* represented a change in the complexion of the Resistance generally. Previously it had been based largely in the occupied zone and located in urban areas. Those involved lived either at home or in safe houses. They remained in their existing occupations and gathered information, which was useful to the Allies. By contrast the *Maquis* lived permanently on the run in remote rural areas, predominantly in Vichy France. Even the mere need to survive brought them into closer association with the populace at large than had been the case with those involved in resistance roles from the start of the occupation. As a group, they were committed to more overt actions against the Germans, and those who collaborated with them, than the Resistance generally.

On 7 December 1941, the same day as the attack on Pearl Harbour, the Night and Fog Decree (*Nacht-und-Nebel-Erlass*) was issued in Paris. Under its provisions the authorities in the occupied territories could arrest and deport anyone whom they considered enemies of the Third Reich. Families were given no details as to the reasons for the detention, the whereabouts of anyone arrested, or their fate. In other words it set aside the provisions of international law including the Hague Convention.

Parallel with these events was a growing awareness among the ordinary people of the treatment being meted out to fellow citizens, in particular the Jews. Early action against Jews in the occupied zone concentrated on those who were not French nationals. The first roundup of Jews in Paris took place on 14 May 1941. 'Yesterday ... 5,000 Jews were taken away ... The working people of Paris who saw these heartrending scenes were full of indignation and shame' (15 May).[21] This roundup was repeated in July of that year. French policemen sealed off an area of Paris and more than 4,000 adult male Jews were arrested. The most notorious roundup occurred in July 1942. Plans had been drawn up for this at a meeting on 7 July. The French police were instructed to carry out the raid with no obvious German involvement. On this occasion the action attracted more public attention for a variety of reasons. The numbers involved were far greater at more than 13,000. The intention was to arrest a greater number but as word had leaked out many destined to be picked up had escaped from the city. Those arrested included women and about 4,000 children, among them natives of France. Up until then only men were arrested and some of the residents of Paris may have believed that they were being taken away to forced labour camps. It was now very obvious that something far more sinister was afoot. Some were placed in internment camps, including the one at Drancy, which was usually the departure point from which prisoners were sent to Auschwitz or Dachau. About half were taken to be held in an indoor stadium which, because of its location near the city centre, meant that the population at large were more aware of what was happening. The conditions in the stadium, the *Vélodrome d'Hiver*, were appalling with little water supply and no sanitary facilities available. The glass roof and the fact that windows were sealed together with the summer temperatures meant that conditions were stifling. A limited number of medics were allowed access but not nearly enough to meet the needs of the captives. During the next eight days more than 100 of the captives in the stadium committed suicide and another twenty-four died. An underground newspaper likened it to 'a scene from hell'. Gitla Rosenblum recalled the awful circumstances decades later:

People screamed all night long. Women threw themselves off the top of the stands. I still hear the screams. I can see the scenes today. We stayed there eight days. The conditions were dreadful ... and the filth was pestilential.[22]

She and her sister survived but her parents did not. There was Vichy involvement in these episodes as sanction was given for the French police to participate. It suited Nazi purposes to create the impression that the French police were initiating these measures and it was not until later that German involvement in arrests, and control of places like the camp at Drancy, was more visible. On 27 March 1942 the first trainload of Jewish prisoners held at Drancy was transported to Auschwitz. In total, in excess of

75,000 Jews were deported from France during the course of the war, of whom less than 3,000 survived. Years later President Chirac publicly apologised on behalf of the nation for the role played by French police.

Circumstances for Jews in the free zone became far more difficult from August 1942 onwards. The Vichy government agreed to a request to deliver 10,000 foreign Jews living in the region to the German authorities in Paris. Those already in internment camps were the first target group and more than 3,000 were transported north in mid-August 1942. Then arrests of those living in registered accommodation began. Eventually more than 11,000 men, women and children were expelled from Vichy France to Drancy internment camp in Paris in the latter part of 1942. In due course almost 10,000 were sent to concentration camps, of whom only a very small number survived.

The Pretence Ends

In response to the Allied invasion of Algeria, Hitler instructed his forces on 11 November to enter the unoccupied zone previously controlled by the Vichy government in order to secure access to the French Mediterranean coast. This represented a clear breach of the armistice agreement that had been negotiated with Pétain. 'The Armistice of June 40 was a stupid blunder as well as an act of treachery. All we gained was dishonour' (Guéhenno, 11 November, 1942). Other than a token protest on the radio, Pétain made no objection to the German action. A particular objective of the move into Vichy France was to gain control of the powerful French Mediterranean fleet at Toulon. Ships had remained there after the tragedy at Mers-el-Kébir and took no part in the war in accordance with the Armistice agreement. Prompt action by French naval personnel denied the Germans this important resource when, with just hours to spare, seventy-three ships were scuttled. Pétain nominally remained in power but his regime was even more of a sham from then on than previously.

This new situation with the Germans in control of the south of France had the effect of reducing the possibility of the *Tarana* or the other vessels accessing the coast in safety and it also meant that O'Leary and his colleagues were likely to experience greater surveillance. Even though the area had been nominally under the control of Vichy there had been a strong presence of German security officials in the area since the early days of Pétain's regime. This increased considerably from November 1942 onwards. The freedom to turn a blind eye to various activities that some Vichy officials and police had exercised was now restricted. As regards the Pyrenees, originally German control was limited to an area on the Atlantic coast. From November onwards the French–Spanish border was totally under German control, which greatly increased the risks for refugees and those guiding and assisting them. The Nazi supporters in the area became more die-hard. On the other hand, the perception that the Allies were making progress undoubtedly had the effect of increasing the numbers of French and Spanish citizens who were willing to turn a blind eye to the activities of those assisting fugitives. Moreover the Spanish authorities were now more inclined to let those 'on the run' pass through to Gibraltar with the minimum of hindrance.

A Rescue

Shortly after the German move to take direct control of the southern zone of France, O'Leary, sensing that he was becoming too well-known in Marseille, moved to live in Toulouse, staying initially with Françoise Dissart and then in other locations in the city. In November also a young Australian, Tom Groome, was sent by the authorities in London as a replacement radio operator for O'Leary. He had landed at Canet-Plage, having been brought there by the *Seadog*. His mother was French so he spoke the language like a native. Initially he began transmitting from the Rodocanachis' apartment but, to minimise risk, O'Leary moved him to Montauban, about 50 km from Toulouse, where he stayed with a family named Cheramy. Using the Cheramy house as a base, Groome moved around the area when transmitting. The danger of being identified while transmitting had become greater because of the increased presence in the area of detection vans since the German occupation of Vichy France. A young French girl, Edith Reddé (known as Danielle in the organisation), acted as a courier to bring messages to and from O'Leary.

As well as helping the Pat Line, Nancy Fiocca also began to work with the Resistance in a group based around Toulon. O'Leary was always nervous of using people who were active in a number of organisations feeling that the risks were greater. So, Nancy's role with him and his colleagues had reduced. However, she continued her weekly visits to Ian Garrow in prison at Mauzac, having presented herself as his cousin. He was aware that there was at least one guard in the prison who, it was alleged, could be bribed to assist with an escape but he didn't know which one it was. She calculated that the regularity of visits might prompt the guard to identify himself to her, which is what transpired in due course. The possibility of organising an escape arose and became particularly urgent when Garrow told her, during a visit in the autumn of 1942, of a rumour that he was shortly to be relocated to Germany. O'Leary decided to try to organise an escape. The price for the guard's assistance was a number of multiples of his yearly salary and the plan was for him to smuggle a guard's uniform into the prison. A Jewish couple, Paul and Imelda Ullmann, who lived in Toulouse, had joined the Pat Line in mid-1942. They supported evaders and escapers in a safe house in the city, which had been procured by Françoise Dissart. Also Paul was used as a guide by O'Leary taking those on the run from place to place. On this occasion, however, it was his professional skills as a tailor that were needed. In the space of forty-eight hours he produced the garment.

Coincidentally when the plan was about to be launched the sentries, who were members of the French army, were replaced by Vichy police so Ullmann had to produce a new uniform. This was smuggled in to Garrow by the guard who had agreed to assist. Meanwhile O'Leary and three colleagues, Guy Berthet, Tom Groome and Fabien de Cortes, went to the area and they met up with Philippe (sometimes using the name Jean) Brégi who owned a farm about 30 km distant from the prison in quite an isolated location. The plan was for Garrow to change into the uniform and leave at the changing of the guard at 7.00 p.m. He would change into the uniform in a toilet and prise open a partition into the guard's quarters and begin his walk to freedom. There were two towers containing machine guns and searchlights at either end of the front wall of the prison. Guy hid near one of them and Fabien close to the other, each armed with a revolver which, of course, could not compete in any way with machine guns but if necessary could be used to distract attention. As it happens the need did not arise.

On 8 December 1942 Ian Garrow walked out in the guard's uniform, among others leaving at that time, and the group made their getaway in Brégi's car. They hid in his farmhouse overnight. By chance six supporters of de Gaulle had escaped from prison in nearby Bergerac on the same night so intense police activity followed. Early next morning, while out tending his animals, Brégi was approached by two policemen who informed him of the two events and told him that a widespread search was underway. They were confident the escapees would be caught quickly as all roads were blocked. Having accepted the farmer's assurance that he had seen nothing unusual, they left without searching the house. Soon afterwards the group left Brégi's house to travel on foot cross country to a second hideout they had planned for, in the village of Bergerac. It was difficult going particularly Ian Garrow whose long stay in prison had weakened him. As the search area widened, hiding in Bergerac itself was a clever move. O'Leary left to make plans to take Garrow to Toulouse. On his return on 28 December he took Garrow to the house of Françoise Dissart, who had agreed to hide him and help him recover his strength.

Aware that she, as his regular visitor, would be suspected of having some involvement in the escape, Nancy Fiocca was careful to maintain a very visible presence on a daily basis around Marseille. When a policeman called to advise her of Garrow's escape she expressed delight, which aroused his suspicions. 'Would you be [delighted] if your cousin had just escaped,' she asked. He had to agree, and joined her in the celebratory drink. After he had left, she rang her husband and, conscious that their phone line was probably tapped, he expressed surprise and delight also. It took Ian Garrow three weeks to recover enough strength to face the trek across the Pyrenees. After two abortive attempts O'Leary took him to Perpignan on 25 January and linked up with a group there, which consisted of two US airmen, an RAF pilot and two civilians together with a guide who was willing to take them to Spain. They travelled by train to Banyuls near the border. O'Leary's parting words to Garrow were, 'Can this go on much longer?' Clearly he was sensing the end of the escape line. On the Spanish side, the group had to walk during the hours of darkness for a few days until contact was made with the British Consulate in Barcelona. A car was provided to transport him to Gibraltar and he reached England on the night of 6 February. Garrow reported O'Leary's remark to Neave and Langley when he was being debriefed back in London a few days later. It was a possibility that had occurred to them also. As both had escaped from France via the Pat Line they knew the risks that were being taken on a daily basis.

In the later months of 1942 the Pat Line was a very extensive organisation. It reached all parts of France. In Paris, Jean de la Olla had a very extensive network of helpers. There were similar groups in Normandy, Rouen and the Pas-de-Calais area. In Nîmes, Gaston Negré had been of huge assistance up until the time of his arrest. On the south coast, people such as Louis and Reneé Nouveau, Mario Prassinos and Françoise Dissart were still heroically supporting Pat O'Leary. All in all, there were about 250 volunteers involved. As an organisation it could perform with great efficiency. An airman crash-landing in northern France could be picked up on the same night, supplied with civilian clothing and forged papers, and within less than two weeks was likely to be back in England. In some ways the line had become a victim of its own success. O'Leary worried that it was becoming unwieldy. Unlike in its earlier days, not all the volunteers were known to him. This and the size of the organisation increased his concerns regarding the possibility of an inadvertent breach of security or more particularly organised infiltration by the Gestapo. As well as this, he had more immediate concerns regarding the safety of a number of his closest associates.

He became aware that the security services were beginning to concentrate their investigations on Louis Nouveau. One option was for Louis and his wife to be evacuated but neither was willing to take this course of action. As an alternative, Louis agreed to move north and continue to work for the organisation. So he moved to Rouen, about an hour's distance north of Paris, with a new identity as Hector Nadier and using forged papers identifying him as a long-term resident of the locality and a member of the local football club and public library. His wife Reneé moved to live with Françoise Dissart in Toulouse. Shortly after that O'Leary decided that Mario Prassinos was at serious risk of arrest and he was evacuated through Spain to London in December. There he joined the Secret Service and returned to France.

In a significant blow to the organisation, Groome was caught by the Gestapo in the act of transmitting a message on 11 January from the Cheramy house. He, together with Danielle Reddé and the Cheramys, was taken to Toulouse for questioning. Groome attempted to escape by jumping out a first-floor window. In the confusion which this caused, Danielle Reddé managed to slip away but Groome was recaptured. Despite threats to kill their young baby, the Cheramys refused to answer questions. In due course they, along with Tom Groome, were incarcerated in a concentration camp in Germany. All three survived despite appalling mistreatment. The baby was looked after by the Red Cross and the family was re-united after the war.

Nancy Fiocca's expression of delight at the escape of her 'cousin' Ian Garrow had bought her some time but the policeman who called with the news remained suspicious. The security forces were aware that there was a woman in the locality who was engaged in a lot of activity which they considered subversive and had begun to gather a file entitled 'The White Mouse'. They were in the course of narrowing down the possibilities and had offered a large amount of money for information leading to her arrest. She began to feel uneasy. Often the phone in her home rang and went dead when answered. The owner of the bistro opposite her home, who was one of her closest collaborators, tipped her off that questions were being asked about her by some odd-looking people. Her husband Henri had supported her throughout all her activities, both with the Pat Line and the Resistance, but his concern was becoming acute. On hearing the latest information he insisted that she agree to leave and go to England. She moved out of their home and went to stay secretly in the Hotel de Paris in Toulouse while O'Leary began to make arrangements for her departure. However, she insisted on continuing her work for the organisation in the interim.

On one such trip she was arrested and taken in for questioning. They were investigating an act of sabotage in the local cinema, with which she had no involvement. Other than denying the allegation she offered very little response to the questions, which made them suspicious. Her papers were entirely in order as she was indeed Mme Fiocca of Marseille and so she felt confident that in due course she would be released. She was held for a few days and physically abused but refused to co-operate in any line of questioning. After four days O'Leary appeared at the police station masquerading as a senior member of the security forces with political friends in high positions in the Vichy administration. He explained to the police chief that Nancy's refusal to answer questions was because she and he were lovers and she was afraid word would get back to her husband. Afraid of a strong reaction from O'Leary's non-existent friends in high places, the police chief released Nancy who moved to stay with Françoise Dissart pending an attempt to reach Spain. Increasing security measures and inclement weather made it difficult to secure the services of a guide willing to take groups across the Pyrenees and a number of attempts fell by the wayside.

Following his capture, Gaston Negré had been imprisoned in Castres. Nitelet ended up in a prison at Chambran, near the Italian border and about 250 km north-east of Marseille. Through Françoise Dissart, Pat O'Leary became aware of one of the jailers in Castres who might prove to be helpful. It seems this young man was anxious to escape to England and was willing to help rescue Negré in return for a promise that he would be assisted to cross the Spanish border. A different approach was required in relation to this rescue attempt. The line had no safe accommodation in the Castres area where Negré and his rescuers could lie low while the immediate search resulting from his disappearance was carried out. In addition train travel was now more difficult as the Germans increased the number of checkpoints in the Vichy area once they took control. O'Leary worked out that the weakest time in the prison's security system was in the early hours of the morning. So, a furniture truck was hired but in order to travel by night the driver of such a vehicle needed a special pass. A forged version was created, which was deemed realistic enough to pass inspection, particularly a night-time one. Three quarters of the truck was packed with furniture leaving an empty space between the furniture and the panel behind the driver's seat. This was large enough to accommodate a number of men though not in particular comfort. The helpful jailer, Robert, was instructed to invent a birthday and to take some drink to work for his colleagues to celebrate the event with him. Dr Rodocanachi had supplied sleeping powders, which were added to some of the wine bottles. In due course Robert's three colleagues fell asleep and Negré, two American airmen and one British pilot, a French sailor, and two civilians who had helped the line in the past followed Robert out of the prison. When they reached the lorry the canvas cover was rolled back and each man climbed on to the roof and slid down into the hidden compartment they then began the journey to Toulouse about 80 km away. On one occasion the lorry was stopped at a checkpoint but, after a cursory look at the driver's pass and the furniture in the back, was waved on. At about 4 a.m. the lorry reached Françoise Dissart's shop in Toulouse where Pat O'Leary was waiting. One by one the escapees were moved to an apartment he had rented for the purpose of hiding them until the search died down. Françoise and Nancy looked after them there.

Gaston Negré declined to avail himself of the possibility of leaving the country and so O'Leary moved him up to Paris, where he continued his work. During the next few weeks O'Leary began to arrange for the evacuation of the remainder of the group. All in all, the plan was to move a group of ten across the border in late February, including Nancy Fiocca and those who had escaped from the prison with the exception of Negré. They boarded a train in Perpignan in twos and threes to make the journey to Banyuls, which is very close to the Spanish border. Pat noticed on boarding that there were plenty of German soldiers on the train. Just after the train pulled out of Perpignan a railway worker came to Pat's compartment and warned him that a search was to be made when they reached Banyuls. So word was passed on to the various groups that they would have to jump out as the train slowed down on the way into the station at Banyuls, not an easy task with so many German personnel on board. They were instructed to meet at the shepherds' hut in the mountains, which was to be their departure point for the trek across the Pyrenees. All did as instructed, jumping out into the darkness with some followed by a volley of shots. A search party of German soldiers was sent out from the station as soon as the train stopped. Notwithstanding the difficulties, some of the group managed to come together in the foothills of the mountains but six were missing, including Robert who had freed some of them from the prison at Castres.

By the time they reach their prearranged meeting point the guide who had been awaiting their arrival earlier was gone. Guy Berthet, who had helped with the escape of Ian Garrow, was one of those leading the group with O'Leary. He volunteered to return to Canet-Plage to seek a replacement guide. When he arrived there he was arrested and, despite his perfectly legitimate identity papers, he never returned and presumably he was killed. O'Leary realised that there was no hope of proceeding with the escape so he led the group by nightfall back to the Hotel du Tennis in Canet-Plage, where they were looked after prior to returning to the various hiding places in Marseille and Toulouse pending another attempt.

Jean Nitelet's incarceration was an easier issue to resolve and is another illustration of conflicting loyalties. As the German authorities strengthened their grip on the area following their invasion of the unoccupied zone of France, the Vichy prison commandant, Colonel Malraison, agreed to release a number of prisoners, including Nitelet, whom he deemed most likely to be shot. Nitelet made his way to Toulouse where he stayed with Françoise Dissart until he was evacuated for a second time through Spain courtesy of the Pat Line.

The port of Bordeaux was of strategic importance to the German war effort as it was the base of operations for many of its ships bringing in vital imports. In December 1942, the Royal Marines carried out a commando raid on the port by attaching limpet mines to the ships in port. Of the ten men involved only two, Herbert Hasler and Bill Sparks, survived. They made their way to the village of Ruffec near the demarcation line on 18 December 1942. There they made contact with Marie-Claire Lindell who smuggled them south to Lyon. After hiding in various safe houses there, the Pat Line picked them up and took them to Marseille in early February.

A Fatal Blow?

In the north Nouveau had some months previously recruited Roger le Neveu, who had come to him well recommended by sources in the Resistance. He had already successfully brought a number of groups down south. Having made one trip with a group in early February, he was supplied with a message from Pat O'Leary for Louis Nouveau. In the note O'Leary asked Nouveau to 'join me at once'. There is no record as to what this proposed meeting was to be about. Undoubtedly, O'Leary was becoming increasingly concerned about the viability of the organisation and he was natural that he would discuss the situation with Nouveau one of his closest long-standing collaborators. So Nouveau decided to travel south to meet him and to take along a group of five American airmen who were due to go there. Also due to travel were Jean de la Olla and Norbert Fillerin. They were seen off at the Gare d'Austerlitz in Paris by Roger le Neveu on 12 February.

The first stage of the journey was to St Pierre des Corps, where they were to change to a local train service. They had just got into an empty carriage on the local train when Gestapo officers arrived and arrested them. This was a shattering blow for all in the organisation but particularly Pat O'Leary. Not only was Louis Nouveau central to everything they had achieved but he was greatly loved by all involved. Some days later Roger le Neveu offered to come to meet O'Leary as he had discovered who had been betrayed Nouveau. The meeting took place on 2 March 1943 in Toulouse but, as it turned out, it was a trap and O'Leary was arrested.

Le Neveu was also arrested but this was merely a ruse. Le Neveu was in fact a traitor working for the Gestapo though, like Cole, it's not entirely clear when and how this started. It seems likely that rather than being a double agent all along he was 'turned' by them at some stage. His treachery also led to the immediate arrest of Jean de la Olla, Jacques Wattebled, Fabien de Cortes and others involved in the organisation in Paris and the surrounding districts. Also arrested about this time in Marseille was Dr Rodocanachi. O'Leary had previously offered to arrange for the doctor's evacuation. As his wife Fanny was seriously ill at the time he opted to stay, with fatal consequences. Strangely, a detailed search of his apartment was not undertaken during his arrest and the Gestapo seem to have no information as to his role in the escape line. Just why he was arrested is not clear but he ended up in Buchenwald concentration camp where he used medical skills to treat his fellow prisoners. Like others there, he was treated appallingly and died of a heart attack in February 1944. He realised he was dying and, at his request, those imprisoned in the same cellblock as him sang the *Marseillaise* for him. O'Leary, Nouveau, Wattebled and de la Olla were tortured in prison but did not betray their accomplices. In O'Leary's case, the torture included being placed in a refrigerator for an extended period of time and continuous vicious beatings. They all ended up in German concentration camps, but towards the end of the war were liberated by the advancing Allied soldiers.

Hasler and Sparks actually crossed the Pyrenees with two of Ponzan-Vidal's guides when O'Leary was captured. In a sense, they were the last beneficiaries of the Pat Line. Francisco Ponzan-Vidal was arrested later in 1943 and incarcerated in Toulouse. Just before the liberation of the city in 1944 he was taken in a group of fifty of his fellow anti-fascists to a wood about 30 km away. The Germans shot the entire group and burned the bodies.

Of course there were still people to be evacuated, including some leading members of the Pat Line. More downed airmen, particularly Americans, continued to head southwards seeking assistance in the months that followed. Françoise Dissart stepped into the breach following the arrest of O'Leary warning other helpers of the line to lie low. She had never met le Neveu but he would have been aware that there were other prominent helpers in the O'Leary network. In particular he and the security forces were seeking the 'White Mouse', though they were still not aware of her identity. So Françoise stayed in Toulouse, while Nancy moved to Nice where she remained for some weeks with

Mme Saison who, with her husband, was an active member of the Resistance.

At the end of March 1943 Nancy, together with Danielle Reddé, Reneé Nouveau and the men who had escaped from the prison at Castres made contact with one of the guides who had worked with O'Leary in the past. Avoiding train travel they moved to the border in a coal truck hidden behind the driver's compartment in the same fashion as those escaping from the prison had travelled in the furniture lorry. They passed through a number of checkpoints successfully and were met in the foothills of the mountains by their guides, a young man and woman, Jean and Pilar, together with a mongrel fox terrier that seemed to know the route best of all. Following their move to take control of the Vichy area the Germans had increased security in the mountains, which included patrols by soldiers with dogs. So, the guides instructed the group to discard their shoes and supplied them with rope espadrilles. These were to facilitate them in taking the rockiest paths of all as the German guard dogs with their soft pads tended to avoid these. When the group reached Spain they ran into some difficulties with the authorities there but the intervention of the British Consulate in Barcelona eventually sorted these out and the group proceeded to England.

Nancy immediately joined the Special Operations Executive, where she was trained for action behind enemy lines. She and a colleague were parachuted into the Auvergne region of France in April 1944, where she linked up with the local *Maquis* group. Their role was to sabotage the activities of the German army as they sought to resist the invasion of France by the Allied forces. She was sent to serve as a liaison officer with London to ensure the group were supplied with ammunition in regular parachute drops and to identify targets to be attacked from the air. Very quickly her bravery and leadership qualities came to the fore and she filled a far more prominent role in the group than originally envisaged, which resulted in her being one of the most highly decorated women of the entire war. Her husband Henri had remained in France, feeling that he was safe because he had no significant direct involvement with the escape line or the Resistance. He was arrested in October 1943 and tortured to death by the Gestapo, who were seeking information as to where his wife had gone. She didn't become aware of this until after the war and for the remainder of her life felt responsible for his demise.

The arrest of O'Leary marked the end of the Pat Line as an organisation stretching right from the north of France to the Mediterranean. The authorities presumed they had destroyed it altogether. In this they persisted in their underestimation of the remarkable Françoise Dissart. In Toulouse she managed to rally those remnants of the organisation still at large. Travelling through the south of France she settled accounts that O'Leary had been due to pay. In the meantime, O'Leary and Fabien de Cortes were being moved by train from prison in Marseille. During the course of the journey O'Leary was able to brief de Cortes on the role le Neveu had played. As they reached the outskirts of Paris, O'Leary helped Fabien to jump off the train. Fabien made his way to Lyon where Françoise picked him up. He briefed her on le Neveu's treachery and she arranged for his evacuation to Toulouse and subsequently to Spain. Unfortunately he was arrested by a Gestapo patrol near the Spanish border and sent to a concentration camp in Germany. He survived the war.

She was more successful in organising an escape for Albert Leycuras and George Zafiri, two others she helped to leave the country in April 1943. In the case of a couple of airmen she escorted them to the border herself and arranged for guides to escort them across the Pyrenees. By the end of 1943 she was on-the-run herself and was forced to go into hiding. Early the following year she made available the funds at her disposal and her range of contacts to two other escape lines, the Dutch-Paris line and the Burgundy line, who had also been working in the area and this ensured the safety of many more.

Accounts of the work of escape lines are both incomplete and lack balance. For obvious reasons, records were not kept. Insofar as the experiences of individual escapees are set down in a contemporaneous record, these are usually limited to members of the armed forces. They were debriefed on return home as a matter of course by MI9 for any information that might assist in the ongoing war effort. Many subsequently wrote war memoirs that outline events in which they were involved. So, in the case of the Pat Line we know that approximately 600 servicemen were evacuated. The picture is not so clear in the case of civilians who were not routinely debriefed and, with some exceptions, never wrote an account of their experiences. The result is that the picture emerging is distorted and the impact of the line's activities is not completely clear. So, there is no way of knowing how many civilians were helped to escape. The probability is that overall about 2,000 individuals were assisted. Estimating the numbers who gave their lives in this cause is also difficult. Apart from the absence of records the involvement of individuals in the line varied greatly with the names of many who gave a limited, though hugely important, contribution not widely known. It is estimated that Cole's treachery cost the lives of fifty people. Some will have been involved in other similar work but it is likely that the majority suffered because of their commitment to the Pat Line. Cole was shot after the war while resisting arrest in Paris. O'Leary had arrived there after his release from Dachau and was called upon to identify the body. The other traitor whose actions cost the lives of some in the Pat Line and others in similar organisations, Roger le Neveu, received summary justice at the hands of the *Maquis*.

After the war O'Leary, under his real name, Albert Guérisse, was honoured by a wide range of governments, including that of the UK which awarded him the George Cross. He had led the organisation by his example of bravery and by personal involvement in some of the most risky operations guiding escapees from the north of France to Marseille. The contribution made by his close associates including Françoise Dissart, Louis and Reneé Nouveau, Fanny Rodocanachi, Nancy Fiocca, Francisco Ponzan-Vidal and Donald Caskie was also recognised. The nuanced view the French people had of Pétain meant that he survived the war, living out his remaining years imprisoned on the Île d'Yeu off the Brittany coast, whereas others were executed for their role in the Vichy administration.

CHAPTER 3

Andrée de Jongh was in her mid-twenties at the outbreak of the war. She was the younger of the two daughters of Frédéric de Jongh and his wife Alice, who lived in Brussels. Also living in the family home, at Avenue Emile Verhaeren, were her older sister Suzanne and Suzanne's husband Paul. He was a refugee from Austria, a widower and father of three small children, when he married Suzanne. Frédéric was principal teacher at a local primary school at Schaerbeek in the city. From her father Andrée inherited a great admiration of the First World War heroine nurse Edith Cavell. In that conflict Cavell, who had remained in Brussels after the German invasion, had enabled hundreds of British soldiers to escape home via neutral Holland. When she was arrested by the Germans, Nurse Cavell, as a matter of honour, explained precisely what she had done and why. Found guilty of treason she was executed in 1915, despite many pleas for leniency.

Andrée, better known during this period as Dédée, trained as a commercial artist and was working in that capacity when war broke out. In addition, she had undertaken some first-aid training at a hospital in Brussels. When Belgium was invaded in May 1940, she immediately volunteered her services in that hospital. Her brother-in-law, Paul, knew that the invasion meant problems would arise for him and he went to England, where he joined the anti-Nazi propaganda effort. Through her work in the hospital Dédée got to know many wounded army personnel, fellow Belgians as well as British. On their behalf she began to send letters home confirming to families the whereabouts of their loved ones. The example of Edith Cavell must have been foremost in Dédée's thoughts because she very quickly began to gather information on the wounded in various hospitals and to identify possible safe accommodation for them when they were ready to be discharged. Her father Frédéric, while naturally concerned that his daughter might be placing herself at risk, quickly became involved in her mission.

Realising that moving the men to safe houses would be an onerous and time-consuming task she began to identify others who might become involved. Her friend Arnold Deppé was an early volunteer. Andrée Dumont, then in her late teens, met Frédéric de Jongh and joined the organisation under the codename 'Nadine'. Charlie Morelle and his sister Elvire also became involved at an early stage. Charlie was a lieutenant in the French army. In 1940 he was captured by the Germans but managed to make his escape to Belgium where he was sheltered by the Marechal family, who were friends of the De Jonghs. Dédée supplied him with false papers which enabled him to safely return home to Valenciennes and he promised, in return, to help her efforts in future. So by March 1941, a series of 'safe houses' in Brussels had been enlisted. Apart from the De Jongh family home, these included that of Ann Duchene, an Irishwoman, and Jean Dupourque. Money, clothes and food were supplied by local supporters.

The group recognised, at an early stage, that when the Allied personnel left hospital, safe houses in Brussels could be used as refuges but not on a long-term basis. It would be necessary to move them on fairly quickly. The safety of the families providing accommodation was paramount but other considerations were also significant, such as the scarcity of food. In Nurse Cavell's time Holland was the escape route but in the Second World War that country was occupied so was not a realistic option. The Belgian coast is adjacent to Britain but, like all such areas, it was particularly closely guarded. A journey to Switzerland would require travelling through Alsace, which was then part of the Third Reich. In any event, the Swiss were taking particular care to protect their borders from penetration by those on the run from the Nazis. So, the only realistic option was to travel south from Belgium to France, along the Atlantic coastal region controlled by the German authorities, or through Vichy France to the Mediterranean. Arnold Deppé knew south-west France well so was sent to explore possibilities there. Frédéric de Jongh had suggested that the De Greef family, whom he had known in Brussels, might be useful contacts. Fernand de Greef had been a businessman there prior to the war. His wife Elvire had been employed by one of the national newspapers. When Belgium was invaded, the family travelled south with a view to moving to England. As it happens they arrived too late to secure a passage on a boat so they eventually rented a villa in Anglet, a couple of kilometres inland from the coastal town of Biarritz, and settled there. Fernand secured a job as a translator in the local German headquarters. There was by then quite an extensive number of Belgian families living in the general locality. Soon, the De Greefs became well-known among this group and the wider community.

When Arnold Deppé approached them in June 1941, his
request was fairly simple. He was seeking to identify a local
guide who would take young men, who wished to reach
England via Spain, across the Pyrenees. The De Greefs were
happy to help and soon the whole family including the teenage
children, Freddy and Janine, became actively involved in the
work. Arnold then travelled to St Jean-de-Luz, which is located
about 5 km from the foothills of the Pyrenees, in the south-
west corner of France. Friends there helped him identify three
possible routes across the mountains and some guides who
would be available. The prompt response by the De Greefs and
others to the appeal for help, and the information gained in
St Jean-de-Luz, confirmed that the escape line could operate
down western France. When Arnold returned to Brussels
and relayed the information, the group adopted that as the
route of their proposed escape line. Of course this involved
travelling through the occupied zone of France. This may seem
to have been an odd decision. However, the reality was that
the German control of the area was, by and large, confined
to well-populated centres. By regular parades and shows of
military strength, they ruled by fear which, of course, impacted
on everyone including those in the rural areas. Executions
were used to reinforce this dominance. But for Dédée and her
colleagues, insofar as they could avoid cities and towns, the
prospects of success were reasonably good. Avoiding the Vichy
area meant that the passes required for those seeking entry
there were not needed. Aside from that, crossing the Pyrenees
near the Atlantic coast, though extremely arduous, was easier
than in the Marseille-Perpignan area as the mountain passes
were somewhat lower and the weather tended to be less severe.

However, there was the challenge of crossing the River Bidasoa. When in full spate the river was difficult, and sometimes impossible, to cross. There was an alternative crossing available by way of a suspension bridge over the river. To use it added to the length of the journey. In some ways it was more dangerous as it was floodlit and within sight of a border post, though on a couple of occasions it was successfully used when the position was lightly guarded. Fernand de Greef's role in the local German HQ meant that he had a pass that allowed for free movement around the area at all times of the day and night. More particularly, in the HQ he was able to acquire blank passes and rubber stamps. While his role was important, Elvire, his wife, proved to be the most significant recruit. Her extraordinary commitment was crucial in enabling the group to establish an escape line right through from Belgium, down western France, to Spain.

Initial Steps

The first venture by the group, in summer 1941, was to take ten Belgian soldiers and one Englishwoman, a Miss Richards, to Spain. The Englishwoman seemed to have no idea of the nature of the expedition ahead as she arrived dressed for a normal train journey, sporting a panama hat and bringing quite a lot of luggage with her. Such a large group was likely to attract attention on the train. So they travelled from Brussels in two groups, one led by Arnold and the other by Dédée. They left the train at the Belgian border village of Quiévrain to go through border control, where their forged passes proved sufficient for them to enter France. After a couple of local train journeys, they reached La Corbie near the River Somme. The official crossing at the river was strongly manned by the Germans, and the group's forged documents were likely to be subject to robust scrutiny there, so the plan was to cross elsewhere under cover of darkness. Even this was risky as the Germans also had mobile patrols travelling along the river bank. As darkness fell, Dédée and Arnold led the group from La Corbie to the banks of the River Somme. By arrangement with a local helper, Renée Boulanger whose codename was 'Nenette', a small boat had been left there to allow them cross the river. Unfortunately when they arrived near the appointed spot, they found a group of holidaymakers had pitched their tents there so it was not possible to access the boat for fear the alarm might be raised. The only option open to the group was to swim across at another point, which would be relatively easy for those who could do so as the Somme is a quite gently flowing river. It transpired, however, that six of the men and Miss Richards were non-swimmers. Arnold searched the neighbouring countryside to see what he might find that could prove useful and returned, at about 2 a.m., with a length of wire and a tyre tube. In the intervening period Dédée and the group had hidden from the passing patrols. Arnold swam across the river with the wire and when he reached the far side he tugged as a signal for others to follow. The tube was attached to the wire and each non-swimmer clambered aboard in turn. Dédée discarded her outer clothing and the first man to cross on the tube carried the bundle at head height to ensure she had dry garments on the other side. This was obviously a practical decision but she was concerned that if a patrol arrived and arrested them she would look quite ridiculous. She swam behind the tube, pushing it, as Arnold pulled the wire to bring it across. She swam back and repeated the process for each of the others non-swimmers. Miss Richards, the last to cross, was reluctant to discard her outer clothing but eventually did so, to reveal a pair of large white bloomers. Dédée was afraid these would be visible to any patrol that might pass when they were in the water. As it happened this did occur and Miss Richards had to slide from the tube into the water to avoid being seen. Over a period of about an hour and a half, all of them had crossed to the other side. 'Nenette' took them to her nearby farmhouse where they had something to eat, dried their clothing and recovered from their exertions. This first episode, while it had a comical side, was significant in that it proved to Arnold and Dédée that they could guide a group even when faced with unanticipated difficulties. It also illustrated Dédée's exceptional physical strength and commitment as she swam back and forth across the river.

The rest of the journey to Spain was fairly uneventful although getting across Paris was always risky. Public transport was the only option available to move through the city quickly as the use of private cars was strictly controlled. The German authorities supervised the issue of licences and mounted checkpoints to ensure no violations occurred. So the group travelled from Paris by train, down through occupied France. When the group reached Anglet, Elvire de Greef, by this time known by the code name 'Tante Go' (after her pet dog, Go-Go), had arranged accommodation in the locality for each of them. A few days later they journeyed further south to the Atlantic port of St Jean-de-Lux. There two Basque guides hired by 'Tante Go', Tómas Anabitarte and Manuel Iturrioz, picked them up and took the group across the Pyrenees.

As it was mid-summer the Bidasoa River did not constitute much of an obstacle. Unfortunately for the majority of the group, their planned journey to England ended abruptly when they reached Spain. The Belgians were arrested by the frontier police and some were imprisoned in the concentration camp at Miranda del Ebro. Five others, who were all officers, were returned to the German authorities in the south-east of France. Miss Richards was allowed to proceed unhindered. Her nationality may have contributed to this decision. It is reasonable to assume, also, that her gender and somewhat eccentric demeanour contributed to the perception that she could not possibly constitute a danger of any sort. In this she had fooled not just the Spanish police but Dédée, Arnold and her fellow escapees. She was in fact a Belgian secret agent, Frédérique Dupuich, who was bringing important intelligence which she had gathered in Brussels to MI6 in London. Later in the conflict she was dropped back into German-controlled France where her expertise and involvement was recognised by the award of various honours after the war.

These events in Spain with the first group alerted Dédée and Arnold to the fact that there was an issue they needed to address in the case of future evacuees. It would be necessary to extend the organisation's reach through Spain to ensure their safety. What they did not realise at that time was that one of the five captured Belgian officers had given information to the German authorities who were now aware that an escape line had begun to operate in the area and also had a description of the two leaders. By August 1941 another group of eleven, eight Belgians and three British, were ready to be moved. The night before departure, two of the Britons were recaptured. So Dédée set out with the remaining one,

Jim Cromar, a Gordon Highlander from Aberdeen, and two Belgians, Robert Merchiers and Ernest Sterkmans, on 17 August. Private Cromar's experiences up to that point had been fairly typical. He was captured with his unit at St Valéry-en-Caux on 11 June. Because he had been wounded he was moved to hospital at Aalst in Belgium, from where he escaped on 25 June. The Langlet family in Hofstade sheltered him for several weeks before he made his way to Brussels, where he was accommodated in a safe house by Andre Michaux and his wife for a period, before being moved on to other helper families.

The plan with this group was for Arnold to go with six of the group by a separate route to meet at La Corbie. On the train from Brussels to Lille they were arrested by the Gestapo who were using the description of Arnold that had been passed on from their colleagues in south-east France. But for the fact that she was on a separate train, the same fate would have befallen Dédée and her three charges. When he failed to turn up at La Corbie, Dédée left them with 'Nenette' and returned to Lille to find him. When no trace could be found there, she travelled to Valenciennes. There she called at the home of Charlie Morelle and asked him to investigate. She then returned and resumed her mission with her charges. There were no hitches on the way south, as they travelled by train via Paris and Bordeaux to Anglet. In Anglet they called on 'Tante Go'. When there was no news there of Arnold, Dédée concluded that the likelihood was that he had been arrested. She and the three men then travelled to St Jean-de-Lux to meet up with the Basque guides. On this occasion, Dédée had decided to cross the Pyrenees with the group to see what she needed to do to ensure that difficulties on the Spanish side were resolved. The Basque guides, Tómas and Manuel, were a bit taken aback at the notion of this small, slightly-built young woman undertaking such an arduous journey but she insisted. From St Jean-de-Lux they walked to the farm of Francia Usandizanga in Urrugne. She was the wife of a French POW detained in Germany and known by her code name, Frantxiska. They ate a meal there prior to setting out. Depending on conditions, the crossing took about eight hours and any doubts about Dédée's ability to overcome such a challenge quickly dissipated as she set an example which Jim Cromar and the two Belgians were obliged to follow. The guides took the group to a Spanish farmhouse. The guides were unwilling to travel further into Spain as Tómas, in particular, was at risk of arrest as a result of his activities during the Civil War. From there a local man, Bernardo Aracama, who was to become a key helper on the Spanish side, took them to his house in San Sebastian where they recuperated.

Official Support

Next day Dédée caught an early train for Bilbao where the nearest British Consulate was based. Travelling in the early morning meant that it was unlikely that police would board the train to check documentation. The consular official whom she met, Arthur Dean, was initially sceptical about her story. The British intelligence services had always considered that escape from Belgium down the west coast of France into Spain was a possibility. However, until Dédée arrived in the consulate, there was little evidence of many escapers willing to explore that option. There was, of course, the danger that she was an agent working for either the Germans or the Spanish and this was likely to be foremost in Claude Dansey's thinking when he was advised of her story. Her slight figure and youth seemed at odds with the arduous journey she had undertaken. At the same time it was so unlikely that it was quite possibly true and a separate conversation Arthur Dean had with Private Cromar convinced him that she was genuine. She explained that it was intended that her group would bring a lot more to freedom by the same route but a shortage of money was a major obstacle. Most of her colleagues and helpers were young and none were from wealthy backgrounds. She calculated that the cost of bringing each person from Belgium to Spain was about 7,000 Belgian francs including a payment to the Spanish guides. It also included the cost of first-class train travel as checks were less frequent in those carriages. Dean explained that the priority was to rescue members of the armed forces and payment, if his superiors in London agreed to co-operate, would be made in respect of such individuals only. Dédée had no objection to this arrangement as her group was anxious to move British soldiers and airmen out of the safe houses they were in, to minimise the dangers to those hiding them, and to enable them to rejoin the war against the Axis powers. She also emphasised that other than money no assistance was required in the operation of the line. She and her colleagues were determined that this was to be a distinctly Belgian initiative and had developed as a response to the German invasion of their country. While convinced of her story and supportive of her plans, Dean made clear that it was a matter for the authorities in London to make a decision as to whether to become involved. He asked her to stay in San Sebastian while he awaited a decision.

Meanwhile Michael Creswell took Private Cromar to Gibraltar and he returned to Britain in the first week of October.

The deliberations in London took more than a week as Claude Dansey of MI6 was extremely suspicious of the proposal and threatened to veto it. Arthur Dean persisted to make the case that to reject her offer was akin to looking a gift horse in the mouth. He was supported by Creswell, who came to meet her and was convinced her intentions were genuine. Donald Darling, the MI9 agent based first in Lisbon and then in Gibraltar, expressed similar views. In checking her story, the fact that she had sent letters home on behalf of British personnel in Belgian hospitals emerged and this served to convince Dansey that the offer she had made was worth exploring. Dean asked her to go back to Brussels and bring down some escapees and he committed to the necessary financial support. She was to be assigned the codename 'postmistress' but, in response to her objection, this was changed to 'postman'. Those she was escorting were described as 'packages'.

On her return journey over the Pyrenees, Dédée was somewhat dispirited by the lack of enthusiasm for her scheme among the British authorities in London. She stayed with 'Tante Go' in Anglet and the two of them debated the issue. It was clear to her friend that Dédée was determined to prove her doubters wrong. In the house at Anglet, on that occasion, Dédée met Albert Edward Johnson for the first time. Universally known as 'B', the Londoner had worked in Brussels as a chauffeur, where he became acquainted with the De Greefs. Shortly after the outbreak of the war he moved south to live with them and proved to be a most valuable acquisition for the escape line. That evening, Charlie Morelle arrived at the De Greef house to inform Dédée about Arnold's fate. He confirmed her fears that he had indeed been arrested. He had been imprisoned, first in Lille and subsequently at St Gilles, before being moved to Germany. Despite being subjected to torture, he refused to give any information about the escape line he had helped to establish. He was rescued when the US forces liberated the concentration camp at Dachau.

For Dédée, Charlie had more bad news. While she was away, the Gestapo had called at her family home in Brussels, asking questions about her and her whereabouts. It was clear that they had a complete description of her appearance and suspicions as to her activities. Frédéric de Jongh, although frightened by this experience at the time, downplayed her absence. He claimed not to know exactly where she was, suggesting that it was just a case of a young girl seeing a bit of the world. But he asked Charlie to convey an instruction to Dédée that she was not to return to Belgium in the current cirumstances.

This new situation brought about some changes in the structure of the escape line. Frédéric, code name Paul, took his daughter's place as the chief organiser in Brussels. He was assisted by two young people, Andrée Dumont and Jean Ingels, in Brussels, while Charlie Morelle and his sister Elvire acted as guides from there to the French border. Dédée picked up evacuees just over the border in Valenciennes at the Morelle house. There she and Elvire Morelle operated the line down to 'Tante Go' at Anglet, who organised safe accommodation and food for them there. Dédée also continued to cross the Pyrenees with the Basque guides and each group of 'packages' for the remainder of 1941. On the Spanish side, Bernardo Aracama's role was to look after the escapees until Michael Creswell could collect them and take them to Lisbon or, more usually, Gibraltar.

Usually this meant that they stayed with Aracama for a number of days, where more than one reported he 'ate like a lord' before moving through Spain.

While new arrangements in Brussels were being put in place 'Tante Go' herself went up to collect the next lot of 'packages': two Scots, Bernard Conville and Bobby Cowan. Successful evacuation of these two would prove to the doubters in London that the line was a valuable asset. The trip nearly failed at an early stage. As always the two men were instructed, before they set out on 14 October 1941, to ensure that they were carrying nothing that would incriminate them or create problems for the escape line. When the train arrived at the station in Quiévrain passengers were required to alight and pass through a customs checkpoint and walk to rejoin the train, which had travelled a short distance across the border in the interim. The presence of the German military police on the platform meant that the Belgian customs officials were determined to appear to be taking an assiduous approach to their role. Conville and Cowan, who were identified on their papers as Flemish labourers, were pulled aside by a customs officer to be searched. Allan Cowan was carrying a large quantity of cigarettes which should, in the normal course of events, have led to him being questioned when the truth would probably have emerged. However the custom official did not do so. One of the German MPs spotted the cigarettes but laughed it off, presuming it to be a routine case of smuggling. When he turned away, Conville and Cowan left to rejoin 'Tante Go'. As they hastily left the station, the customs official caught up with the group and offered some fairly useful advice to

'Tante Go'. 'When you take birds like this about, don't wait for the Customs to empty their pockets. Do it beforehand. Good luck!' From then on, escapees were required to empty their pockets before any journey. Dédée joined the group in the Morelle house, and they crossed the Somme in a small boat, and set off on the next stage of their journey.

In Paris following the introduction of curfews, evacuees had to be escorted in daylight. Often extended curfews were introduced at short notice, usually in response to a local incident. For example, a booby trap killed some German soldiers in a brothel near where Guéhenno lived and the people in that arrondissement, Montmartre, were obliged to remain indoors between five in the evening and five the next morning. In his diary entry for 8 December 1941, Guéhenno recalls standing at a window looking out and seeing the people opposite also looking into the empty street like him. 'We wave to each other, but suddenly ... the sound of a loud bugle call; a cocky Parisian kid is thumbing his nose at our servitude.'[1] In many ways for those helping refugees travel south, the journey through Paris was a time of greatest risk. The German secret service in the city was particularly effective and successful but on this occasion no difficulty arose. The group travelled by train from Paris to Bayonne and thence by bus to St Jean-de-Lux. Dédée and the Basque guides escorted Conville and Cowan across the mountains into Spain and reached Bernardo Aracama's house in San Sebastian on 16 October. The three travelled some days later to the British Consulate in Bilbao from where Cowan and Conville were moved to the embassy in Madrid and subsequently to Gibraltar and freedom.

Priorities

Dédée stayed in Bilbao to discuss future plans with Donald Darling, whom she met for the first time on that occasion. She asked for funding to pay for housing, transport and other necessities for the evacuees and Darling agreed to this. He urged that in future she, and her colleagues, prioritise the cases of airmen as distinct from members of the ground forces. The scarcity of airmen, the length of time involved training them and the cost were factors in this approach. So the next mission consisted of three pilots from the RAF, one Canadian, John Ives, and two Poles, Michel Kowalski and Stefan Tomici. Ives had been shot down on 18/19 August 1941, flying over eastern Belgium. He hid in a wood for four days, during which time he developed dysentery. A farmer found him and Ives stayed on the farm until he was fit to cycle to Hasselt, on 27 August, where he caught the train to Brussels. There he was the first of many 'guests' who found refuge with Julian and Anne Brusselmans. The two Poles were shot down near Marche-en-Famenne and became separated. Like Ives both were cared for by locals before reaching Brussels, where they were picked up by the Comet Line (*Réseau Comète* was the name by which the group had become known). Frédéric de Jongh collected the two Poles on 6 November and took them to Gare du Midi where Elvire Morelle was waiting with John Ives. Elvire was to be the guide on the first part of the train journey. She got them through the disembarkation procedure at Quiévrain where they were met by Dédée. The four proceeded south and crossed the Somme by boat before getting a train to the Gare du Nord in Paris. While Elvire returned home, the three airmen and Dédée stayed in a safe house until crossing Paris in the evening on 8 November, before curfew. They boarded a train to Bayonne at the Gare d'Austerlitz. By chance, all the carriages, save the one they were in, were occupied by German soldiers. Fortuitously, the lights in the compartments fused as the train left the station and the journey was completed in darkness. The soldiers disembarked in Bordeaux. On arrival at the station in Bayonne the group were met by 'Tante Go' and 'B' Johnson. He introduced to them to a tactic which became known as 'operation water closet'. On the platform there was a door into the toilet as normal. Inside the toilet block there was a door, always locked, which opened to the street. Johnson had obtained a duplicate key so his 'charges' were always able to leave the station without being checked. After spending the night with the De Greef family, the group got the train to St Jean-de-Luz, then walked for a couple of hours to reach the farm of Francia Usandizanga at Urrugne. The four crossed the mountains on 10/11 November with their guides and were picked up by a Spanish supporter who took them to Irun, where they caught a train to Bilbao. The three airmen arrived by boat in Glasgow on 4 January 1942.

The next group left Brussels on 10 December. It consisted of two members of the RAF, the first pilot of the RAAF to be helped across, and a civilian, Gerard Waucquez. He had been helpful to the line in the past but was also an agent of the British Secret Service who needed to report back to the authorities in London. The journey south through to the foothills of the mountains was uneventful. However, the River Bidasoa was in flood and the group had to wait a few days in the farmhouse at Urrugne before crossing.

The largest group Dédée escorted across the Pyrenees in 1941 consisted of seven men: five pilots, a Belgian army officer and one of the line's helpers, Leo Gierse. They went over on Christmas Day, obviously chosen because security in the area was likely to be more lax than usual. While delighted to devote her Christmas Day to this task Dédée was, at the same time, experiencing some homesickness. It was unsafe for her to enter Belgium so the only family member she met for months was her father on his occasional trips into northern France. The snow was falling in Brussels one evening in January 1942 when she turned up at the family home, unannounced, to what must have been an emotional reunion. The next day while they were gathered in an upstairs drawing room her sister's stepson, sixteen-year-old Martin Wittek, who was keeping watch at the window, raised the alarm as a Gestapo car pulled up outside. Dédée quickly scaled the wall at the bottom of the back garden with Martin's assistance and went to stay with a friend until it was safe to return to France.

Conscious of the fact that she might be picked up by the security forces at any time, Dédée began to involve some of her colleagues in the trips across the mountains. 'B' Johnson accompanied a group in January and on many occasions subsequently. Elvire Morelle and Dédée both climbed the mountains to Spain with a group on 8 February 1942 together with the Basque guides. The journey back was difficult in quite a heavy snowfall and Elvire slipped and fractured her leg. One of the guides went to borrow a mule from a local farmer and this was used to move her, in considerable pain, to a shepherd's hut where they sheltered until nightfall. Then they descended back down on the Spanish side to a farmhouse. Bernardo Aracama came from San Sebastian collected her and took her to a Basque surgeon who operated on the leg successfully. Charlie Morelle accompanied the group which crossed on 30 March 1942 so that he would have the opportunity of visiting his sister, Elvire, who was still recuperating in Spain.

An Efficient Escape Line

By this time the group was operating with great efficiency. The lapse of time between someone seeking their help, having their story checked out and being evacuated was usually just a matter of weeks. It was a very widespread organisation involving many hundreds of people in an area controlled by the German forces. Leaks, treachery and infiltration were a constant concern. A particular worry for Dédée, of course, was the safety of her father. In February the Gestapo called again at the De Jongh house. By chance her father was away, having gone to Valenciennes in the north of France to meet up with some of the helpers there. His elder daughter Suzanne was questioned closely about the whereabouts of Dédée but gave no important information. She was struck by the fact that no mention of her father was made during the interrogation. A neighbour was able to tell her the next day, however, that the Gestapo had been asking many questions about Frédéric in the locality. So, after many months of ongoing concern, he was finally persuaded to move to Paris. The larger city and the fact that he was not known there offered some reassurance although his daughter had hoped that she could persuade him that he had done enough. Her hope was that he would move to England. He left Brussels on 30 April and it was not a moment too soon. An Englishwoman, Anne-Marie Bruycker-Roberts, was one of those operating a safe house for the line in Brussels. During this time she was helped with supplies of clothing by a Spaniard called Florrie Dings. Roberts did not realise that Dings was the partner of Prosper Dezitter, one of the most notorious Nazi collaborators in Belgium. Roberts, in her innocence, took Dings to a meeting in Henri Michelli's house on 6 May. The Gestapo followed quickly afterwards and Charlie Morelle, Michelli and Gerard Waucquez were all arrested. Waucquez had returned to Belgium in early March after his trip to London where had received training as a radio operator. The plan was that he would introduce and operate good communications systems between London and those groups assisting Allied personnel including the Comet Line. All three ended up in concentration camps. Michelli survived but Charlie Morelle became ill and died in Dachau concentration camp on 18 May 1945. Waucquez was sentenced to death in a concentration camp near Munich. Fortuitously for him, a bombing raid destroyed the gas chamber and he survived until the area was liberated. These arrests together with the fact that neither Dédée nor her father could enter Belgium safely prompted those working in MI9 to anticipate the end of the Comet Line.

Albert and Jean Greindl were titled members of a well-to-do aristocratic family in Brussels. Like many other Belgians they had been anxious for some time to become more active in resisting the occupation of their country. In 1941 Jean met Peggy van Lier, who had similar ambitions. Through Jean Ingels, a Comet supporter, they were introduced to Frédéric de Jongh later that year. All became involved in helping the organisation. Then in his mid-thirties, Jean Greindl was running a canteen for poor children in the city, which had been established by the Swedish Red Cross.

His initial contribution to the escape line was to use his role at the canteen to purchase food for airmen living in safe houses locally. After her father's departure for Paris, and the subsequent arrests, Suzanne Wittek (de Jongh) was determined that the work would continue and she turned to Jean Greindl for help. Very quickly he, and Peggy van Lier, became the rallying point in Brussels for the remnants of the organisation, including Jean Ingels, the Greindl brothers and Andrée Dumont. Also becoming more directly involved at this time were two cousins, Edouard and Georges d'Oultremont, and a friend of theirs, Jean-Francois Nothomb. Jean Greindl, known within the group as 'Nemo', by his efforts ensured that the escape line was functioning very efficiently again within a few weeks. Indeed, not content with ensuring the survival of the line, Nemo set about expanding it. Central to his approach was establishing a range of contacts throughout Belgium so that wherever an Allied aircraft came down, there was someone in the area who could arrange that the crew members reached safe accommodation and were quickly put in touch with the Comet Line.

The fate of a bomber mission which took off from England at 11 p.m. on 30 May 1942 for Cologne provided a typical example of how well the line was operating. Over Germany the plane was damaged by anti-aircraft fire but it completed its mission. On the return journey, the plane began to lose altitude. The pilot, Leslie Manser, instructed the crew to evacuate. He held the plane steady to enable them exit. The aircraft crashed quite quickly afterwards and he died. Six of his colleagues parachuted down, reaching various different locations near Antwerp. One, R. J. Barnes, was captured almost immediately. The other five were looked after by friendly locals. In due course they were put in touch with the Comet Line. Two crossed to Spain with Dédée on 13 June and the remaining three followed eleven days later. Remarkably all had reached Gibraltar within a month of their aircraft being shot down and were ready for the journey home to rejoin their unit.

A Legendary Guide

In the early months of the operation of the line, the Basque guides were Manuel Iturrioz and a young colleague, Tómas Anabitarte. In April 1942 Manuel was arrested by the Spanish authorities. He escaped two days later but the experience made him reconsider his position. There is a suggestion that the two men, at that time, sought an increase in the level of payment they were receiving for acting as guides and that this was motivated by greed but this is a harsh judgement. It must be borne in mind that they were running extreme risks. Spotted in the mountains at night they, and those they were guiding, were likely to come under sniper fire. If caught on the French side, there was a strong possibility of execution. Over the border Manuel was on the Spanish 'wanted' list. In any event, by mid-summer, the services of a new guide, Florentino Goikoetxea, had been secured. He and Dédée were an odd pair, the tall and burly Basque man and the slight but determined Belgian woman. Goikoetxea was a huge man of enormous strength who had an intimate knowledge of the mountains. He spoke no language other than his native Basque and was illiterate. From the start Florentino was intensely loyal to Dédée and was destined to become her favourite guide and something of a legend for the role he played in helping so many to escape. She did, however, have to keep an eye on his fondness for Cognac. Not only did he like to consume some before they set out but he tended to secrete supplies along the way. Of course, this could be justified as being necessary to provide sustenance for the escapees. So, he and Dédée reached an understanding that if he dropped his practice of consuming a fairly liberal amount before the start of the journey the supplies en route were justified.

Despite the severe setback of the arrests in early May, the Comet Line was back working efficiently by summer 1942 with considerable assistance from Florentino Goikoetxea. Sixty-nine people were evacuated in the period July to December 1942, usually in groups of four, sometimes accompanied by Dédée and on other occasions by 'B' Johnson. A few were helpers of the line who needed to leave after the May arrests. The vast majority were airmen, of course. Most were British, but there were also some Poles, Australians, Canadians and, on one occasion, Russians. Two Russians had to abandon their plane near Berlin when it was damaged by anti-aircraft fire and they were captured. They subsequently escaped and made their way to Belgium and, having linked up with the Comet Line, were evacuated in October. The first member of the US Air Force brought out was Forrest Hardin, who was one of a group of four evacuated on 20 December 1942.

During one of their meetings in Spain, Creswell suggested to Dédée that using the same route to cross the mountains might lead to their activities becoming too obvious and she began to examine other options. She consulted Pierre Elhorga for advice and assistance. A First World War veteran living in Anglet, he had been recruited initially by 'Tante Go' as a provider of safe accommodation but, with the passage of time, his local knowledge and contacts were to prove helpful. At Dédée's request he began to explore other possible routes across the Pyrenees.

After his departure from Brussels, Frédéric de Jongh quickly established himself in Paris, renting an apartment on the Rue Vaneau where he was joined by his daughter Dédée when she was in the city. Elvire Morelle rented an apartment on the Rue Oudinot. She became acquainted with a neighbour in the apartment block, Aimable Fouquerel, who was happy to accommodate those whom she and Frédéric were hiding. Another source of important support, at that time, came from Robert and Germaine Aylé, who lived nearby on the Rue de Babylone. René Coaches, and his wife Raymonde, organised food and clothes for the refugees and hid many of them in their apartment in the Paris suburb of Asnières. Securing food for evacuees was an ongoing difficulty. Many of the citizens did not have enough for their own needs. Those who had relatives in the countryside relied on them to supplement their rations. With support from locals and making use of the black market, the volunteers somehow managed reasonably well. So Frédéric and his helpers were well positioned to accommodate evacuees in and around Paris while they were awaiting Dédée and Janine de Greef, who would take them on the journey south. With safe locations in various parts of the city, the Paris end of the line operated successfully in the latter part of 1942.

Setbacks

The smooth operation of the Comet Line through France and over the mountains to Spain was achieved against a background of further heavy setbacks for the Brussels end of the Comet organisation. Very early one morning in August, the Gestapo raided the Dumont family home in the city. Despite her father's best efforts to help her escape through a back window, Andrée Dumont was arrested. Both she and her father Eugène were taken away for questioning. Her role in the organisation had been to take airmen from Brussels to Paris, where she linked up with Frédéric de Jongh. By this time she had successfully guided more than twenty across the border between Belgium and France. Her father helped in this work. The main line of questioning by the Gestapo related to Frédéric de Jongh's whereabouts but she denied all knowledge of him. Subsequently a Belgian man whom she recognised arrived and denounced her. She had known him as a member of the Resistance but he was, in fact, acting for the Gestapo. 'Nadine', who was then just twenty years old, was held in St Gilles prison near Brussels where she was subject to interrogation. Despite the brutality used, she yielded no information and was transferred to a German concentration camp about a year later. By chance her father was moved there also and they were able to spend some time together due to the kindness of one of the German guards. Eugène Dumont died in the concentration camp at Gross-Rosen in 1945. His daughter survived and was freed when the Mauthausen camp in Austria was liberated in May of that year. In a display of remarkable courage, 'Nadine's' place in the organisation was taken some months later by her younger sister Micheline, usually known as Aline to her friends. In the escape line she adopted the name 'Michou'. In working for the group she had the active support of her mother.

In November 1942 a further blow to the organisation occurred. Two German agents, posing as American airmen, managed to access a safe house in Brussels, the family home of the Maréchals. Naiveté on the part of the family members meant that it was some time before their suspicions were aroused and even then it took a while before the reality was accepted. Georges and Elsie Maréchal were arrested, together with their children, Elsie aged eighteen and Robert, sixteen. Robert was released some days later but the remaining members of the family were incarcerated. In the meantime the agents had garnered a lot of information, which led to the arrests of many of the Comet Line members in the city. They included Elvire Morelle and Suzanne Wittek, the elder of the two De Jongh daughters. Also picked up for questioning at that time was Peggy van Lier but the lack of evidence linking her to the group led to her being released. Jean Greindl immediately recognised that many of his close colleagues were in danger and arranged for his close collaborators the d'Oultremont cousins, Georges and Edouard, and Peggy van Lier, to be quickly evacuated. They crossed the Pyrenees on 6 December 1942 guided by Florentino Goikoetxea accompanied by 'B' Johnson. With these departures Jean-Francois Nothomb, known as 'Franco', began to take a more prominent role in the organisation. Clearly Jean Greindl would have been aware that he was most at risk but he decided to stay in position. Dédée arranged to meet him in Paris in early January in an effort to persuade him to leave Brussels. Her admonition that 'there are nine chances out of ten that you will never come out of this alive' was to no avail. Eventually the Gestapo identified who 'Nemo' was and Jean Greindl was arrested on 6 February 1943. Tried and condemned to death, he was held awaiting execution in a barracks at Etterbeek in Brussels. By a sad irony, during an Allied bombing raid on 7 September Jean Greindl was killed instantly when a bomb fell on the building in which he was detained. Shortly after his capture other leading members of the Brussels section of the Comet Line were arrested. Eight, including Jean Ingels and Georges Maréchal, were executed by firing squad in Brussels on 20 October 1943.

The arrests of 'Nadine' and her father Eugène and then the Maréchals heightened Dédée's ever-present concerns for her father's safety. In January 1943 he eventually agreed that he would leave for England. On 13 January they left Paris, together with three pilots, on the train for Bayonne. They stayed there in safe houses overnight and travelled on the following day. An extreme storm was raging so crossing the River Bidasoa was impractical. The guide Florentino was proposing to use an alternative route. This involved crossing the bridge further along the river. The location was usually kept under observation by border patrols but he anticipated that in the appalling weather it might be unguarded. The detour added a number of hours to the journey and taking this into account, along with the difficult weather conditions, it was decided that Frédéric could not possibly make the trip this time. Instead he planned to go back to Paris the following morning and guide the next group of evacuees down south and cross into Spain with them. So, Dédée and the three airmen set off for Francia Usandizanga's farmhouse at Urrugne in the foothills of the mountains. The storm had become more violent and when Florentino arrived he pointed out that to attempt a mountain crossing would be very dangerous. It was agreed to defer the attempt for a day, so he returned home.

Some hours later a force of the local police arrived at the house in Urrugne. A local man had tipped them off and received a financial reward after which he disappeared from the area entirely. Dédée, the three airmen and Francia were all arrested. Based on the tip-off the police had expected to arrest six people, so the captives were subject to severe interrogation. None supplied information which would have identified Florentino.

The capture of Dédée on 15 January 1943 was a severe blow for the organisation. Those arrested were initially taken to the local police station in St Jean de Lux and moved on the following morning to the Villa Chagrin, the aptly named prison in Bayonne. 'Tante Go' immediately set about trying to rescue her friend and leader from the Villa Chagrin with the help of 'B' Johnson, Pierre Elhorga and Jean Dassié, the Comet Line's leading figure in Bayonne. 'Tante Go' used her numerous contacts, and information gleaned by her husband in the local German HQ, to come up with an ingenious rescue plan. Unfortunately when they were about to implement it, Dédée was not in the prison as she had been moved elsewhere for questioning. Indeed she was moved a couple of times, which thwarted various rescue schemes that the group devised. In the meantime one of the airmen who had been arrested with her 'cracked' and indicated where he had stayed overnight in Bayonne on the journey south and this led to the arrest of Jean Dassié. Both Jean and Dédée were then moved to a prison in Paris and in due course to concentration camps in Germany. While they survived, Jean Dassié's treatment there damaged his health so severely that he died shortly after he returned home. Francia Usandizanga died in Ravensbrück in April 1945, aged thirty-six. Dédée's interrogation throughout her imprisonment in France focused very much on her father, his whereabouts and activities. It had been clear for some time that he was perceived by the Gestapo as the leader of the escape line. As with the case of Françoise Dissart in Toulouse, Dédée's appearance, in her case her slight build, youth and gender, led the authorities to completely underestimate her. Even when she disclosed to them that she was the leader in an effort to protect her father should he be captured, they dismissed the notion entirely.

All these setbacks seemed to signal the death knell of the Comet Line as it stood. Certainly, Airey Neave and Jimmy Langley in MI9 began to explore the possibility of sending in agents to replace it. Clearly, they underestimated those still committed to the task. From the outset the organisation had displayed remarkable resilience. Each departure was quickly replaced and this pattern continued. Usually what happened was that somebody already helping the Comet Line in a limited way became more directly in the work. At this juncture Jean-Francois Nothomb ('Franco'), then aged twenty-three, became the leader of the group, picking up evacuees in Paris and bringing them south. 'Tante Go' and her helpers there continued as before. Most remarkably of all, Dédée's father Frédéric decided that his best response to her arrest would be to return to Paris and resume the leadership of the group located in the city. The best efforts of Nothomb, 'Tante Go' and 'B' Johnson to persuade him to go to England were to no avail. Back in the apartment on the Rue Vaneau, he resumed his role with help from 'Michou', Aimable Fouquerel and the Aylés. Also prominent at that time were Madeline Bouteloupt, Martine Noel, Valerie Lefebre, Max Roger and Rosaline Thérier. Of course the greatest damage had occurred in Brussels, where the organisation suffered the loss of many prominent members. This occurred at the same time Allied flights were becoming more frequent with a consequent growth in the number of downed airmen seeking assistance. Count Antoine d'Ursel, known in the group as 'Jacques Cartier', stepped into the breach left by the arrest of 'Nemo' and others, and he began to rebuild the organisation in Belgium.

Resilience

Jean-Francois Nothomb crossed to Spain with Florentino on 16 January, the day after the arrests at Urrugne, to meet up with Michael Creswell and update him on the recent developments. He was taken to Gibraltar and smuggled past the Spanish border post concealed in the boot of a car. Donald Darling had arranged for Airey Neave to go over from MI9 to meet him. The object from the point of view of Neave and Darling was to acknowledge what the line had achieved, but given the huge risks involved, persuade Nothomb that it should cease operations. It quickly became clear that this was not going to happen. Then Neave offered more help and Nothomb was open to this but only on the strict understanding that the escape line was Belgian and would continue to operate as such. Anyone sent over from England would have to comply with instructions from the local leadership. As it happened, Jacques Legrelle, working on behalf of MI9, who was sent after these discussions to help the line in Paris, was a Belgian native.

On his return over the mountains Nothomb consulted Pierre Elhorga who had, as requested, identified other routes and additional guides willing to help. The availability of alternative guides was opportune as it was decided that Florentino should take a low profile for a period. Nothomb explored one of these routes, known as the Bidarray crossing, on his own with Jean Elizondo as guide on 6 February. The first evacuation after the arrests took place on 12 February 1943 over the Bidarray route guided by Martin Orhategaray, a nephew of Pierre Elhorga. The group consisted of three airmen, two American and one Canadian, and Albert Greindl, who had to leave Brussels quickly after the arrest of his brother. They were accompanied by Jean-Francois Nothomb and 'B' Johnson. The crossing was successful despite atrocious weather conditions. Unfortunately, on the Spanish side difficulties arose. The group had been collected by car just over the border but had travelled only a short distance when they reached a police checkpoint. Johnson and Greindl leapt out of the car and escaped into the hills but the remainder of the group, Nothomb and the three airmen, were arrested. Imprisoned overnight, they were interrogated the next day. The police were convinced that they had captured four escaping airmen. In the meantime Johnson and Greindl had reached San Sebastian and raised the alarm in the British Consulate. By this time, the Spanish authorities had altered their stance and were quite open to approaches by British diplomats seeking the release of members of the Allied forces so all were released. However, the experience raised concerns about the Bidarray route and it was never used again.

Following his release, Nothomb despatched Johnson to Paris to persuade Frédéric de Jongh to come south join the next group of evacuees and go to England. Arriving back in the station at Bayonne he was met by 'Tante Go' and her friend Yvonne Yribarren who hoped Frédéric might be with him but the mission had proved fruitless. The three decided to go on the local train to Ustaritz with a view to exploring that locality for possible escape routes across the mountains. Shortly after the journey started the train was boarded by police who checked identity papers. Johnson had documents on him that would prove incriminating. Yvonne Yribarren pretended she was about to get sick and Johnson, with permission from the police, opened the window for her and, at the same time, surreptitiously discarded the documents. His own papers identified him as Belgian but the officers were suspicious as his appearance suggested otherwise. The believed him to be a British airman. The three were arrested and taken to the town of St Jean Pied du Port. Johnson was placed in a separate prison from the others. By a combination of belligerence and bravado, pretending that her connections with the local senior German personnel were very close, 'Tante Go' secured the release of all three. It had been a close-run thing and the decision was taken that 'B' Johnson, who had been involved in the escape line from the start, would leave France at the next opportunity. There was concern also for Yvonne Yribarren and her husband Germain Lapeyre, who helped 'Tante Go' by providing accommodation at their home in Bayonne to airmen on the run. The airman who cracked after the arrests had stayed overnight with Jean Dassié but during the day had been taken to stay with the Lapeyres. The arrest of Dassié, a relative by marriage, meant that they were at high risk of a similar fate. So the next crossing of the Pyrenees, on 14 March 1943, consisted of the two Lapeyres and 'B' Johnson guided by Florentino. Indeed the guide carried Yvonne across the river on his shoulders as it was flowing quite quickly.

Yet the line continued to operate notwithstanding these setbacks. Alfie Martin, a native of Belfast, was a member of a crew that took off in April 1943 in a Halifax bomber to attack a Skoda works in Czechoslovakia. Having completed the mission, they were returning home when shot down by enemy aircraft on the French–Belgian border. All but one of the crew bailed out and survived but became separated in the darkness and confusion. Walking along a country road Alfie met two policemen who asked for his papers. His pretence of being dumb was unconvincing so he was asked if he was '*Anglais*'. He nodded in the affirmative and was about to make a run for it when one officer told him to '*Allez vite*' which he did.

Martin was found by a twelve-year-old boy who took him to his home, where he rested before commencing a walk westward. After two days he met a family by the name of Coolen who hid him for six weeks while contact and arrangements were made with the Comet Line. In the meantime his ginger hair was dyed black, as were his RAF trousers. On 26 May he was taken to a safe house in Paris owned by Madeline Bouteloupt where he was supplied with false identity papers. Also there was the pilot of his plane, Wally Lashbrook, and an American airman, Douglas Hoehn. The three went by train to Bordeaux, escorted by Jean-Francois Nothomb and Rosine Witton. From there they travelled on to Dax and completed the remainder of the journey to Bayonne, where they were provided with a meal and accommodation by 'an incredibly fat and jovial Frenchman'. The next morning they resumed their journey to St Jean-de-Lux, where a guide was waiting to take them to a house in the foothills of the mountains. They crossed the

Pyrenees on 5 June in the company of Florentino Goikoetxea, whom they described as 'astonishingly fit and agile'. A month later, Alfie was back with his regiment. He and members of the Coolen family maintained a friendship and contact until he died in December 2017.

Jean Masson

Concerns about the Bidarray route prompted Pierre Elhorga to continue to seek alternatives. He identified another escape route via Larresore and later in 1943 a second one at Souraïde. This involved the help of other guides for the remainder of the line's existence, but the original route across the Bidasoa remained the favoured one and Florentino the most frequently used guide. While the line had suffered severe setbacks it was up and running again by spring 1943. Robert Aylé introduced Frédéric to a member of the local Resistance, Jean Masson, in April of that year. He was ideally placed to help with the task of guiding charges from Brussels to Paris as he came from the village of Tourcoing, which is located on the border between France and Belgium, and he knew the area well. By now the border was more strictly controlled so the task was more difficult than it had been previously.

At their first meeting Masson produced a supply of passes and a copy of the stamp used to authenticate them, which he explained had been supplied to him by a local contact. His first group of seven airmen were brought from Brussels on 15 May and passed on to Madeline Bouteloupt, Robert Aylé and Frédéric. In early June, Masson contacted Frédéric to say he was ready to bring another large group across the border. He would need help to bring them in separate groups on the train to Paris, so Madeline Bouteloupt and Raymonde Coaches were dispatched to meet him in Lille. Each was given one airman to guide. Both were arrested separately by the Gestapo before the train left the station. When Masson arrived with the remainder in Paris, Frédéric, Robert and Germaine Aylé were on the platform at the Gare Montparnasse to meet him. All were quickly arrested including Masson and the airmen. The arrest of Masson was merely pretence. From the early days of the war he had been working for the Gestapo, infiltrating the Resistance and then the Comet Line. Madeline Bouteloupt and Raymonde Coaches were sent to a concentration camp. Both survived until liberation but Madeline's health had deteriorated there and she died on VE day, 8 May 1945.

Yet again the line survived, though with help from the outside on this occasion. Count Jacques Legrelle, a Belgian who had made his way to England some time previously, volunteered his services to MI9. In the autumn of 1943 via Gibraltar and Spain, he made his way to France and took up the leadership role for the Line in Paris under the codename 'Jerome'. So, the Comet Line continued to function successfully throughout the second half of 1943. From the time of the arrests of Frédéric de Jongh and his colleagues on 7 June to the end of the year, more than 160 evacuees were guided to Spain in thirty-eight crossings of the Pyrenees.

Ray de Pape and his colleagues were actually over Germany when they had to bail out following an attack by enemy aircraft. He was the only one of the eight-man crew to evade capture. He walked eastwards for four nights before reaching Belgium. Eventually reaching a small village, he sought help. Of Belgian extraction, he was a fluent Flemish speaker and was taken to a local group who questioned him closely. Satisfied that he was genuine, the Comet Line was contacted and 'Michou' came to pick him up. Over the next few days she took him to Brussels, staying in various safe houses on the way. The line was arranging to move a group south, including Ray and three others. Splitting into two pairs, Ray and a compatriot, Reg Cornelius, were guided by 'Michou' to the house of the Thomé family close to the French border. Monique Thomé was a guide for the Comet Line. She, with the help of a Belgian border guard and a local doctor, successfully took them across the border, hidden under blankets in the doctor's car. Monique took them to a safe house in Paris, where they stayed for four days. From there they travelled south by train and then bicycle, where Janine de Greef took over. She lodged them in a café in Bayonne, where they remained overnight. They were joined there by the other pair they had been with in Brussels, two American airmen, and a Belgian pilot anxious to reach the UK to join the Allies. They were taken the next day to a safe house in Urrugne and crossed the mountains with Florentino Goikoetxea on 15 November 1943.

Most assisted during the period were airmen but some were helpers of the escape line who needed to flee. One of these was Count Antoine d'Ursel who went by the name 'Jacques Cartier'. He succeeded 'Nemo' as leader of the group in Brussels but by June it was clear that the security forces had identified him. He went into hiding in order to continue his work but it became obvious in the autumn of 1943 that he would have to leave Brussels. He was included with the group of five Americans scheduled to cross on Christmas Eve by the Bidasoa route. Unfortunately Florentino was ill and two other guides were

Above left: *Aristides de Sousa Mendes (19 July 1885 – 3 April 1954) became the Portuguese Consul General in Bordeaux in 1938. Despite orders from António de Oliveira Salazar's regime, he continued to issue visas and passports to refugees, including Jews, who were fleeing the Nazis.*

Above right: *Chiune Sugihara (1 January 1900 – 31 July 1986) worked in the Japanese consulates in Manchuria, Finland and Lithuania.*

Below: *Jewish refugees in Kobe, Japan, who escaped from Lithuania with visas signed by Sugihara.*

Above: *Gertrude (Trudy), left, and beside her, Carl Lutz, at an official dinner in Budapest in 1955. During the Second World War, they were among those who strove to save refugees. Carl Lutz (30 March 1895 – 12 February 1975) served as the Swiss Vice-Consul in Budapest, from 1942.*

Left: *Raoul Wallenberg (4 August 1912 – disappeared 17 January 1945) was a Swedish architect, businessman and diplomat. He played a major humanitarian role in Budapest, Hungary, in 1944.*

Jews queuing at the Swiss office in Vatasz Street, Budapest, hoping to get a protective letter which would (hopefully) exempt them from deportation.

Above left: *An Italian by birth, Giorgio (Jorge) Perlasca was living in Budapest and operating an import-export business when he applied to Angel Sanz-Briz for a Spanish passport. They worked together to assist refugees. After the Spanish government recalled Angel Sanz-Briz for his own safety, Perlasca continued the humanitarian work of the legation despite lack of accreditation as a diplomat.*

Above right: *Studio picture of Wilf and Bronia Kokotek and their eldest daughter Rachel taken in 1936. She was hospitalised in 1942 with scarlet fever when the major roundup of Jews in Paris took place. Her parents Wilf and Bronia and younger sister were arrested and subsequently died at the hands of the Nazis in Auschwitz. When she was ready to leave hospital a kindly neighbour Mme Registel collected her and placed her in the care of an order of nuns and subsequently with a family in rural France. She explained to Rachel that the family had to leave Paris in advance of the roundup. Rachel learned the full story after the war was over.*

Fleeing ahead of the army of the Third Reich.

Albert Guérisse (Pat O'Leary) in uniform on the day the George Cross was bestowed on him in 1946, together with his future wife Sylvia and two veterans of the escape line, Fabien de Cortes and Albert Leycuras.

Captain Ian Garrow, a South African of Scottish descent, was a member of the Seaforth Highlanders and led his men towards Dunkirk but did not get there in time to be evacuated. He and other officers set up an escape line based in Marseille, where Garrow continued to assist a steady stream of escapers and evaders.

Above left: *Andrée (Dédée) de Jongh (30 November 1916 – 13 October 2007) was inspired by the example of Nurse Edith Cavell. After German troops invaded Belgium in May 1940, Dédée became a Red Cross volunteer in Brussels. To assist escaped Allied soldiers and airmen, she organised safe houses and later created the Comet Line. (Le Réseau Comète) so they could be escorted through occupied France to reach Spain and Gibraltar.*

Above right: *Micheline Aline Dumont (20 May 1921 – 16 November 2017) was known as 'Michou' and was a key player in the Belgian resistance whose work on the Comet escape line helped to save many stranded airmen.*

Nancy Wake was born in New Zealand and raised in Australia. After working as a freelance journalist, she met and married Henri Fiocca, a wealthy Marseille industrialist. Based in the French port, Nancy helped thousands of downed Allied pilots and Jewish families elude German and Vichy officials to reach the Pyrenees and neutral Spain. She became known as 'the White Mouse' because of her ability to elude capture.

Above: *The De Greef family, with Elvire ('Tante Go') on the left, with her pet dog. When Belgium was invaded, the family travelled south, intending to more to England but, unable to get a passage on a boat, they rented a villa in Anglet, inland from the coastal town of Biarritz in south-west France. From 1941 the whole family were involved in assisting young men who wished to reach England by crossing the Pyrenees into Spain.*

Below left: *Frédéric de Jongh (1897 – 7 June 1943) was the father of Andrée (Dédée) de Jongh, (see previous page). He worked as a school principal and now the school he worked at bears his name. He and his family assisted many airmen in occupied Belgium.*

Below right: *Père Marie-Benoît (3 March 1895 – 5 February 1990) was was born Pierre Péteul. As a CapuchinFranciscan friar, he helped smuggle approximately 4,000 Jews to safety from Nazi-occupied Southern France.*

Gino Bartali. A photo of an autographed card which Gino gave, in 1939, to Giorgio Goldenberg, the son the family he was hiding.

Gino Bartali in 1945. (Wiki Commons).

Left: *Airey Neave (23 January 1916 –
30 March 1979) was the first British
Prisoner of War to succeed in escaping
from Colditz Castle. He later worked
for MI9. After the Second World War,
he served with the International Military
Tribunal at the Nuremberg Trials.
(Courtesy United States Holocaust
Memorial Museum)*

Below: *Prisoners in Buchenwald,
photographed five days after their
liberation. (NARA)*

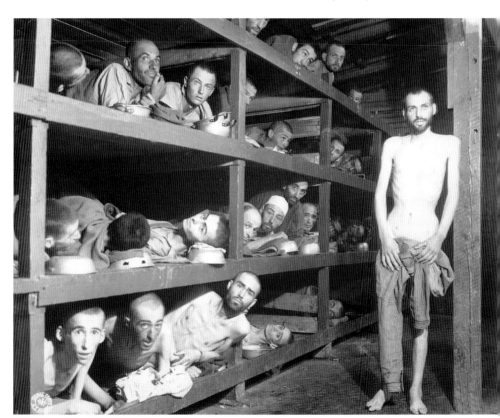

recruited to bring the group across. They were also accompanied by Jean-Francois Nothomb. When they reached the river, it was in fairly full torrent. It was deemed passable but Nothomb realised that each of the group, none of whom had any experience of fording a river, would need assistance. 'Cartier' got into difficulty crossing and became separated from the guide but managed to return to the French bank of the river. Jean-Francois Nothomb went back and tried to persuade his colleague, by now wet through and shivering with the cold, to return to the farmhouse they had just left and await the next crossing scheduled for later in the week but 'Cartier' wanted to try again. On the second crossing shots rang out as the border guards became aware of what was going on. The two became separated and 'Cartier', lacking the strength to reach either bank, drowned. In the panic caused by the firing of shots the airmen on the far side sought to make their escape and one of them, James F. Burch, a native of Texas, also drowned.

In Decline

Despite the continued operation of the escape line through the latter part of 1943, leading members sensed that time was running out and that the Gestapo, with assistance from Jean Masson, had penetrated the organisation. Yvon Michiels using the name Jean Serment had taken charge in Brussels after 'Jacques Cartier' left. On 7 January 1944 her apartment was searched, although nothing incriminating was found. Jacques Legrelle had already decided to leave Paris but delayed too long. On 17 January he was arrested at his apartment on the Rue de

Longchamp together with a colleague, Jacques de Bruyn. Jean-Francois Nothomb arrived there on the following day and was also arrested. During that month the Comet Line as it existed in Brussels and Paris was almost completely destroyed. Anne Brusselmans, who had to lie low for a period when security was breached in late 1943, became active again in the spring of 1944 organising accommodation for evaders in the city. 'Michou' guided charges from Brussels to Paris but it quickly became necessary for her to move to France. She was replaced by Henri Maca who, with his wife Marie, had been operating a safe house in Brussels. He guided evaders to Paris until he was arrested on 27 May 1944. Imprisoned in Belgium, he survived the war as did his wife who had escaped to Switzerland when her role became known. In May 1944 Yvon Michiels also had to evacuate and was replaced as leader of the organisation by Gaston Matthys, a policeman based in Brussels and long-time ally of the Comet Line.

From Paris 'Michou' guided groups to the south-west. Her chief allies in this were a French couple, Virginia and Philippe d'Albert-Lake. The line continued to operate from Paris down to the border where 'Tante Go' arranged accommodation for evacuees and organised their journeys to Spain. The lack of a safe mechanism for moving evaders into France meant that Anne Brusselmans, with help from 'Michou's' mother Françoise Dumont, had to hide increasing numbers in Brussels and keep them there. By May she was hiding forty-nine airmen in the city and in July this increased to fifty-four. Virginia d'Albert-Lake was caught escorting Allied airmen on 12 June 1944 and ended up in Ravensbrück concentration camp. She was liberated on 21 April 1945 in an emaciated condition weighing little over five stone but she made a full recovery. After her arrest, her husband Phillipe was evacuated and crossed the Pyrenees with the guide Florentino Goikoetxea on 25 June 1944.

In Paris 'Michou' met a man named Pierre Poulin who was anxious to revive the organisation in the city. He also claimed that he had been commissioned to eliminate the traitor Jean Masson. 'Michou' explained to him that she was going to Spain to consult the British authorities and she arranged to meet again on her return. In February she crossed the Pyrenees to meet Michael Creswell who was a bit sceptical but agreed to keep an open mind. On her return to Anglet, 'Tante Go' informed her of the arrest of more helpers in Paris including Martine Noel. It was obvious to both that the escape line in the Paris area had been completely compromised and that there must be a spy within the group. Despite the risks involved, 'Michou' returned to the city in March 1944 determined to establish the identity of the culprit.

She made straight for Fresnes Prison where Martine Noel was held. Having identified where the women's section was she stood at the wall shouting, 'Martine, Martine, who is the traitor?' hoping that she would be heard and eventually she was. The answer came back, 'It is Pierre Poulin.' As she was leaving she was stopped by a policeman who took her to the prison commander for questioning. The diminutive 'Michou' looked younger than her years and her identity card indicated she was fifteen. She explained that Martine Noel was the family's dentist. When they got word that she had been arrested, 'Michou' had been sent out to determine where she was held so that they could send a food parcel to her. The prison commander accepted this story and, considering her actions to be naughty rather than anything more serious, cautioned her as to her future behaviour. On leaving the prison, 'Michou' took the train for Bayonne and made her way to the de Greef house in Anglet. She warned 'Tante Go' that Poulin was a spy and thus ensured the continued safety of the Comet Line in the area. Some helpers in Paris were sceptical, as the man they knew as Pierre Poulin had proved to be helpful and they felt that 'Michou' may have been mistaken in identifying him as a traitor. So a meeting was arranged for two of them, Baron Jean de Blommaert and Albert Ancia, on 7 May, with the man. De Blommaert had been involved with the line in 1943 but had to be evacuated in August of that year. He was dropped by parachute into France in April 1944, together with Ancia, to undertake work on behalf of MI9 as the war moved into a new phase. They came in contact with Poulin and were convinced that he was trustworthy. The plan was for them to meet him, with 'Michou' observing from a distance. By chance Poulain spotted her and she had to lie low herself so she travelled down to Anglet. However, she now knew Poulain was Masson himself, and was able to alert others. 'Tante Go' insisted she head for Spain so she crossed the mountains with Fernando on 11 May 1944. During the first four months she, with help from 'Tante Go', had arranged the evacuation of more than thirty people. Back in London the Secret Service quickly concluded that Poulin was a false name being used by Jean Masson. It emerged later that the traitor's real name was Jacques Desoubrie. He managed to evade capture until 1947.

By this time the war was heading towards a new phase. Planning for an invasion of France was well underway. Neave, and his colleagues in MI9, realised that even if escape lines like Comet remained operational, moving downed airmen through France once it became an active war zone would be impractical. The focus would have to be on ensuring their safety in situ until

Allied forces arrived. So 'Operation Marathon' was devised, under which large numbers of men could be hidden and supported in various areas of France. It was this sort of work that de Blommaert and Ancia were to undertake. The need to recreate the Comet Line in Brussels and Paris was declining. In the south, 'Tante Go' and her team were still fully operational. Downed airmen who made their way south were still guided to Spain. Helpers who needed to escape were also evacuated. While staying at her post, 'Tante Go' evacuated her children and those of Charlie Morelle on D-Day, 6 June, on the instruction of Michael Creswell. All this time, no news was received about Frédéric and those arrested in Paris the previous year and there were some hopes that the developing war situation might improve their prospects. Tragically these proved to be unfounded. On 28 March 1944, Frédéric, Dédée's father and closest supporter, was shot by firing squad in Paris along with his friends and colleagues Robert Aylé and Aimable Fouquerel.

In July 1944 Goikoetxea crossed into Spain. By this time the need for evacuations had passed but he and 'Tante Go' continued to serve the Allied cause by bringing information across regarding the disposition of German forces. Returning during the night, he had crossed the Bidasoa and was descending to Urrugne when he was fired upon by German border guards, leaving him with a shattered leg. He was taken to the police headquarters but declined to answer any questions. After some hours, he was moved to hospital in Bayonne. The news reached 'Tante Go' very quickly. Not only that but, within a day, her wide range of contacts ensured that she knew where he was in the hospital and the name of a young Frenchman in the neighbouring bed. She visited the hospital the next morning on the pretext of bringing a parcel of food to the young man. She ignored Florentino in the next bed and he displayed no sign of knowing her. That afternoon three men arrived in an ambulance with an authorisation from the Gestapo to move Florentino to Biarritz. They removed him on a stretcher despite the protests of the nuns running the hospital. The Basque made no protest as he had recognised that one of the three was 'Tante Go's' husband Fernand. He had forged the authorisation, used it to procure an ambulance and, with two friends, executed the rescue plan. Florentino was moved to a safe house in Anglet and was looked after there.

Recognition

Meticulous research in the decades since has provided us with a more complete picture of the Comet Line than any other similar organisation.[2] Almost 300 Allied servicemen and 100 civilians were evacuated to Spain in 100 journeys across the Pyrenees. Nearly fifty airmen were passed on to other lines to be evacuated. Slightly more than 170 Allied personnel whom the Comet Line were intending to evacuate were recaptured as a result of breaches in the group's security. Well in excess of 200 were hidden by the group as part of Operation Marathon in 1944 and more than 100 remained in safe houses until the Liberation. There were about 2,000 who were involved in the line's activities in one role or another. Of these, more than 150 made the ultimate sacrifice. Some were executed, others died or were killed in concentration camps and a number died soon after Liberation as a result of their treatment there. Happily there were some survivors, including Arnold Deppé (who established the line with Dédée), Elvire Morelle, Germaine Aylé, Elsie Maréchal and her mother, Andrée Dumont ('Nadine'), the elder of the de Jongh daughters Suzanne Wittek, Martine Noel, Jacques de Bruyn and Jacques Legrelle.

As in the case of Dédée, the Germans did not suspect that Jean-Francois Nothomb ('Franco') was at the time of his arrest the leader of the Comet Line. His relatively young age saved him from immediate execution. He returned home in April 1945 with a severe case of tuberculosis and hovered between life and death for some months before recovering. He later served in the priesthood before leaving to get married.

Also very dangerously ill when liberated was the founder and moving spirit of the Comet Line, Dédée (Andrée de Jongh), but she also recovered and subsequently spent her career as a nurse in Africa.

The traitors, Prosper Dezitter and Jacques Desoubrie, whose actions led to the deaths of so many of the Comet Line's helpers, were both tried, found guilty, and executed after the war.

Many of those involved with the line were honoured in their own country and by Allied governments after the war. The primary school in which Frédéric de Jongh served as principal now bears his name. His daughter Dédée was awarded honours by the Belgian, British, American and French governments. The George Medal is the second-highest honour the British government can award to a civilian. In addition to Dédée, the George Medal was conferred on Aline Dumont ('Michou'), Elvire de Greef ('Tante Go') and Florentino Goikoetxea. In the case of the latter, some potential difficulties had to be surmounted. He was a known opponent of the Franco government and was wanted for questioning by them on charges of smuggling. In some circles it was feared that an award of a British government honour might cause diplomatic difficulties. Airey Neave, Michael Creswell and Donald Darling ensured that opposition to the awarding of the George Medal in this case was overcome. Indeed, Darling was so committed to this case that if the award were denied he intended to make a classic English protest: resignation of his position followed by a letter to *The Times*. In the event, this proved unnecessary but Darling was given the task of composing the commendation which was to include some background information on the recipient including his occupation. Any possible embarrassment was avoided by describing Florentino Goikoetxea as an 'import and export merchant'.

CHAPTER 4

The First World War was a bitter episode for the Italian people. From the time they joined the conflict until its end, the Italian armies were in battle on the Austrian front, displaying great heroism, without gaining a hugely significant amount of ground. Tragically, they lost 600,000 men in a three-year period. Despite the fact that the country was on the victorious side, Italy benefitted very little from the outcome of the war. Britain and France divided the main spoils between them and Italy's only significant gain was a small piece of territory that had formerly been part of Austria. In addition, in 1921, when the US and Britain agreed to fix limits on the size of the fleets that the various Allied powers were to operate, Italy was forced to accept restrictions which resulted in them being permitted only the same naval strength in the Mediterranean as the British Royal Navy. Many Italians interpreted this as a direct insult to their national pride.

Throughout this period Italy was fairly unsettled. There was a clear disparity between what they felt they were entitled to as members of the victorious Allied side, most particularly in light of the huge level of human sacrifice involved, and what had been assigned to them. Veterans, their families and others, mainly in the working and lower-middle classes, were deeply dissatisfied with the situation. In addition, this was a time of recession and high unemployment, accompanied by a rise in extreme nationalism. Strikes and rumours of revolution were the order of the day. These uncertain conditions proved to be an ideal breeding ground for the rise of fascism. In 1922 the king, Victor Emmanuel III, invited Benito Mussolini, leader of the National Fascist Party, to form a government. Within four years Mussolini had effectively established a dictatorship, outlawing all other political parties, undermining civil liberties and imposing a totalitarian regime. At the same time, he managed to gain popularity by astute propaganda efforts, public works projects, and, most particularly, by creating the appearance of order.

Given the origins of the fascist movement it is not surprising that Mussolini and his colleagues adopted an expansionist foreign policy based on aggression. In the mid-1930s the Italian army invaded and conquered Ethiopia, and in 1936 Italy sent troops to support Franco in the Spanish Civil War. Later that year Mussolini and Hitler established the Rome–Berlin axis. In 1939 Italy occupied Albania and the two dictators, Hitler and Mussolini, concluded a military alliance known as the Pact of Steel.

The Second World War began on 3 September 1939. By that time efforts were already underway to keep Italy out of the war. President Roosevelt of the United States and Pope Pius XII were very actively involved in the process. During this period the Italian Foreign Minister was Count Ciano, who was married to Mussolini's favourite daughter Edda. He was one of a number of the fascist leadership who were trying to persuade Mussolini not to join the conflict. Under the original Axis agreement, the Italian understanding was that the war, if it were to happen, would not commence before 1943. Although Ciano shared Mussolini's expansionist policies, he was acutely aware that Italy was in no position to engage in a prolonged war effort. He was also sensitive to the fact that among the public there was little enthusiasm for such a policy. Unfortunately, his advice, as well as the diplomatic efforts being made by the Vatican and various foreign governments, fell on deaf ears. The Allied diplomats and the Vatican authorities who were working to keep Italy out of the war did not foresee the quick collapse of France and the British withdrawal from Dunkirk in late May 1940. Mussolini was, most likely, influenced by the fact that France had fallen and he thought that he was joining the winning side. On Monday 10 June 1940, he announced to the Italian people that they would be at war the following day as partners of Germany.

The partnership between Germany and Italy was never one of equals. Italy's economy could only support a fraction of the military expenditure of Germany. The armed forces had been allowed to decline in numbers since the previous war and emigration to the US had greatly increased. Much of the equipment available to the armed forces was seriously outdated. As regards public opinion, there was a major question. The Italians traditionally had little or no enmity towards the various Allied countries and had supported them in the First World War. For a long time, there had been a close connection between the Italian and English upper classes and there was a high level of

Anglophilia among the various noble families in Rome. The Italian working class had a high regard for the US. They were aware, from relatives and friends who had emigrated to America, of the negative view of Nazism held in that country.

After the establishment of closer relations with Germany in the mid-1930s, it is noticeable that Mussolini began to move towards a similar attitude to the Jewish people as held by Hitler. Previously there was no sign that the presence of a Jewish community in Italy was something that greatly concerned him. A document produced in 1938, claiming to be a scientific and academic analysis of different racial characteristics, sought to establish that there were superior and inferior races. The Italians being Aryan were deemed to be in the former category, whereas the Jews were not. This was followed some months later by the establishment of a new state agency, the Office of Demography and Race, which carried out a census of all Jews living in Italy. By September 1938, Jewish children were banned from attending state schools and Jewish teachers were prohibited from employment in them. Later that month, Jews who had moved to live in the country since January 1919 were ordered to leave within six months or face expulsion. As a result, approximately 10,000 of a total of about 60,000 Jews emigrated, though some were replaced by others who arrived in Italy from areas occupied by the Third Reich. Later in 1938, intermarriage between Italians of Aryan origin and other races was prohibited, and Jews were not allowed to work in various forms of employment. Any land or businesses above a certain size owned by Jews, were confiscated.

Many of the ordinary Italian people were not supportive of these regulations and, from the outset, sceptical of the wisdom of Mussolini's decision to support Hitler's war policies. As the war progressed, this scepticism about the merit of Mussolini's policies began to grow. The latter months of 1942 and early 1943 saw the beginnings of a re-evaluation of Italian involvement in the war by some in positions of authority. By March 1943, there were signs in army circles that many were willing to consider the possibility of a coup d'état. A message was transmitted to Mussolini by the Vatican authorities emphasising concern at the damage that was being caused to Italy by the conflict and indicating that the Pope was available to act as peacemaker. Mussolini, however, still thought victory was possible and so did not explore this offer of assistance. At the same time, suggestions came to him from the king and those around him that a change of policy would be appropriate. He responded that it would take three months to prepare for a possible peace initiative. Meanwhile it was becoming increasingly clear that the Allied forces, following their successes in North Africa, would shortly be in a position to invade Italy. Hitler anticipated this and offered Mussolini five additional German divisions, but this was declined. It is clear that Hitler was anxious to stiffen the resolve of the Italian leader in view of his strategic importance to the German cause:

> In Italy we can rely only on the Duce. There are strong fears that he may be got rid of or neutralised in some way. The Royal family, all leading members of the officer corps, the clergy, the Jews and broad sectors of the civil society are hostile and negative towards us ... the broad masses are apathetic and lacking leadership.[1]

On 10 July 1943, Allied forces invaded Sicily and within four or five weeks had taken the island. This prompted further reflection among many sectors of Italian society as to the advisability of Mussolini's alliance with Hitler. Shortly after the invasion of

Sicily, Hitler had flown to Italy to meet with Mussolini. Mussolini promised the king that in the meeting with Hitler he would raise the possibility of an Italian withdrawal from the war. He failed to honour this commitment which prompted the king to contemplate withdrawing his support. In the meantime the Fascist Grand Council had requested Mussolini to call a meeting. Traditionally this group had merely served as a rubber stamp for his actions so he did not anticipate that there would be any difficulty with his colleagues. The meeting was held over two days in late July. On 25 July the council adopted a motion of no-confidence in Mussolini by nineteen votes to seven. Included among those speaking and voting in favour of the motion was his son-in-law Count Ciano. Despite this setback, Mussolini, in the mistaken belief that he still had the support of the king, expected to retain power. He was due to have a meeting with King Victor Emmanuel later that day but when he arrived he was quickly arrested. Marshall Pietro Badoglio was appointed as his replacement. Thomas Kiernan was serving as Irish ambassador to the Vatican at this time. He recalls the outpouring of joy at the collapse of the Mussolini regime:

A few minutes before midnight we were raised from our beds by wild shouting of exaltation. Broken-down cars loaded with young men were careering through Rome shouting their heads off. Mussolini is arrested ... People who have been waiting like a condemned-to-death prisoner reacted now with all the wild abandon of reprieve; not only reprieve, but complete liberty.[2]

Another observer, a Swiss journalist named de Wyss, was alert to the political significance.

Hearing the news people rushed into the streets just as they were, in nightgowns, nightshirts, pyjamas, some in trousers bare to the waist, some in slippers, some barefoot, all howling, yelling, screaming space ... They shouted '*Abasso Mussolini*' (down with Mussolini) ... the publishing office of *Il Tevere* (a rabidly fascist newspaper) was set on fire ... I often heard anti-German shouts ... many times, on seeing Germans, they shouted 'out with the foreigners' ... I also saw them applauding a bonfire of fascist insignia.[3]

A Refuge

In the early years of the Second World War, Assisi, which is almost 200 km north of Rome, was relatively unaffected by the war. Of course, this was not the case for individuals serving in the armed forces and their families but the area itself remained largely undisturbed. The city for centuries was a place of pilgrimage, particularly for those devoted to, or with an interest in, the lives of St Francis and St Clare. However in military terms it had no particular significance. Unlike Monte Cassino, for example, Assisi had no strategic value and in addition it possessed no industrial base. So, other than those members of the German or Italian military who came to visit the area as tourists, little attention was paid to the city and its environs. In civic terms from 1928 onwards it, like other Italian cities, was controlled by representatives of Mussolini's fascist government. The local leadership as well as being fascists were also, in the main, devout Catholics. So, for example, the mayor, Arnaldo Fortini, a local lawyer and a long-time supporter of Mussolini, was also president of the International Society for Franciscan Studies and had authored many books on the saint's life and teachings.

Events elsewhere in Italy, however, had meant that a number of people, approximately 2,000 in total, had come to the area as pilgrims and sought refuge there as it was viewed as a safe haven. As a result, the local bishop, Giuseppe Placido Nicolini, had established a committee for refugees under the leadership of Don Aldo Brunacci, a canon stationed at the Cathedral of San Rufino.

Rufino Niccacci was born in 1911 in the village of Deruta some 10 km or so outside Assisi. In his early twenties he commenced studies to become a Franciscan in the seminary of San Damiano, in Assisi. In 1942, having completed his studies and served in various monasteries of the order, he was appointed as Father Guardian and head of the seminary. The collapse of Mussolini's government in 1943 had brought about some changes in the local administration in Assisi. The Fascist house and the OVRA, the fascist equivalent of the Gestapo, were disbanded but Fortini remained as mayor. So life in Assisi continued, more or less, as before.

German Control

In public Badoglio's government stated that it would remain at war on Hitler's side but essentially this was a diversionary tactic. The new Prime Minister entered secret negotiations with the Allies. On 8 September the Allies and the Badoglio government announced the signing of an armistice. An American-born nun, Mother Mary St Luke, was working at that time in the

Vatican information bureau in Rome. Her diary entries of 8 and 9 September captured the mood:

> At half past seven the news of the armistice broke. The Rome radio broadcast Eisenhower's statement and Badoglio's short dignified addressed to the Italian people. ... in the papers there was a chorus of approval for Badoglio's measures. The German radio let loose a flood of invective against the 'vile treason of the Italians' ... people overflowing with optimism began to talk English freely on the telephone. Yes, it was all over. The Italians would have to hold out for just one week and then the Allies would be here; they dropped leaflets to that effect. ... a lot of Italian soldiers hastily put on civilian clothes. The Roman barracks were evacuated.[4]

The German Army commander in Italy, Field Marshal Albert Kesselring, moved quickly in an effort to take control of Rome. By 11 September he had overcome brave but futile Italian resistance. The king and Badoglio abandoned the city and Hitler went on Radio Rome to make an address to the Italian people. Martial law was introduced and steps were taken to suppress any dissent against German rule. Less than twenty-four hours later, the Germans managed to snatch Mussolini from captivity and he was subsequently moved to the town of Salo at Lake Garda in the north of Italy. There he set up a government, the Social Italian Republic, which was usually referred to as the Republic of Salo. It had no real power and merely acted as a front for the German occupation.

These altered circumstances were destined to have serious consequences for the people, including those living in Assisi and, in particular, for Padre Rufino. A couple of hours after he heard about the German occupation of Rome, he was awoken at about midnight by one of his colleagues. The local bishop, Giuseppe Placido Nicolini, wanted to see him immediately. Padre Rufino dressed quickly and hurried to meet the bishop with no clear idea as to what to expect. When he arrived the bishop came straight to the point:

> *Cor ad cor loguitur* [Heart speaks to heart]. What I am going to say to you, Padre, must remain sub rosa, in strict secrecy between us. I want you to take care of some refugees who are now sleeping under my roof.[5]

The request mystified Padre Rufino and he asked why they were not being looked after by the Committee for Refugees under Canon Brunacci. The response surprised him:

> They are no ordinary refugees. They are Jews who escaped from Rome today. There is a rabbi among them. I want you to take them to Cardinal Elia Della Costa, the Archbishop of Florence ... (he) will send them on to Genoa where Cardinal Pietro Boetto might manage to get them out on a neutral ship as he has done in the past with other Jews and political refugees.[6]

The bishop supplied Padre Rufino with a letter, signed and sealed by him, which testified that the group involved were Christian pilgrims returning to their homes from Assisi. He instructed that they be taken to Florence by the first train at approximately 6 a.m. the following morning. Rufino slept on the couch in the bishop's quarters for a few hours and was woken the following morning and introduced to the group of nine Jews by the bishop.

This was his first time ever to meet a Jew. Before they left the rabbi handed over some sacred Jewish documents to the bishop for safekeeping. If he failed to return the rabbi requested that the bishop would ensure that the documentation was passed on to the Jewish community. 'But why should you fail to return?' the bishop asked. The rabbi mentioned the rumours about Auschwitz and Dachau. 'But you are in Italy ... The Italians wouldn't stand for it. It couldn't happen here, not in the land of Dante, Manzoni and Petrarch.' The rabbi's reply was one that Padre Rufino never forgot. 'That's what the German Jews kept saying ... not in the land of Goethe, Schiller and Heine.'[7]

Having left the bishop, the group went to a basilica near the station. Rufino's plan was that he would go to buy the tickets for the journey and take the group to the station just as the train was about to leave so as not to attract any unwanted attention. In the basilica he was requested by Father Sebastian, who was in charge there, to buy an additional ticket for a Franciscan monk, Fra Felice. This news encouraged Rufino as he felt the chances of success were greater if two were shepherding the group rather than one. It turned out that Fra Felice was not quite what he seemed. Some weeks previously a young Jewish man had made his way to the basilica seeking sanctuary. The real Fra Felice had recently died so the monks dressed the young man as a friar, instructed him to grow a beard and gave him the identity papers of the recently deceased colleague. So, rather than nine, Rufino was now guiding a group of ten Jews.

About a quarter of an hour before the train was due to depart, Rufino led his charges from the basilica. Before he left, he had borrowed a supply of breviaries, one for each member of his group. They had a narrow escape shortly after the journey began.

In Perugia station the train was boarded by some members of the Gestapo who began to check for papers. Rufino handed over the tickets and the bishop's letter identifying the group as Christian pilgrims. These were not deemed sufficient and individual identity papers were demanded. An arrest of the original group of nine seemed inevitable. Just then the air raid siren activated and the Gestapo unit abandoned the train to make for the safety of the nearby fields and the train was instructed to pull out of the station. Rufino looked out the window and saw that the planes overhead were displaying the RAF insignia. The journey after that was uneventful and all managed to get out of Italy. Having successfully completed his mission, he returned to Assisi, which was then under Nazi control. In Assisi, Fortini continued as mayor, the fascist house was reinstated and the OVRA resumed its role of searching houses and checking for documentation.

Another Episode

Rufino's life went back to normal and he began to take it that the bishop's request to him was just a one-off episode. A favourite pastime for him was to meet up with an old friend, Luigi Brizi, the local printer, for a game of checkers on a Wednesday afternoon in café Minerva. On one Wednesday afternoon in late September the bishop's niece arrived at the café with a message that her uncle wanted to see Rufino immediately. It became clear to Padre Rufino at the meeting that the bishop had another mission for him. This case involved twenty Jews who had escaped from Rome to Perugia and were seeking assistance. The narrow escape of the previous group had underlined the fact that identity papers were now of huge importance as the Germans were making far more thorough checks than had previously been the case. So, the first challenge was to come up with identity papers that would withstand scrutiny. While this issue was being addressed, it was decided that the group should be moved to as safe a location as possible.

The Poor Clares is an enclosed order of nuns. They maintained, at their convent, San Quirico, a guesthouse for pilgrims to Assisi. It was agreed that this offered the best prospect of relatively safe accommodation. So a local taxi service, using side roads, took the group in three taxis from Perugia to Assisi on 29 September 1943. A young man, Giorgio Kropf, acted as spokesman for the group. His parents, who were also in the group, had come to Italy after the First World War, having previously lived in Vienna. He was raised in Italy and could pass for a native. The group entered the guesthouse, where they were met by the extern nuns who began to show them to their rooms. These extern nuns were a group of three members of the order whose duties were to attend the outside affairs of the convent. One of the nuns asked Giorgio, as the leader of the group, to collect up their identity papers. It was a legal requirement at the time that those managing guesthouses would check and record the identity details of all those being accommodated in the premises. Padre Rufino explained that there would be no identity cards supplied and asked to see the abbess, Mother Giuseppina. He explained the predicament to her and, at her request, outlined the circumstances in a sermon to the entire congregation at prayers later that evening. After that he went upstairs to the accommodation to meet his new charges.

There were a number of family groups ranging in ages, including children, their parents and, in one case, a grandparent.

It emerged that they were from various parts of Europe and only two of the family groups were Italian. He sensed that this might present problems in due course as it would be difficult for the remainder to pass themselves off as Italian pilgrims in Assisi and suggested that they minimise any conversations they might be having in the presence of others. He clarified for them that the registration issue had been resolved with the abbess and they expressed gratitude for what had been done for them. One of them produced a bottle of wine which they had saved until they had cause for celebration. Padre Rufino, always partial to a nice drop of wine, joined them in the celebration. In the course of conversation it emerged that this day, 29 September 1943, was the eve of Rosh Hashanah, the Jewish New Year. On hearing this, Padre Rufino requested one of the extern nuns to organise some more bottles of wine from the cellar. Flowers from the convent garden were also brought into the room in order to have a proper celebration. And so it came to pass that Rosh Hashanah, in the year 5704 of the calendar, was celebrated by a group of Jews, a Franciscan priest, and some Poor Clare nuns, in a Catholic convent in Assisi. In the course of the conversation, Padre Rufino confessed to the group that he knew little of the Jewish people and their religion. One of them, Otto Maionica, gave him a copy of a history of the Italian Jews and told him that he would find that people of their faith had played a prominent and valuable part in the history of the country over the years.

A few days later, a large congregation including the civic and religious leaders was gathered on Sunday 3 October for a ceremony to celebrate the feast of St Francis, which was due to fall the following day. The bishop was presiding and Mayor Fortini was participating as the civic leader of the community.

The proceedings were interrupted by the arrival of a German lieutenant who announced that a Captain Stolmann wanted to see the mayor and the bishop immediately. Fortini began to leave the basilica but Bishop Nicolini explained that he was in the middle of a ceremony and nominated Padre Rufino to represent him.

When they stepped outside the church they were confronted with the sight of a German tank in the middle of the piazza with its gun pointed at the basilica. Fortini and Padre Rufino were taken across the square to the Hotel Subasio where Stolmann and a group of German officers had established their headquarters. He advised them that the area was now under the 'protection' of the Third Reich and that a detachment of military police had taken up residence. Mayor Fortini assured him that a good fascist administration was in place in the area and that the OVRA were very efficient. Stolmann welcomed this as evidence that co-operation would be forthcoming and he produced a poster to be erected in all public places immediately. It specified that all citizens were required to surrender any arms they possessed within twenty-four hours. The penalty for failure to do so was death. A night curfew was to be observed from dusk to dawn and anyone found outdoors would be shot. Similarly anyone engaging in an act of sabotage, obstruction or attack would be shot on the spot. When the captain saw that both men had read this, he asked Fortini to ensure that OVRA arrested twelve men in the area most under suspicion for harbouring anti-Nazi opinions. He advised that they would be held as hostages. In the event of any attack on German soldiers, the hostages would be executed. Fortini protested at this request but to no avail. Stolmann requested Padre Rufino to reassure the bishop that the church's properties and institutions would be respected. Indeed, he expected that many of his colleagues, being of the Catholic faith, would participate in church ceremonies in Assisi. As the meeting ended, he asked Fortini how many Jews lived in the area. The mayor replied that there were none and that no Jew had ever lived in Assisi throughout its history.

Tightened Security

Fortini decided that rather than comply with Stollmann's instructions he would resign as mayor, a position he had held for over two decades. He was succeeded by Alcide Checconi. As distinct from his predecessor, Checconi's sole devotion was to the fascist cause. The people of Assisi became aware of the new reality on the following day, 4 October. At sunset, units of the SS and the Gestapo were moved in to carry out a raid. They sealed off the seven gates of the city and together with the local police and OVRA personnel, they began to carry out a house-to-house search. Large rewards were offered to anyone who gave information which would help them in identifying suspects and those who failed to co-operate in this endeavour were threatened with execution. The raid caused panic at the convent of the San Quirico. The sisters began to pray for divine intervention, whereas the Jewish refugees prepared themselves for the worst. Padre Rufino rushed to the convent and asked to meet Mother Giuseppina immediately. Speaking to her through the grille between the outside world and the enclosed area, he instructed her to open the cloister to which only she and one colleague, the doorkeeper, had the key.

The admission of others, particularly men, to the cloister would be a complete breach of the order's rules and traditions.

Mother Giuseppina vehemently refused Rufino's request. Padre Rufino decided he needed the bishop's help and raced to seek it. Bishop Nicolini decided he better intervene directly and they returned to the convent. On the way they were questioned by a policeman as they were in breach of the curfew. They were allowed to proceed when the bishop explained that a nun in the convent was ailing and she had asked to see him. As they passed through the streets they saw a Benedictine monastery being raided so it was obvious that religious institutions were not exempt. At the convent the Mother Abbess's first response to his request was that, according to the rules of the order, only the Pope or a cardinal could instruct her in this matter. Nicolini's response, 'I'm the Pope's representative in this diocese and carrying out the Pope's order', had the desired effect. The cloister was opened and all the Jewish refugees, now numbering thirty because of some more recent arrivals, gathered their few belongings and hurried in and were moved into the various rooms. The abbess locked them all in the cloister, including the bishop and Padre Rufino, just as an Italian policeman arrived at the entrance and asked to see the guestbook. There were no entries as one of the extern nuns, in response to his question, explained that there were no guests in the convent at the time. He was quickly joined by members of the Gestapo who seemed intent on entering the enclosed area but relented when Mother Giuseppina protested strongly.

After this narrow escape, Bishop Nicolini decided that a system of alerting the people to an impending raid was necessary. In an area like Assisi with many religious houses the sound of bells ringing was a regular feature of life. The Gestapo were based in the nearby town of Bastia. The entrance to Assisi from that direction was opposite the Basilica of Santa Maria degli Angeli. A lookout was permanently on duty in the belfry there. The signal for a raid was five peals, a pause, and five more.

In the pre-war era, Emilio Viterbi was a distinguished professor in the School of Physics at the University of Padua. In accordance with a proclamation issued by Mussolini in 1938 he, like other Jewish academics, was dismissed from his post. The changed circumstances in the northern part of Italy following the German occupation meant that he and his family had to seek refuge like so many others. He was a friend of Arnaldo Fortini who, by this time, was no longer mayor or indeed involved in politics at all. Viterbi approached him for assistance, firstly to hide all his scientific papers, which Fortini did, and then to help him find safe accommodation. Fortini approached the bishop for help and he, in turn, referred the matter to Padre Rufino. In the meantime Viterbi and his wife and two daughters had moved to live in a local hotel, which of course was far from being a safe location. Happily, Padre Rufino, having anticipated the arrival of an increased number of Jewish refugees, had already made arrangements with some of the other convents and religious houses to assist in the effort and he was able to place the Viterbi family in safe accommodation.

Just before retiring from the post of mayor, Fortini had started a campaign to persuade the German and Allied authorities to agree that Assisi should be declared an open city, in view of its historic and religious significance. If all of the combatant countries agreed this would render Assisi free from attack by the armed forces of either side. He alerted the Vatican to his proposal so they could relay it to the Allied authorities. Fortini made some significant progress on this issue, as he was able to tell Padre Rufino shortly after the discussion on the Viterbi case. Not surprisingly the Vatican authorities had agreed readily to help but the Germans were less enthusiastic. However, while not accepting the open city proposal they had agreed to assign the area as a convalescent centre to treat their wounded personnel in the local hospital. That was conveyed through Vatican channels and the Allies respected the situation by avoiding any attack on Assisi.

The Printers

While developments on that front were being awaited, the urgency of being able to move refugees out of Assisi was underlined by the raid on the convent of the Poor Clare order. Various possibilities were open. Cardinal Boetto was still able to get some out on neutral ships through Genoa while Cardinal Della Costa had organised, with help from parish priests, a route into Switzerland. However, it would not be possible to take advantage of these options without providing those involved with alternative and convincing identity cards. His friendship with the printer Brizi was one that Padre Rufino knew he would have to explore and the issue was now becoming urgent. He also knew that involving Bishop Nicolini would be to no avail, as Brizi was not a religious man. On the other hand, he was aware that Luigi Brizi came from a family that was quite distinguished in its patriotic endeavour, both nationally and locally. The Padre took this approach. He used the knowledge which he had gained from reading the history of the Italian Jews, which Otto Maionica had given him, to point out to his friend the prominent role many had played in supporting Garibaldi and Mazzini. Some of Brizi's ancestors were similarly involved. He also pointed out that descendants of some of these noted Jews were among those in hiding in Assisi. The padre's argument proved successful, although the printer emphasised that he did not want his son, Trento, involved as he was aware of the risks attached of what was proposed. Trento was at that time recuperating from wounds received while serving in the Italian army. He was not easily fooled and soon became aware of what his father was doing, late at night, in the back room of his printing shop. Despite his father's protestations, he became involved in the work.

The task facing them was no easy one. Padre Rufino calculated that he needed 150 documents altogether, some for those who were in hiding in Assisi and others for refugees elsewhere. The identity cards in use at the time varied in design and typeface from region to region. Once the identity card was printed and the photograph attached, a seal had to be stamped on it and these again varied from area to area. They had to create a lot of of these stamps because if the various 'pilgrims to Assisi' were identified as coming from just two or three areas, suspicions would have been aroused. The work had to be carried out at night and Brizi decided that at the end of each session he would have to break up the typeset for fear that if his premises were raided, what they were involved in would become obvious. On the other hand the fact that part of the country was occupied by the Allied forces was of some help. This meant that identity cards could be produced for those areas which could not be checked through official channels by the authorities in areas under Nazi control. Padre Rufino's immediate clerical colleagues became involved in helping. Some accessed directories for the southern provinces to gather the names and addresses of people who actually lived there. Then these could be used in the false identity papers and if the authorities sought to check in the directories they would be reassured that such a person existed. So some cards were in the names and addresses of real people, while others were fictitious. Others gathered postage stamps. Aside from the seal, each identity card had to have postage stamps attached and the friars, by buying a few at a time and from a range of shops, were able to gather all that were necessary without alerting the authorities to what was afoot. Luigi Brizi was a perfectionist, with the result that the process took some time, but the advantage was that the cards, when complete, were unlikely to be detected as false. The need for the cards was growing as more Jews and other refugees seeking to avoid Nazi arrest were now arriving in Assisi. The bishop, Rufino and Brunacci placed them in religious houses throughout the area. Padre Rufino's own seminary of San Damiano was catering for about 70. Adopting the tactic that had worked in the case of 'Fra Felice', Rufino had dressed them in monks' habits and was teaching them some prayers from the Catholic liturgy so that they could pass themselves off successfully. The work of putting the identity cards together, typing in the details and affixing the seals and stamps was carried out by the Jews in the cloister area at San Quirico.

With that process in hand, Padre Rufino travelled to Florence on 23 November 1943 to meet Cardinal Della Costa in order to arrange for the transport of the first group of refugees from Assisi to either Genoa or into Switzerland. When he arrived in the city it was clear that a raid was underway. During the course of that day approximately 1,000 Jews and others were arrested and deported. Included among them was the chief rabbi of Florence and a Catholic priest Don Leto Casini. Among the institutions raided was a Dominican convent where the nuns were taking care of Jewish orphans. Fifty were removed and only two were saved as the Mother Superior had managed to hide them under her habit. When eventually Padre Rufino sat down with the cardinal, he received further bad news. The escape route to Genoa had been uncovered and stopped. The Swiss were limiting refugees; they would admit babies, pregnant women and old people. However, Della Costa was not about to give up easily and was prepared to explore other possibilities. In order to have any chance of success, given the increasing checks being carried out, convincing identity papers were vital. He acknowledged that those being produced in Assisi were outstanding and he suggested to Padre Rufino that a system be set up whereby those cards could be supplied to all those in hiding throughout the region. This plan was not without its difficulties. While the Brizis could print the blanks, photographs and personal details of the intended recipients would have to be supplied to those completing the process in the Poor Clare convent before affixing the official stamp. It would then be necessary to return them to those in hiding in Florence, Perugia and the region generally. Della Costa undertook to set up a secret courier system to overcome these challenges.

While this increasing role would present a great challenge to those working in Assisi to help the refugees, and was a cause of concern and worry to Padre Rufino, good news was forthcoming a couple of weeks later. The decision of the German authorities to designate the area as a convalescent centre was being implemented. Lieutenant-Colonel Valentin Muller arrived in December as the new senior German officer. He was a doctor and, it emerged within a few days, a Catholic. Padre Rufino decided a visit to the city centre might be worthwhile to try and find out a little more about the new German commander. While sitting in his usual place at the café Minerva he was approached by Giovanni Cardelli, an ex-cavalry officer in the Italian army. In the course of a discussion it emerged that Cardelli was involved in the local Resistance movement. It also became clear that he had at least some idea of the work that Padre Rufino was doing. He raised the possibility of some co-operation between those caring for the refugees and the Resistance. He asked that Padre Rufino would find accommodation for two officers who had deserted the army. One of these was a Colonel Gay, who was a member of the General Staff of the Italian Army and much sought after by the German authorities. The other was a Lieutenant Podda. Padre Rufino agreed to look after these two in return for which Cardelli promised to use sources the Resistance had in the local police and civic offices to keep them informed of any significant developments. Just as the conversation finished, they were approached by Mayor Checconi who was accompanied by the new German commander, Colonel Muller, whom he introduced to both. Muller expressed an interest in visiting various locations in the area associated with St Francis and Padre Rufino agreed to show him around. He called a few days later and Padre Rufino took him to all the holy and historic locations in the area. As a result, a valuable relationship developed between the two men, though they were unsurprisingly slightly wary of each other.

A Sporting Icon

Gino Bartali was born in July 1914 in the small village of Ponte a Ema, a few kilometres outside Florence. His family background was a modest one and the accommodation which he, his three siblings and his parents lived in was quite cramped. Although he possessed a somewhat delicate constitution, Gino spent as much time as possible out of doors, playing with neighbouring children. He proved to be a fairly unsuccessful student during his school years. An early fascination for him was his father's bike, which he longed to ride. His small size and slight build meant he was forbidden to do so. However he managed, on occasion, to break this rule. In his teenage years he spent as much time as he could at a bicycle shop in Florence where his cousin Armando Sizzi worked. While soccer was the main sport in Italy at the time, during the summer months bicycle races attracted huge attention. The shop in Florence was a meeting place for bike enthusiasts and, as a result, Gino's interest in the sport grew. He subsequently secured a part-time position in the bicycle shop located in his own village as a means of supplementing family income. As was the case in Florence, the shop was a meeting place for those interested in the sport and many customers and the owner went for training spins together.

Invited to participate, it soon became clear that Gino had a particular talent for the sport. His employer there, Oscar Casamonti, tried to persuade Gino's parents to allow their son to enter some amateur races. For a while they resisted but eventually gave permission. Very quickly Gino began to experience success. While the races were for amateurs, the prize money for winning was quite significant, with the result that his parents were happy for him to become very active in the sport. He turned professional in 1935 and again made a significant and early impact. In that year he finished seventh in the Giro d'Italia, which was then, as now, the major multi-stage road race in the country. His high finish in the general classification together with the fact that he won the King of the Mountains category attracted a lot of attention. In that year also he experienced success on foreign soil, winning the Tour of the Basque country. The promotion of success in sport was central to Mussolini's propaganda policy. So, while Gino, like others of his age group, was conscripted into the army in 1935, he was exempted from many of the normal duties of soldiers to allow him develop his career. His exceptional ability as a cyclist became clear when he won the Giro d' Italia in successive years, 1936 and 1937, and he became one of the best-known sportsmen in the country. His easy way with people meant that he was soon a popular sporting icon.

The two main movements in Italy at that time were the fascists and Catholic Action. Gino, a very devout Catholic, was an active member of the latter group and indeed was held up as an example by its leaders for the young people of Italy to follow. Sport at the time was dominated by political considerations as Mussolini sought to use it to reflect glory on himself and his administration, locally and internationally. The Italian Cycling Federation, who controlled the sport and the programmes of the individual cyclists, was an instrument of Mussolini's policy. So, while Gino was reluctant to enter the 1937 Tour de France, having suffered a bout of pneumonia, the Federation forced him to do so because they considered he was the best hope of an Italian success. In the course of the race he suffered an accident but struggled on to finish that stage. He felt fit to continue but the Federation, fearing his eventual placing would not garner credit for Italy, withdrew him from the race. It was a decision that he greatly resented. They forced him to enter when he didn't feel ready for it and then when he was willing to continue, they removed him. The next year the

Federation, acting on behalf of Mussolini, was even more anxious for an Italian victory in the Tour de France. On that basis they refused to allow Gino to participate in the Giro d'Italia that year, notwithstanding the fact that he had won it in the previous two, as they claimed it would interfere with his preparation for the French race. So the Tour de France was his main target for 1938. The early stages were fairly uneventful for Gino. The race was due to enter the challenging Alpine stages on 16 July. The night before, he was surprised to have a visit from his father who had never previously left Italy and now had made his first trip ever to see his son race. Probably that contributed to the fact that on the next day Gino rode like a man inspired and finished the stage five minutes before the second-placed rider and more than a quarter-of-an hour ahead of the race leader. This secured the yellow jersey of race leader for him, which he retained to Paris and the end of the race without any great difficulty. Mussolini's propaganda machine was claiming this as a great victory for fascist Italy. Gino, in his acceptance speech, pointedly ignored this interpretation and settled for thanking his fans in Italy and France.

Gino was second in the Giro in 1939 and ninth the following year, winning the King of the Mountains classification on both occasions. The impending war resulted in no Italian entries for the 1939 Tour de France. Both of these events in France and Italy were then suspended until the war was over. Other more local and one-day classic races were held and Gino experienced a good deal of success.

In late 1943, Gino received a phone from Cardinal Della Costa. The men were friends and indeed the prelate had celebrated Gino's wedding to Adriana in 1940. The archbishop wanted to see Gino urgently. Aware of the possibility that phone calls might be monitored, Gino asked no questions but cycled into Florence immediately. When they met, the cardinal outlined some of the work that he was doing, with others, to assist refugees. Bartali was not surprised at this as his friend was known to be an ardent opponent of Nazism and Fascism and indeed had snubbed the visit of Hitler and Mussolini when they met in Florence in 1938. Della Costa requested that Gino become one of his couriers.

In many ways Gino was an ideal choice. The sight of the famous sportsman cycling through the region on training sessions was a familiar one. He was less likely to be challenged than others, though such a possibility clearly existed. If he were caught the dire repercussions for him and maybe for his wife and son were clear. The cardinal emphasised the risks involved and insisted that Gino would have to keep these activities secret from everyone, including his wife. Understandably, this was a decision that could not be taken quickly so Bartali took some time over it.

During that period a different request for assistance came to him. When he was working in the bicycle shop in Florence he got to know Giacomo Goldenberg, a member of a local Jewish family. Subsequently the Goldenbergs moved to another part of the country but rumours of what was happening to their Jewish friends prompted them to head back towards Florence, where they felt might be safer. However, they had no accommodation available to them. Even renting accommodation was dangerous as huge rewards were available to anyone betraying the location of Jews.

In desperation Giacomo made contact with his old friend Armando Sizzi, but he had no solution to hand. However, he knew that his cousin Gino had used some of his considerable earnings as a professional cyclist to invest in a number of houses and he approached him with a request to help the Goldenbergs. So, instead of one extremely risky decision Gino Bartali found himself facing two. He decided to respond positively in both cases. He moved the Goldenbergs into one of the properties he owned, but as raids became more frequent, and given the ever present threat of somebody selling information to the authorities, he had to move them again. Eventually he housed them in the cellar of one of the buildings he owned. It was a small, dark area with no windows and only one door. No electricity or running water was available. Only Giacomo's wife Elvira ventured out as her complexion was Italian and Gentile in appearance. They relied on Gino and his extended family for food and supplies.

His role as a courier was fairly straightforward, notwithstanding the huge risks involved. Photographs and document that he transported from place to place were stored in the bicycle frame. All he needed to do was roll up the documentation like a scroll and insert it in the frame. On his journey, a cyclist like him ostensibly on a training session carries little baggage. Quite often he wasn't even stopped at checkpoints. If he was, there was little to search. He often found that those stopping him just wanted an autograph.

Most of the journeys he undertook were quite lengthy, such as that from Florence to Assisi of about 120 kms, so on occasion he would break and sleep overnight in a local church. His wife Adriana knew that his training pattern had changed from what it traditionally had been and so she became somewhat suspicious. However, concerned for her safety, he never explained to her what he was involved in. More significantly, one of the fascist officers in Florence, Major Carita, began to wonder why Bartali was engaged in such extensive training when there was little or no competitive racing taking place. Carita had a fearsome reputation for his techniques of interrogation and when Gino was called in for questioning over a period of a few days he feared the worst. He thought maybe his own activities had been uncovered or perhaps the existence of the Goldenbergs had become known to the authorities. The fascist press often mocked Bartali's devotion to his religion by referring to him as Gino the Pious. This reputation actually came to his assistance during questioning. When he denied any wrongdoing some of his interrogators were inclined to believe him as a man of honour, though Carita remain sceptical. He was released after three days questioning and returned home to his wife, who was by then in a state of panic.

Having successfully established a courier system, of which Gino Bartali was just one member, though perhaps the most noted, Cardinal Della Costa began to turn his mind to possible escape routes for refugees. As the Allied forces made progress in southern Italy, for the refugees going south rather than north as previously, began to make more sense. From Sicily into Italy, the Allies made reasonable progress, to such an extent that they were expected to take Rome early in 1944. They were in fact held up for a considerable period of more than four months at Monte Cassino south of Rome where a long and drawn-out battle took place. Yet the option of heading towards their lines was a realistic one.

A Change of Direction

Bishop Nicolini sent for Padre Rufino on New Year's Day 1944. By that time Cardinal Della Costa's helpers had made contact with some who were willing, for a fee, to smuggle refugees across to the Allied lines. When they met on the first day of 1944 Bishop Nicolini was then accommodating in his own palace a group of 15 Jews, including one rabbi. His request was for Padre Rufino to take them south to the village of Pescocostanzo, in the Abruzzo region of Italy, which lies east of Rome. There they would be met by a couple of local men who were engaged in smuggling goods across the river. They would assist the refugees across the Sangro River to the Allied side, before making a return journey with smuggled goods. The challenge involved in completing this task was considerable and the risks enormous. The trains to the Abruzzo from Assisi were no longer operating, so a journey by road was the only possibility. It was virtually certain that checkpoints would be encountered over the distance involved, which was approximately 250 kms. The padre's initial reaction was that the task was impossible.

By this time Col Muller had begun to make a favourable impression on the inhabitants of Assisi. His approach was far friendlier than that of his predecessor, as he mingled with the local people on a daily stroll through the city. Just after Christmas he chanced upon Padre Rufino who was at the café Minerva waiting for his friend Luigi Brizi. He sat down and had a quick game of chess with the padre, at the end of which he invited his opponent to a return match at his headquarters in the Hotel Subasio. Now, faced with a seemingly insoluble problem, Padre Rufino decided on a high high-risk strategy. Later that New Year's Day, after his conversation with the Bishop Nicolini, he called into the Hotel Subasio, ostensibly to seek his return chess match with the German colonel. He explained to Muller that he was trying to help a group of Christian pilgrims from Pescocostanzo who had come to Assisi to celebrate Christmas but were now having difficulty returning home. He had been unable to access any form of transport to assist them. He also mentioned that he had to make the same journey himself on church business and was wondering if the colonel was in a position to help. This strategy worked. Not only did the colonel supply vehicles but also an armed escort. The following day the German army truck arrived together with a driver and a corporal. Padre Rufino and his charges climbed aboard the truck and both Bishop Nicolini and Col Muller attended to wish them well on their journey. When they were stopped along the way at checkpoints they were rarely delayed because of the presence of the German army personnel and the letter which the bishop had supplied identifying the group as Christian pilgrims. Eventually, in the early evening, they reached their destination, a small church in Pescocostanzo. They were taken in there and had a meal, organised by the local priest. The German soldiers departed to their overnight accommodation and indicated to Padre Rufino that they would be back in the early morning to collect him for the return journey.

Shortly after they left, one of the smugglers, Luigi, arrived. Padre Rufino handed over 3,000 lire to cover the cost of guiding the 15 refugees to safety. However, Luigi responded that was not enough. He maintained that as it was snowing at the time, footsteps would be visible and so the danger greater. He wanted 6,000 lire to be shared between himself and his fellow smuggler Vittorio. The rabbi organised a quick collection among his group but it wasn't enough to make up the deficit. Just then, evening prayers were about to begin in the church. At the invitation of the local priest, Padre Rufino delivered the sermon and announced that a collection was being made to assist poor and destitute refugees. Luigi and Vittorio had joined their families who were in attendance at the ceremony and contributed, as did the rest of the congregation. Between that and the collection among the Jewish refugees, 2,600 lire was raised and the local priest raided an alms box to secure the balance.

After the congregation left Luigi and Vittorio took the group, in a small truck, a further 10 or so kilometres via back lanes and through the forest above the banks of the Sangro to a small hut in a clearing. There they were introduced to Francesco the forester. Padre Rufino remained in the hut with Francesco while the smugglers led the refugees on foot down a steep incline to the bank of the river and across in two small boats to safety. Some hours later a single gunshot confirmed that Luigi and Vittorio had made the return journey. Padre Rufino and Francesco with his two mules went down to the banks of the river to assist in bringing up the smuggled goods. This took about an hour as they had quite a haul, filling both boats, and because of the steep incline, which was muddy. Back at the hut some of the goods had markings that indicated the source, which was US Armed Forces, and these had to be removed. Then Luigi and Vittorio took Padre Rufino back to the church, which they reached about 5 a.m. Before leaving they gave him a barrel of oil and bags of sugar and salt which they described as his share of the goods. About an hour later the German truck arrived to pick him up and the soldiers helpfully loaded up the provisions, which he explained had been acquired for the poor of Assisi.

The journey home was to be a happy one for him. Not only had he achieved his objective and secured the freedom of 15 refugees but he had also garnered some useful supplies. When he returned to San Damiano, however, a Gestapo officer was waiting to meet him. Ostensibly this officer, Captain Von den Velde, was just calling to introduce himself to the local community leaders as the person responsible for security in the entire region. It is clear from the conversation, however, that he had some suspicions as to Padre Rufino's reasons for his recent trip and regarding his activities generally. Unsettled by this, the priest went into the city to call on Colonel Muller who reassured them that Von den Velde liked to throw his weight around but could be easily handled. However, the colonel made it clear that, in providing the army vehicle to the Padre, he had erred and he would not be in a position to do so again.

The success of the Padre's trip to Pescocostanzo had raised hopes among those in hiding in Assisi, including those in the Poor Clare convent, that they might be able to escape also. On the other hand, Padre Rufino was very unsettled by his conversation with Von den Velde. Bishop Nicolini invited those directly involved in organising assistance for refugees to a meeting. At that time there were almost 1,000 Christian and Jewish refugees being looked after in Florence, Perugia and Assisi. The options being discussed were to make an effort to assist more to cross the Sangro River or to increase the accommodation available in Assisi. At this stage the monasteries in the city were all fairly full.

It was decided to send Gino Bartali on a scouting mission to Pescocostanzo to assess whether further use of that escape line was viable. During the course of the meeting a message came to the bishop that two American airmen had been shot down, and had been found in the forest by a young boy of ten or eleven. He had brought them to the basilica where there were in hiding, wearing monks' habits. One of them needed medical attention, which was provided by Dr Carlo Maionica, who was in hiding in the Poor Clare convent. They remained hidden in the basilica although the authorities, being aware that plane had been shot down, carried out extensive searches.

Bartali returned a few days later with grim news. A German patrol had intercepted the smugglers and Luigi had been killed, Vittorio had escaped, and Francesco the forester had been taken by the Gestapo. The only option therefore was to keep the refugees in hiding and hope that the Allies quickly brought hostilities to an end. The Christian refugees were accommodated by and large in private houses while the Jews were in hiding in monasteries, convents, and churches in the city and surrounding area. In an effort to increase the number of places available to Jewish refugees Padre Rufino and his colleagues began to call on those who were already accommodating Christian refugees. In many cases they agreed to take in extra 'guests' although it would have often been obvious to them from their facial features these were Jews. Every couple of days he visited the various religious houses. In the convent of St Colette, when he called one day the nuns were singing in the chapel their daily Gregorian chants. Musical accompaniment to a very high standard was being provided, hardly surprising as the organist was Professor Fano.

Life in Assisi continued as before. The Brizis continued their printing of identity cards by night. The original group in the Poor Clare convent continued to process these and, through couriers, they were distributed to refugees. The numbers involved were such that Bartali could not handle all of this work. Local young men, including Jews who could pass as native Italian Gentiles, were used to take documents from place to place, usually concealed in their shoes. Col Muller maintained good relationships with the local people as he set about the task of opening convalescent centres for his wounded colleagues, numbering about 2,000. Dr Maionica ministered to those refugees in need, although, in cases when prescriptions were required, a local doctor was called to the patient. In mid-February one of the group in the Poor Clare convent, an elderly Jewess, Clara Weiss, died. This presented a new problem as anything other than a Christian burial ceremony would attract attention. So, Canon Brunacci, who looked after Christian refugees, presided at the funeral of one of 'his flock', named as Signora Clara Bianchi. Padre Rufino took particular note that a member of OVRA, the security service, was in attendance at the funeral ceremony.

In February 1944, Giorgio Kropf made the journey to Perugia to transport some identity cards destined for refugees there. He had regularly fulfilled this sort of mission without any difficulty. On this occasion he was joined by Pali Jozsa, a fellow resident at San Querico, and Professor Fano's son Bruno who was living at the convent of St Colette. At the last minute they were joined also by Col Gay and Lieutenant Podda. When they reached Perugia they went straight to the parish church of San Andrea where they handed over the documentation to the contact there, Padre Frederico Vincenti, who arranged for the identity papers to be distributed. Subsequently, they went into a café where they were considered suspicious by one of a group of OVRA members there and all were arrested, with the exception of Col Gay. He managed to avoid arrest only because he was in the toilet. He made his way back to Assisi to convey the bad news. Padre Rufino went quickly to the Hotel Subasio to seek Col Muller's assistance for the four who were in captivity, whom he described as Christian refugees. Muller undertook to see what he could do, provided they had committed no criminal offence. Padre Rufino reassured him on this point. As curfew was about to start the priest didn't have time to alert the bishop by calling on him. Instead he rang and the bishop immediately decided to appoint Arnaldo Fortini to act as their legal representative. Before finishing the phone call, the bishop advised Padre Rufino to visit Sister Clara as she was not well. It took the Padre some time to work this out, before realising that in all probability the bishop's phone calls were monitored and, in reality, he was referring to the convent of the Poor Clares at San Quirico. The identity papers of three of those arrested in Perugia listed them as Christian refugees staying at the guesthouse operated by the Poor Clares. As such, in the event of a raid, it was likely to be the first target.

The priest went there directly and advised the nuns and the refugees that everyone needed to be on the alert, as a raid might be imminent. He also sent messengers out to the other religious houses with the same information.

A Raid

When the warning bells rang in the in the early hours of the morning, arrangements were made to evacuate San Querico as quickly as possible. The escape route was an old concealed tunnel that led from the cloister through to the gardens of the convent and then into the open country outside the city walls towards the mountains and forests. There were many caves in the mountains where the refugees could shelter. The local resistance was located there and could provide some protection and food. The refugees gathered their belongings and the nuns began to strip the beds and take the linen and blankets down to the laundry. Shortly after the warning bells sounded, two vehicles arrived at the convent and a

Gestapo officer sought to gain admittance. In the meantime the refugees and Padre Rufino escaped through the tunnel. Outside, those who were able to, began to climb into the mountain and Padre Rufino took a group of older men to his own monastery, where they were quickly dressed as friars. Meanwhile inside the convent the raid was proceeding under the direction of Captain Von den Velde. Col Gay had remained in the guest house. He was Italian and his false identity papers were perfect. He had his real papers also, and as the rest were making their escape, he had intended to give them to Padre Rufino for safekeeping. Unfortunately, in the rush he had passed over the counterfeit ones. So, when asked for his papers the ones he handed over were the real ones, which identified him as Col Gay. Von den Velde quickly realised who he was and arrested him immediately. His men completed the search of the guesthouse and then, despite the protestations of the abbess, continued on into the cloister, but nobody else was located.

Padre Rufino was celebrating mass at dawn the next morning in his monastery, San Damiano. Among the congregation, all in Franciscan garb, were Jews, including those who had arrived overnight. They were interrupted by the arrival of Captain Von den Velde, accompanied on this occasion by Col Muller. The padre protested about the interruption and the proposed search. Col Muller referred to the fact that religious houses had been hiding refugees and complained that Rufino had abused his trust. The search proceeded but nothing was found. The task for the rest of that day for Rufino and his colleagues was to relocate the refugees who were now in the mountains. Other offers of accommodation were forthcoming. Those who were Gentile in appearance were located with families in the immediate locality and the remainder were taken out to locations in the countryside. In addition, thirty were taken into the bishop's accommodation, which was quite extensive, including gardens and Roman ruins.

Meanwhile, in Perugia, the interrogation of the four captured originally, and of Col Gay, concluded in late February 1944. Nothing of great significance was disclosed. The conclusion was that Gay should be tried for high treason and Podda for desertion. Kropf, Jozsa and Fano were to be prosecuted for carrying false documentation. However, some circumstantial evidence had emerged to link them with Padre Rufino. Von den Velde had long held suspicions regarding the priest's activities and decided to bring him in for questioning. Padre Rufino was held for four days and subjected to a series of interrogations. He was also compelled to witness an execution. On the fourth day, Vincenzo Texeira arrived in his cell and introduced himself to the priest as his new legal representative. It wasn't that he had any particular legal skills over and above those of Fortini. However, he had a significant contact, who enabled him to secure the padre's release.

It seems that his sister-in-law, a very beautiful Neapolitan princess, was a particular friend of General Octavius Bube, German Chief Judge in the province. At the request of Cardinal Della Costa, Bube agreed to consider the case of Padre Rufino as a matter of urgency. He instructed that the priest be released immediately because of lack of evidence against him. In due course, he also examined the files of the other refugees in jail in Perugia. Some time later, Kropf, Jozsa and Fano were released as Bube considered the allegations against them to be without foundation. Some judicious bribery of the prison officers ensured that, in the interim, they were not ill-treated while in captivity.

Col Gay and Lieutenant Podda were sent forward for trial – the advancing Allies, on arriving in the area, released them.

In mid-May 1944 a new Allied offensive at Monte Cassino began to meet with some success and eventually, the German commander Kesselring recognised that he would have to retreat further north. Mother Mary St Luke, in a diary entry for 14 May recorded the significance:

> ... the offensive has put new life into us, a new hope into the Italians. The Allies are progressing slowly, but as long as they do progress, all is well.[8]

In early June Allied forces entered Rome and at the same time, the D-Day offensive was launched. Clearly this was a significant turning point in the war and it was obvious that Kesselring would have to withdraw his troops to the heavily fortified Gothic Line, which was north of Assisi. The humanitarian work of Padre Rufino, Bartali, the Brizis, and so many courageous individuals in Assisi and the surrounding areas, was coming to an end. However, on 18 May, Bishop Nicolini sent for Padre one last time to intervene on behalf of a refugee. Daniel Levi, a teenager living with his family in the grounds of the bishop's palace, was caught by the police after curfew and immediately recognised as being Jewish. Leaving the bishop, Padre Rufino went straight to the police headquarters where the young boy was being held. There he met the chief of police who had received orders to hand the captive over to Captain Von den Velde. Padre Rufino pointed out to the police chief that the Allies were advancing towards Rome and would soon control all of Italy. In the circumstances, it might be wise for him to redeem actions he had taken in the past on behalf of the Nazis with a significant gesture. The boy was released. Clearly convinced that currying favour with the padre was a good idea, the police chief contacted him again on the last day of May with the information the German engineers had arrived into the town to plant mines under various public buildings. The priest immediately went into the city and saw the sappers at their work guarded by members of the SS. He pondered whether it would be worthwhile to make an approach to Col Muller, given that their relationship had broken down somewhat. As he stood in front of the hotel Subasio a German military vehicle pulled up. He was surprised to see Paolo Jozsa, one of his refugees who had been imprisoned in Perugia, get out of the vehicle.

Paolo explained that through the good offices of the Neapolitan princess he had secured a civilian post working for the German army and he had been sent to Assisi with an important document for Col Muller. The document declared, over the signature of Kesselring, that Assisi was to be treated as an open city. When he emerged from the German headquarters Paolo told him that orders had been given to the sappers to dismantle any mines that had been installed and leave the area. Padre Rufino was inclined to credit the Vatican with this important development. The explanation was rather more prosaic. In the course of this work Paolo had secured some blank documentation in General Bube's office, which had been pre-signed by Kesselring for use in an emergency situation. Paolo just filled in the blanks. Just then Col Muller emerged and the two months hiatus in the relationship between him and Padre Rufino ended as they both went up to announce this important news to the bishop. As they left, Von den Velde appeared and protested against the new orders, but Col

Muller told him that he and his men were to leave the city within an hour. A few days later, Muller asked Padre Rufino to go along with him as he bade his final farewell to the bishop and Assisi. He advised them that he had given instructions that the warehouse in the city, which he had established and which contained a wide range of medical supplies and instruments, was to be left as a gift to the people of Assisi. At dawn the next day advance troops of the Allied Forces came into the city to a rapturous reception.

From Bishop Nicolini's initial request in September through to June 1944, not a single Jewish person who sought refuge in Assisi had been deported or killed by the Nazis. The people of Assisi returned to normal life. It is difficult to estimate how many were saved by Rufino and his colleagues. In addition to the Jews who were hidden in Assisi, others passed through having taken temporary refuge and been supplied with forged documentation. Aside from Jewish people, there were others who for one reason or another were on the run and they were helped also. The probability is that in Assisi itself around 500 individuals benefitted and others in Perugia and Florence were saved by the false papers supplied by Luigi and Trento Brizi.

A Postscript

The lack of professional bicycle races during the war period seriously depleted Gino Bartali's income and savings. Although, in normal circumstances, he would have been at his peak in the intervening years, it was necessary to return to competitive cycling after the war in the hope of securing the financial future of his family. He had no alternative professional trade to which to turn.

More particularly, there was the matter of his pride as people began to dismiss his chances in the major races and turn attention to the new rising star of Italian cycling, Fausto Coppi. In 1946 the Giro d'Italia resumed and a titanic struggle ensued between Bartali and Coppi. The race leadership changed hands on numerous occasions and, to the surprise of many, Bartali was successful, beating his main opponent by less than one minute. In the following year the positions were reversed with Coppi emerging as the winner. Many took this as a sign that he was the new dominant force in Italian cycling. However, when it came to entering an Italian team for the 1948 Tour de France, Bartali was chosen as leader. This was the country's first participation in the event after the war and, given his greater experience, Bartali was deemed the more suitable choice. In protest, Coppi withdrew from the team. Gino fared reasonably well in the early part of the tour, winning three stages. However, disaster struck on 13 July when a nail penetrated one of his tyres. With none of his teammates nearby he had to replace the tyre himself and inflate the new one. He arrived in Cannes more than 21 minutes behind the race leader, Frenchman Louis Bobet. In the view of many experts at the time, Bobet was expected to emerge as the overall winner of the event. Even among Italian journalists covering the event, Gino's chances of recovering from the setback were dismissed.

Italy at this time was a political powder keg. It had become a sort of battleground between the Soviet Union and the US in the aftermath of the war as both of them sought to achieve world domination. Relationships in the parliament between the governing party, the Christian Democrats, and the main opposition, the Communist Party, were extremely bitter. On 14 July an attempt was made to assassinate the leader of the

Communist Party, Palmiro Togliatti, near the entrance to Parliament. Speculation was rife as to the motivation of the assailant and what group, if any, was behind the attempt. Unrest was widespread and the breakdown of law and order, including the possibility of a civil war, was distinctly possible.

The 14th was a rest day on the tour as France celebrated Bastille Day. During the course of the afternoon Bartali received a phone call from the Italian Prime Minister, Alcide de Gasperi. The two had known each other from their time together in Catholic Action. The Prime Minister referred to the unrest and dangerous situation in Italy and expressed the hope some success in the tour might have a settling effect. The cyclist promised that he and his team would do their very best on the next stage of the race. This was from Cannes on the coast, to Briançon in the Alps, a distance of about 300 kms. It involved three mountain climbs, the smallest of which was more than 2,000 metres above sea level. Conditions in the Alps were extremely difficult as snow fell and was accompanied by a freezing wind. On the descent from the second climb, Bartali took the lead. He rode alone on the final climb up the Col d'Izoard before the descent into Briançon. The leader of the tour, Louis Bobet, reached the finish 18 minutes later, with the other main challengers even further behind. This allowed Bobet retain the race leader's jersey but with a vastly reduced lead over Gino of just more than a minute. The momentum had swung to the Italian and he won the next two stages. For a cyclist to win three mountain stages consecutively was unprecedented in the history of the tour. Having established his dominance, he rode to victory in Paris. This was the pinnacle of his career, albeit coming fairly late. He rode on for the next few years with some success but without achieving a victory, coming second in both major tours to Coppi in 1949. As with his father's unexpected visit prior to the decisive stage in his 1938 victory, de Gasperi's phone call was undoubtedly a factor. For his part, Bartali's performance served to lessen tensions in Italy.

It is likely that the major contributory factor to his success in 1948 was pride in his own courage and ability, coupled with a determination to silence his critics who had dismissed his chance of success. The same courage and determination was even more evident in his wartime work. However, as regards this aspect of his life, he remained self-effacing and indeed secretive. Details of his role emerged only from the accounts of others, and this some decades later.

Keeping a promise to Padre Rufino, Col Muller returned with his family to visit Assisi in September 1950. He was warmly greeted and an official reception was held for him. He attended a mass celebrated by Padre Rufino at San Damiano. There is no record to suggest that the priest ever sought to find out what the German colonel knew of his clandestine activities. Asked about his many years later, Col Muller's son Robert replied, 'he suspected it and if he was deceived ... it is because he wanted to be.'[9] There is good reason to believe that this is an accurate summation.

CHAPTER 5

Pierre Péteul was born on 30 March 1895. His family were in the milling business in the village of Le Bourg-d'Iré, which is about 50 kms north-west of the city of Angers. Unfortunately, business difficulties meant that the family had to sell up and move to Angers where his father, also Pierre, secured a position as a candle maker. As a result Pierre and his siblings were raised in modest circumstances. The family were active in church affairs and Pierre attended a local Catholic primary school where he proved to be a very bright pupil. In 1907 he decided to prepare for the priesthood. Pierre wished to join the Capuchins, and so went to Belgium to continue his education there at the age of 12.

The outbreak of the First World War led the French government to introduce conscription. Living abroad Pierre could probably have avoided this. However, while politics never really interested him he was a patriotic Frenchman. So he journeyed home to sign up and in 1915 he commenced service as a stretcher bearer in an infantry regiment. He served with great distinction in that position and received citations for bravery on five occasions. Following demobilisation in 1919, he returned to the Capuchin monastery to continue his studies for the priesthood. The most gifted of the recruits to the order worldwide were usually sent to their college at Brindisi in Rome and Pierre was transferred there in October 1921.

There was political turmoil in Rome when Pierre arrived as the fascists and socialists struggled to become the dominant force. Like all combatant nations, Italy had suffered very significant loss of life among its young men during the First World War. There was resentment that, in the division of the spoils of war, the Italian contribution to the Allied victory was not fully reflected. The fascists under Benito Mussolini played on these feelings to establish a dictatorship.

Pierre Péteul had, in the meantime, been ordained to the priesthood, taking the name Marie-Benoît. (In Italy he was known as Padre Maria Benedetto). In 1925 he was awarded his doctorate in theology and was appointed assistant professor in the college at Brindisi. He taught there for the next fourteen years. The outbreak of the Second World War brought that to an end.

In September 1939, still eligible for military service, he returned to France and was assigned to an infantry regiment in the south of the country. His role was to use his knowledge of Italian to act as an interpreter. It was widely assumed that Mussolini would join forces with Hitler and there was anticipation that, in response, France would invade Italy. As it happened, Mussolini hesitated for a time and Pierre's regiment was relocated and his services were not needed. Too old for an active military role, he was demobilised in December 1939 and returned to Rome. Of course, some months later, the German offensive in Western Europe commenced and Marie-Benoît felt it necessary to return home as he was still liable to be called up by the military authorities. He relocated to the Capuchin monastery in Marseille.

Following the invasion of France, Marie-Benoît, like many others, probably welcomed the armistice between the French government of Pétain and the occupying Nazi forces as the lesser of two evils. Aside from that, Pierre had served under Pétain at Verdun and presumably retained some affection and admiration for his former commander. Residents of Marseille, being located in the area of France under the control of Pétain's government in Vichy, would have been hoping that they would avoid the worst horrors of war. Indeed for some time this was the case, although it was not long before they began to see the effects of the conflict. Refugees from Holland, Belgium and northern France began to head south in huge numbers as the Nazi armies advanced. Included amongst these were tens of thousands of Jews.

The first steps taken by the Vichy regime in summer 1940 were aimed at foreigners in general. Various positions in the professions and public service were restricted to native-born individuals whose fathers were also French. Subsistence payments, which had been provided to recent refugees, were terminated and immigrants could be interned or obliged to become involved in labouring on public works, such as building roads. In August an early indication of the administrations' attitude to Jews came when legislation prohibiting attacks on individuals on grounds of race or religion was revoked. This was followed by a prohibition on Jews filling positions in the public service, journalism and teaching throughout France. Serious though these steps were for natives, foreign Jews were at even greater risk. A law introduced in October 1940 provided authorisation for the internment of Jews of foreign nationality. Another measure targeted at all Jews was introduced in June 1941. In it the list of occupations they were not allowed to follow was extended and a census of Jews was introduced. This was a response to a similar provision carried out in the occupied zone of France the previous autumn.

In Vichy France about 140,000 registered themselves as Jews, which represented perhaps 90% of the total. Probably a mixture of fear and naivety contributed to this relatively high proportion. There were undercover Gestapo officials circulating in southern France as a means of ensuring action was taken against anyone who was deemed to be an opponent of the Third Reich. This resulted in pressure on local officials to implement measures introduced by the Pétain government. It is important to allow for the fact that steps taken by the Vichy government to curry favour with their Nazi masters were not always comprehensively implemented at a local level. Despite this, many thousands of people were living in fear, with good reason, throughout the so-called free zone.

Becoming Involved

It is not absolutely clear when and how Père Marie-Benoît began to take an active role in helping people, particularly Jews, who were at risk from the authorities. Early on, he campaigned locally in Marseille against anti-Semitism. Indeed his views on attitudes to Jews, especially among his fellow Catholics, were already abundantly clear. As a young priest in Rome in the latter part of the 1920s he became active in a Catholic action group known as *Amici*. It had been established to promote dialogue and reconciliation between Catholics and Jews. He also studied Hebrew and had many friends in the Jewish community in Rome. His early initiatives in Marseille involved dealing with some cases of Jews and others who had the necessary documents and resources to allow them emigrate and he assisted them in their dealings with the local bureaucratic structures. Some cases were referred to him by the Sisters of the Notre Dame de Sion, who had a convent and school in Marseille. The order had been established originally to pray for the conversion of Jews. Over the years the order worldwide had broadened its mission to promoting good relations between Catholics and Jews. This included offering assistance to members of that faith who were in need, and it had become known for this work.

Marie-Benoît's immediate task was to find safe accommodation where those he was trying to assist could remain for a short period until he could arrange for their departure. He was able to place people with religious communities in the area and some private citizens. In the meantime, he organised papers that would enable them to travel to Spain or Switzerland. Blank official documents were obtained through favourably disposed public servants. The Notre Dame Sisters also used former pupils as a source of supply. Marie-Benoît used guides to help those in need leave France. Some of the guides were motivated by humanitarian considerations while others undertook the task in return for payment.

The need to do more came about when the Vichy authorities began to actively round up Jews in August 1942, ostensibly to be interned in Paris. This was as a result of a Nazi 'request' and the target group were Jewish immigrants to France who had arrived in the country since the start of 1936. There were some exclusions, such as those older than sixty years of age, unaccompanied minors, war veterans and parents of children younger than five. But these categories and the cut-off date of 1936 were soon changed. During August, thousands of Jews were arrested and transported north. Subsequently they were moved to concentration camps, and very few survived. The numbers seeking help from Marie-Benoît increased dramatically as a result of the actions of Pétain's government in Vichy, and the need for safe accommodation and documentation became more acute. At the same time, the police had become far more active in their searches and in trying to establish who was helping escapees. Luckily for Père Marie-Benoît, at this time he became acquainted with Joseph Bass.

Joseph Bass

Bass was a Russian-born Jew who moved to Paris where he qualified as both an engineer and as a lawyer. The professional practice he established was very successful until 1940, when Jewish owned property came under threat of confiscation by the Nazis. To avoid this he transferred the ownership of the firm and its offices to a trusted Gentile colleague and moved to Lyon to open a second practice. He did not register this as Jewish-owned. As it happens, the reason the authorities became suspicious of him was not his religion but because he was known to have anti-government sympathies. After the Germans broke their treaty with the Soviets he was arrested as a Russian national in the summer of 1941. He was placed in an internment camp at Argeles, near the Spanish border, but managed to escape and make his way to Marseille. There, operating under the pseudonym André, he began to establish an organisation to help those who were on the run from the authorities.

Initially the group was limited to his fellow Jews. These included Adrien Benveniste, Sammy Klein, Maurice Brener and Raoul Lambert. Also among his early recruits was Leon Poliakov who in later life became well known as a historian. Bass quickly realised that he needed help from outside his own community and others became involved in what became known as *Le Service André*. These included quite a number of Protestant clergy such as Jean-Séverin Lemaire, Marcel Heuzé and Roland Leenhardt. André Trocmé, who performed an extraordinary role in protecting children in the remote area around Le Chambon-sur-Lignon, also assisted. There were Catholic clergymen involved, including the prior of the Dominican monastery Père de Perceval, his colleague Frère Marcolin, Alfred Daumas, and Père Brémond of the Jesuit community in Nice. Thus, having worked largely on his own, Père Marie-Benoît now became part of a well-organised group of about three dozen committed men and women from various walks of life.

Funding was provided by an American Jewish organisation, as well as some local groups and wealthy individuals. The primary focus of their efforts were Jews but others needing assistance, such as Allied soldiers or political opponents of the regime, were also helped. Refugees were hidden in religious houses or private properties until some form of documentation could be provided. The organisation was functioning well by the autumn of 1942, which is when its services were most needed. The Vichy authorities had intensified their efforts to capture refugees in the

Marseille area in September and October. The situation became even more critical in November when the Germans took over most of the unoccupied zone that had previously been under the control of the Vichy government. At the same time, parts of the Vichy-controlled area to the east of the River Rhone were occupied by Italy. In early 1943, the German authorities destroyed the port area of Marseille and conducted intensive searches throughout the city. It was not possible for *Le Service André* to move all those seeking their help out of France quickly enough to avoid this roundup so they began to relocate fugitives to remote countryside areas. In doing this the assistance of people such as Père Marie-Benoît and Pastor Trocmé was critical as they were able to use their clerical contacts in these areas to find safe accommodation.

Marie-Benoît also worked with Joseph Bass in securing accommodation for refugees in the Italian-controlled zone. The attitude of the local Italian authorities to the Jewish people was different from that of the Nazis. In order to impress their allies in the Third Reich regulations were promulgated and enforced, but not with the same rigour as in the areas under German control. Some steps were never introduced. For example, the Vichy authorities had ordered in 1942 that the documents of Jews in the unoccupied zone were to be stamped *Juif* or *Juive*, as had been the case in the Nazi-controlled area since 1940. The Italians did not implement this provision. To a degree they monitored the situation, in that many Jewish immigrants were in supervised residences. They had to report to police twice a day and their right to travel was restricted. Of course, many more were in the Italian-controlled zone unbeknownst to the authorities. The most significant element of the Italian policy in the area was that even when they arrested and imprisoned fugitives, they did not make them available to be transported to concentration camps. Indeed, on occasions when the Vichy police had entered the Italian zone to arrest Jews, the local authorities insisted on their release.

Le Service André was able to move many Jewish fugitives to the Italian zone using Marie-Benoît's clerical contacts, particularly in Nice and Grenoble. A particularly useful friend in Nice was an elderly Jesuit, Father Brémond. He was a long-time resident there and over the years had become acquainted with many of the city's influential citizens. He introduced Marie-Benoît to Angelo Donati, a wealthy Jew who was head of the Franco-Italian Bank. Very quickly Donati was able to establish a list of houses where escapees could remain in safety while arrangements were put in place to assist them to travel abroad. Using his contacts with organisations and individuals in the city, he was also able to supply them with the necessary resources including money, clothing, food and documentation. There is evidence that the civic authorities also assisted this effort by providing false identity cards and food ration passes to thousands of them.

While working with his colleagues in *Le Service André*, Marie-Benoît continued to act on his own initiative when he came across a case he could address directly. Fernande Leboucher, a young fashion designer, was one such case and she has written an account of his role in trying to help her. Ludwik Nadelman, a Jewish engineer from Poland, moved to live in Paris when his country was invaded by the Nazis. There he met and married Fernande in the early years of the war. Following the invasion of France, they moved to live in the unoccupied zone. Just before the Germans moved to take over the Vichy-controlled area, Ludwik disappeared. Fernande approached Marie-Benoît for help and a couple of days later it was confirmed that Ludwik had been interned in the camp at Rivesaltes, some 10 kms from Perpignan. Fernande made the journey to the camp, which was quite arduous as the final part had to be made on foot. She introduced herself to the Catholic chaplain there with a letter of recommendation from Marie-Benoît. Strictly speaking, visits were not allowed. The chaplain made the case that Fernande was unaware of this regulation and, in light of the difficult journey she had made, persuaded the camp commandant to allow her meet Ludwik. Subsequently the commandant, clearly less than fully committed to official policy and regulations, relented and agreed to allow further visits. At the first meeting Ludwik explained to his wife that the camp was very lightly guarded. However, as each internee arrived any documentation he possessed was confiscated. So, while getting out of the camp could be achieved fairly easily, the lack of papers meant that as soon as the escapee tried to use public transport, sought to buy food or indeed was casually questioned by a policeman he would be re-arrested. Returning to Marseille late that night, Fernande immediately went to the Capuchin monastery and briefed Père Marie-Benoît. Within a few days he had produced the necessary papers. A baptismal certificate using a common Christian forename and surname, stamped by the church authorities, established that Ludwik was a Catholic as were his parents. Through his contacts the priest obtained a blank ration card with the appropriate seal and stamps on it. Fernande filled in her husband's alias to match the baptismal certificate and attached a photograph of her husband. Stitching these documents into her skirt, she made her second visit to Rivesaltes. Ludwik was impressed with the documentation but explained that his need to escape was not the most urgent. Moving around the camp was fairly easy and he introduced her to four fellow prisoners who had been listed for deportation to the Third Reich. He impressed on her that it was essential to assist them to escape before that happened.

Again the Capuchin produced the necessary documents. In the case of two of the men, their families were located and photographs secured. In the case of the other two, Fernande, relying on her memory of her meeting with them, picked out photographs of two similar looking people. On her next visit she delivered the papers. Ludwik briefed the men who escaped a few days later. On arrival at the Marseille railway station they went straight into the restaurant and used an unguarded door there, which led directly onto the street to avoid the identification checkpoint at the main exit. From there they went directly to the Capuchin priory on Rue Croix-de-Régnier. Some days later they were dispatched to Nice and supporters there subsequently managed to get them into Switzerland. This successful tactic was used to assist others to escape from Rivesaltes over the next few weeks. Eventually the authorities brought pressure to bear on the camp commandant and he began to rigidly implement the regulation prohibiting the admittance of visitors. Ludwik had always promised his wife that if there was any sign he was listed to be deported he would endeavour to escape. Sometime later a Resistance source alerted Marie-Benoît that Ludwik's name was on the list of those due to be deported, so Fernande again made her way to the camp. On being refused admission, she returned to Perpignan where a friend of the Capuchin, working in the civic authority there, issued her with an official pass to the camp. This ensured that she was allowed a 10-minute meeting with her husband. Alerted to the imminent danger, he escaped that night and travelled to Marseille. However, Ludwik was betrayed by an informer there and re-interned, this time in a camp at Gurs near Pau. Marie-Benoît and Fernande immediately set about replicating the system they had used when Ludwik was in Rivesaltes and documentation was supplied to enable some of those in Gurs to escape across the border to Spain, which was relatively close. This lasted only a short while before disaster struck. Ludwik was taken to Drancy prison in Paris, although not listed for any move. It seems German soldiers arrived and, by chance, he was picked to be moved in order to fulfil the quota they had been instructed to collect. Drancy was usually the location from where prisoners were moved fairly quickly to concentration camps. Ludwik was transferred to Auschwitz within a few days and did not survive the war.

Notwithstanding this tragedy, Fernande Leboucher continued to work with Père Marie-Benoît by acting as a guide to move fugitives from place to place. She had by this time opened a shop in Marseille and was using her skills as a fashion designer to make garments and hats that proved quite popular with the wealthier women in the city. The income from the shop, and occasional fashion shows, proved to be a useful source of funds to support the fugitives.

Increasing Demands

In the early months of 1943 the number of Jews seeking assistance increased at a rapid rate. At the same time the Nazi leadership were becoming impatient with the Italian reluctance to make available internees to be transported to concentration camps. At a meeting in February, the Foreign Minister of the Third Reich expressed their dissatisfaction to Mussolini. To deflect German criticism, the Italian dictator took a number of steps. In relation to the area of France under Italian control, Mussolini appointed a police chief from Bari, Guido Lospinoso, to establish a Commissariat for Jewish Affairs in Nice. He was required to expedite the internment of all Jews living in the region. By a stroke of good fortune, Lospinoso was a friend of the Jesuit Father Brémond, who arranged for Marie-Benoît and Donati to meet him shortly after he arrived in Nice to take up his position. At the end of their meeting Lospinoso advised the two men that he was going to take a humane approach to his role. True to his word, this is what transpired. Lospinoso had consulted senior colleagues before he left Italy and they would have suggested that he apply a liberal interpretation to regulations. So, how much of his approach to his role is due to the intervention by Donati and Marie-Benoît is not clear but the meeting would have certainly reinforced his intentions and helped him to understand how best to help those Jews who were fugitives in the area. For the rest of the time, until Mussolini was removed from power in July 1943 and the German-Italian alliance collapsed, there were no mass deportations from the area.

In September German forces occupied the area of France formerly controlled by the Italians. While Angelo Donati may not have foreseen precisely how the conflict would unfold, he had anticipated that the fairly lax approach of the Italian authorities, and Lospinoso in particular, would not last forever. From the autumn of 1942 he had been working on a scheme to evacuate Jewish fugitives from Nice and the surrounding areas into mainland Italy. His contacts in the Italian administration ensured that there was openness to the idea. Donati's greatest fear was for those in supervised residences. In the event of a change in policy, they could be located and arrested quite quickly. Marie-Benoît was aware of Donati's plan and a change in his own circumstances meant he could play a part in trying to bring it about.

In July 1942 Père Marie-Benoît had been notified by the head of the Capuchin Order that he was to be appointed head of Theology at the International College in Rome. The probability is that the decision to move him from France was for his own safety and that of his fellow Capuchins in Marseille. He was becoming too well known for his work and inevitably the Gestapo would have caught up with him. Indeed, some of those who had helped *Le Service André* had already been caught. These included a senior French policeman, Antoine Zaratta, who had supplied blank identification forms. He died in Buchenwald. Some of the clergy who were involved were also arrested and deported, including Pastor Lemaire who survived Dachau with his health gravely affected and Pastor Heuzé who died in captivity. The Dominican friar Marcolin just managed to avoid captivity and joined the Resistance. Père de Perceval was arrested and held in prison for months until a plea from his bishop secured his release, whereupon he resumed his clandestine role. While stressing his obligation to obey his superior, Marie-Benoît resisted the move, citing the importance of the work he was undertaking in France. This led to some delay but eventually the new appointment was confirmed and he arrived in Rome in June 1943. During the following month he had an audience with the Pope and briefed him on a range of issues, including the Donati plan. Later that same month Mussolini was deposed and replaced by the Badoglio administration. This improved the chances for Donati to put his plan into action and, of course, increased the urgency of doing so, as the Germans moved to take control of south-eastern France. While Italian officials were supportive of the Donati plan, they were realistic enough to know that the country would be unable to cater for upwards of 30,000 additional refugees.

As awareness grew of what was being planned, the numbers of people wishing to participate grew quite quickly. So Donati revised his intentions and sought to move the fugitives through Italy into North Africa. To do this he needed the support of the American and British governments. The relevant diplomats, Harold Tittmann of the US and D'Arcy Osborne representing Britain were, by then, living in the Vatican. When Italy joined the war, they had moved into the neutral territory of the Papal State. Monsignor Joseph Hérissé lived in the same section of the Vatican complex of buildings as the two diplomats and knew them well. He was a friend of Marie-Benoît and was able to set up meetings for him and Donati with each of them during late August 1943. Both agreed to support the plan and they persuaded their governments to consider it favourably. However, it was overtaken by events as the Germans moved to occupy Italy in September. Whether it was ever more than a pipe dream, albeit a very noble one, is a moot point. To move so many people such a distance successfully, even in the best of circumstances, would have presented considerable challenges.

The fact that it proved impossible to evacuate Jewish fugitives from the area of France previously under Italian control had appalling consequences for many, though not to the extent originally feared by Donati and Marie-Benoît. A team of German SS under Captain Alois Brunner arrived during September and commenced a search for Jews. However, the local people rallied round and provided safe accommodation for the vast majority of them. Less than 2,000 were arrested and deported, of whom very few survived. The humanitarian actions of the local people ensured the safety and survival of well in excess of 20,000 Jews.

Rome

Following his return to live in Rome during June 1943, Marie-Benoît spent the summer months renewing some long-standing friendships. These included members of the Jewish community. The German restoration of the Mussolini regime as a puppet government and their move to take control of Rome in early September 1943 greatly increased fears among Jews living in the city and the surrounding areas. The Swiss journalist de Wyss summarised the atmosphere in her diary entry of 21 September:

> Life is really queer now. Thousands upon thousands are in hiding, many of them never daring to show their faces. They listen tensely to every noise in the street, to every step passing on the stairs, incessantly turning over in their minds the possibility of escape – if it should become necessary. In this way live the English war prisoners, the Italian officers, the soldiers, the clerks appointed to go north, even the women belonging to their families, for Germans as well as Fascists began to throw wives into jail when they could not get hold of the husbands. One half of the population is in

hiding and the other half helps the former: so all are involved in
illegal activity of one kind or another, and all live in fear and dread
of the Germans.[1]

She also observed the particular targeting of Jews, describing how
Germans and Fascists raided apartment blocks:

They come at random, force the porters to reveal how many Jewish
families live in the building, blow doors open with hand-grenades,
and by beating, kicking and brutal treatment, they hustle the
unfortunate Hebrews – small babies as well as old persons – into
closed cars and take them to an unknown destination.[2]

Inevitably Marie-Benoît became involved in offering assistance
by making himself available to the Jewish welfare organisation
Delasem (*Delegazione per l'Assistenza degli Emigranti Ebrei*).
This was a national organisation based in Genoa. The director
of the Rome office was Settimio Sorani, whose assistant was
Giuseppe Levi. By a strange coincidence the first group of
fugitives Marie-Benoît assisted were refugees from the area of
France previously controlled by Italy and it included a number of
people who were already acquainted with him. Stefan Schwamm,
whom the Capuchin had known in Marseille, was part of the
group. Schwamm was an Austrian lawyer who left his native
Vienna after the *Anschluss* and, in a sense, kept moving ahead of
the advancing Nazis, first to Paris, then Marseille and from there
to Grenoble. He was to become a close collaborator of Marie-
Benoît's in the next few months and, subsequently a life-long
friend. The group reached Rome by train in mid-September and
made contact with Delasem. Sorani and Marie-Benoît arranged

for them to be dispersed to boarding houses and small hotels throughout the city, but both understood that this could only be a temporary measure. As the Germans and the fascist police gained control of the city, further difficulties were likely to arise. Indeed Delasem itself, which had previously been allowed to operate openly, was likely to come under threat and Sorani began destroy all records in the Delasem offices that might lead the authorities to those whom the organisation was supporting by paying for accommodation and food.

Towards the end of September the organisation relocated to the Capuchin monastery on the Via Sicilia. A vast building, including both the living quarters of the Capuchins and the college they ran, it was ideally suited to the purpose. The hope was that people entering and leaving an institution of this nature would be unlikely to arouse undue suspicion. Soon the numbers coming for help, which included Allied servicemen on the run, civilians whom the Gestapo were seeking for political reasons, as well as Jews, increased rapidly. As a result, arrangements were made to set up a number of additional points of contact throughout the city for those in need of support. As feared, a major roundup was carried out in the city in October when more than 1,000 Jews were arrested and transported to Auschwitz. Very few survived. By chance only a small number of those whom Delasem had begun supporting in recent times were picked up. Most of those arrested were native Italian Jews who had living in the city for years, rather than recent immigrants. Clearly the authorities were not fully aware of this latter group, though there were some close calls on that day and in the following weeks. The usual instruction to those living in boarding houses was to leave early and return late at night as it was deemed less likely that they would be arrested on the streets or in the cities' parks or churches; and that was why so many escaped arrest.

A couple of weeks later, the organisation suffered a potentially serious setback. The director of Delasem, Settimio Sorani, was arrested. He was calling to see Cyril Kotnik, a supportive Yugoslavian diplomat. Kotnik had been arrested the previous day and when Sorani arrived at the apartment, the Gestapo were actually searching it. Sorani was questioned for over a week but, despite being tortured, stuck to his story that he had mistakenly called at the wrong door. With the Gestapo unable to pin any specific charges on him, Sorani was released, but this episode meant that he had to adopt a lower profile from then on, with the result that Marie-Benoît had to take a more prominent role. Stefan Schwamm and Aron Kasztearsztein, a Polish refugee, who had arrived on the train to Rome with him, were now also playing important roles in Delasem.

By this time the organisation was facing a number of difficulties relating to accommodation, identity papers for refugees, and money. It was clear to Sorani and Marie-Benoît, following the October roundup of Jews, that it was necessary to identify alternative, safer locations in which to lodge refugees. Père Marie-Benoît began approaching the superiors of the many religious houses in the city, seeking accommodation for the refugees. Most proved supportive, so many of those who had approached Delasem for help were relocated into these institutions, or the homes of locals, or in rented accommodation in private apartments. Under the terms of the Lateran Treaty, the Vatican City and all Papal institutions elsewhere in Rome, such as convents and seminaries, were protected as neutral territory.

In addition to accommodation, there was the ongoing need to provide false identification papers and ration cards. Marie-Benoît recalled that during his previous time in Rome one of his Capuchin colleagues had used a printing press to produce documents for the order and the local parishioners. After a search in a storeroom, it was found and he arranged to have it refurbished. Luckily, one of the fugitives whom he was helping had the necessary skills to operate it. As a result, it was used to supplement the blank forms that were being passed on by sympathisers within the local administrative and police services. Having blank forms available was merely the first step. As well as identification documents that concealed the fact that they were Jews, the refugees needed papers certifying their nationality. A decree issued in early December had established that, from then on, no foreigners would be granted residency. As many spoke with clearly foreign accents, even if they knew Italian, it would be obvious that they were not natives. To circumvent this, Delasem needed to provide backdated documents certifying nationality. So identity forms were filled in with false names and photographs of fugitives and stamped with French seals created by a supportive engraver. To be doubly sure, many forms were taken to be certified at the Swiss Embassy, which was acting for French interests in Rome at the time. A diplomat there, Marc Chauvet, certified French nationality for hundreds of cases. When Chauvet came under pressure from his superiors to cease this practice, Victor Szasz, the Hungarian Consul-General, took over the task. These false identity papers and nationality documents meant that applications could be lodged for residency permits, which in turn established a right to ration books. The responsibility for issuing residency permits lay with the police authorities, who did not have the resources to process applications quickly, which delayed the availability of urgently needed ration books. So Marie-Benoît and Stefan Schwamm arranged to meet with Luigi Charrier, the senior police officer responsible for rationing, to discuss the problem. Luckily he was well-disposed towards them. While no mention was made of the fact that the vast majority of refugees were Jewish, in all probability he was aware of this. It was agreed that Père Marie-Benoît would establish a Committee for the Assistance of Refugees (*Comitato Assistenza Profughi*) known as CAP. Père Marie-Benoît would issue to each person a document signed by him, which would specify that the holder was a genuine refugee who had arrived in the city before the December decree, certified as such by CAP, the Red Cross and the Swiss Embassy.

In a clever move the Capuchin secured the counter-signature of Monsignor Dionisi, a senior official in the office of the Bishop of Rome, the Pope. All Dionisi was doing was certifying that the signature in each case was that of Marie-Benoît but, to the casual observer, it added an implied Vatican authority to the document. This process satisfied Charrier and allowed him to issue ration books. Between them Monsignor Dionisi and Père Marie-Benoît persuaded Charrier's counterpart in charge of issuing residency permits to agree to the same arrangement. These efforts ensured that 500 or so refugees had a full set of documentation to allow them live reasonably openly in Rome, although being careful not to do anything which would attract the attention of the authorities.

By the end of 1943, in addition to these 500, Delasem was supporting approximately 2,000 others. This was placing heavy demands on the financial resources of the organisation, particularly as at that time the cost of basic foodstuffs and other necessities was increasing dramatically. The American Jewish Joint Distribution Committee was likely to be willing to help but finding a means of transferring the money was a challenge. Through diplomatic channels, the American diplomat Harold Tittmann relayed a request on behalf of Marie-Benoît. As a result, $20,000 was lodged by the Joint Committee in a London bank in January 1944. Marie-Benoît was able to raise loans from wealthy Roman citizens on this basis as both Tittmann and his British counterpart D'Arcy Osborne vouched for the existence of the fund in London and repayment post-war. Written evidence of the loans was retained by Monsignor Hérissé in his apartment. This scheme, together with a second contribution from the Committee of $100,000 some months later, was of great significance but cumbersome and slow to operate.

A source which might make funds available more quickly was the Italian headquarters of Delasem in Genoa. With the German occupation of northern Italy, the Delasem director in Genoa, Lelio Valobra, had found it necessary to go into hiding. Before doing so he had transferred the funds and records of the organisation to the Catholic Archbishop of Genoa, Cardinal Pietro Boetto, for safe keeping. The cardinal and his secretary, Don Francesco Repetto, were already heavily involved in helping to support Jewish and other fugitives and had worked closely with Delasem. In the circumstances of the country at that time, the only way to move money from Genoa to Rome was to actually go and collect it. So, Marie-Benoît and Stefan Schwamm set out on the journey north. The plan was to travel to Milan first, in order to explore the possibility of moving some of the refugees to safety in Switzerland through there, and then to call on Genoa on the return journey.

They reached Milan in mid-April and went their separate ways to explore possible escape routes for refugees. When they met up in a restaurant some days later to compare notes, Schwamm rang the telephone number of a local woman who might be able to help and asked her to come to meet him. As it happens the police were actually searching the woman's apartment when he rang and it was a female police officer who answered the phone. A couple of minutes later, the police arrived at the restaurant and arrested Schwamm. Immediately the police departed, Marie-Benoît returned to the hotel and checked out, saying he was returning to Rome. In fact, he went to the local Capuchin monastery. Shortly afterwards, the police arrived at the hotel to arrest him. Believing he was going to travel to Rome, they monitored the railway station for a few days before concluding he had eluded them. The priest actually stayed in Milan for about a week in order to avoid arrest and also to try to establish what had happened to his friend. He then travelled on to Genoa, collected a million lire of Delasem funds from Cardinal Boetto and returned to Rome. As a precaution he immediately moved Stefan Schwamm's parents to live with a Protestant pastor. Stefan was imprisoned in Milan for some months and then sent to a forced labour camp in Poland. He and his colleagues incarcerated there were freed by the advancing Soviet army in early 1945. Meanwhile Marie-Benoît's return to Rome with the million lire meant that it was possible to continue supporting the refugees there. In this sense, May 1944 was a successful time for the organisation.

On the other hand, they experienced serious losses at that time. Given the nature of the group, the numbers of refugees it was supporting, and the active measures taken by the Gestapo and the fascist police, setbacks were inevitable. The fascists did not feel compelled to respect the terms of the Lateran Treaty and so raids on pontifical properties outside the Vatican began.

Delasem suffered its most serious breach in May 1944, just weeks before the Allies arrived in Rome. While the focus of the group was to assist Jews, others sometimes came to Delasem for help. Often these were Allied servicemen who had found themselves behind enemy lines in the northern part of Italy. Some remained at large while others, even though they were arrested, managed to escape. For many, Rome was an obvious place to go looking for help. Usually their objective was to return to their units and Delasem helped many to achieve this. In early 1944 two Frenchmen who said they had been conscripted into the German army came looking for help and were supported in the city while false documents were prepared for them. While there, they quickly learned a lot about the work Delasem was engaged in and the individuals who were leading it. Unfortunately, they betrayed the organisation to the fascist police, presumably in return for money. One of Delasem's leaders Aron Kasztersztein was arrested and, sometime later, deported to Auschwitz. He survived the war. His arrest placed Delasem on alert and arrangements were made to relocate those whose whereabouts and circumstances may have been betrayed. This was a major task and inevitably some were caught. Over the period of the German occupation about 60 refugees were arrested, the greatest single loss being 20 betrayed in May 1944.

Meanwhile Marie-Benoît, Sorani and Levi went into hiding until Rome was liberated by the Allies on 6 June. The evidence suggests that during his time in Rome, Père Marie-Benoît and his colleagues played a major role in saving the lives of more than 2,500 people. An accurate estimate for his time in Marseille and Nice is less easy to make because the organisation there was somewhat looser in structure. The probability is that something of a similar order is a reasonable guess. It is not entirely clear how influential he was in persuading Guido Lospinoso to take a low-key approach to his role when he arrived in Nice. We know that as a result of Lospinoso's attitude, many thousands were probably saved, so this may have been, in numerical terms at least, Père Marie-Benoît's greatest contribution.

BIBLIOGRAPHY

Braddon, Russell, *Nancy Wake* (London: Pan Books, 1958).

Brome, Vincent, *The Way Back* (London: The Companions Book Club, n.d.).

Burns, Jimmy, *Papa Spy* (London: Bloomsbury, 2009).

Burrin, Phillippe, *Living with Defeat: France under the German Occupation,* 1940–1944, (trans. Janet Lloyd) (London: Arnold, 1996).

Caskie, Donald, *Tartan Pimpernel* (Edinburgh: Birlinn, 1999).

Clutton-Brook, Oliver, *RAF Evaders* (London: Bounty Books, 2012).

Cobb, Matthew, *The Resistance: The French Fight Against the Nazis* (London: Simon and Schuster, 2009).

Dalin, David G., *The Myth of Hitler's Pope* (Washington DC: Regnery Publishing, 2005).

Darling, Donald, *Secret Sunday* (London: William Kimber, 1975).

Derry, Sam, *The Rome Escape Line* (London: George G. Harrap & Co., 1960).

De Vicente, Patricia Martínez, *La Clave Embassy* (Madrid: La Esfera de los libros, 2010).

De Wyss, M., *Rome Under the Terror: A Diary of Events in Rome from April, 1943 to June, 1944* (London: Robert Hale, 1945).

Diamond, Hanna, *Fleeing Hitler* (Oxford: Oxford University Press, 2007).

Downing, Rupert, *If I Laugh: The Chronicles of My Strange Adventures in the Great Paris Exodus, June 1940* (London: Harrap, 1941).

Du Cros, Janet Teissier, *Divided Loyalties* (Edinburgh: Canongate Classics, 1992).

Eisner, Peter, *The Freedom Line* (Glasgow: Harper Collins, 2005).

Fittko, Lisa, *Escape through the Pyrenees* (trans. David Koblick), (Evanston, Illinois: Northwestern University Press, 1991).

Fleming, Brian, *The Vatican Pimpernel: The Wartime Exploits of Monsignor Hugh O'Flaherty* (Cork: The Collins Press, 2008).

Fogelman, Eva, *Conscience and Courage* (London: Cassell, 1995).

Foot, M. R. D., and Langley, J. M., *MI9: Escape and Evasion, 1939–1945* (London: Biteback Publishing, 1979).

Fralon, José-Alain, *A Good Man in Evil Times* (London: Penguin, 1998).

Franco, Manuela and Fevereiro, Maria Isabel, *Spared Lives: The Actions of Three Portuguese Diplomats in World War II* (Lisbon: Portuguese Ministry of Foreign Affairs, 2000).

Gilbert, Martin, *The Righteous: The Unsung Heroes of the Holocaust* (London: Doubleday, 2002).

Guéhenno, Jean, *Diary of the Dark Years* (trans. David Ball) (Oxford: Oxford University Press, 2014).

Gushee, David P., *The Righteous Gentiles of the Holocaust* (Minneapolis: Fortress Press, 1994).

Goodall, Scott, *The Freedom Trail* (Banbery: Inchmere Design, 2005).

Grunwald-Spier, Agnes, *The Other Schindlers* (Stroud: the History Press, 2010).

Hart-Davis, Duff, *Man of War* (London: Arrow Books, 2013).

Ho, Feng Shan, *My Forty Years as a Diplomat* (trans. Dr Monto Ho) (Pittsburgh: Dorrance Publishing, 2000).

Jackson, Julian, *The Fall of France* (Oxford: Oxford University Press, 2003).

Janes, Peter Scott, *Conscript Heroes* (Boston: Paul Mould Publishing, 2004).

Katz, Robert, *Fatal Silence: The Pope, the Resistance and the German Occupation of Rome* (London: Orion, 2003).

Keegan, John, *The Second World War* (London: Pimlico, 1997).

Kiernan, Thomas J., *Pius XII*, (Dublin: Clonmore and Reynolds, 1958).

Langley, J. M., *Fight Another Day* (London: Collins, 1974).

Leboucher, Fernande, *The Incredible Mission of Father Benoît* (London; William Kimber, 1970).

Kurzman, Dan, *The Race for Rome* (New York, Doubleday & Co., 1975).

Levine, Hillel, *In Search of Sugihara* (New York: The Free Press, 1996).

Lewin, Isaac, *Remember the Days of Old: Historical Essays* (New York: Research Institute of Religious Jewry, 1994).

Lochery, Neil, *Lisbon: War in the Shadows in the City of Light, 1939–1945* (Philadelphia: Public Affairs Publishing, 2011).

Long, Helen, *Safe Houses are Dangerous* (London: Abson Books, 1989).

McConnon, Aili and McConnon, Andres, *Road to Valour* (London: Orion Publishing, 2012).

Mosely, Ray, *The Last Days of Mussolini* (Stroud: Sutton Publishing, 2006).

Nabarro, Derrick, *Wait for the Dawn* (London: Cassell., 1953).

Neave, Airey, *They Have Their Exits* (London: Hodder & Stoughton, 1953).

—— *Little Cyclone: The Girl Who Started the Comet Line* (London: Coronet Books, 1954).

—— *Saturday at M.I.9* (London: Coronet Books, 1965).

Nichol, John, and Renell, Tony, *Home Run: Escape from Nazi Europe* (London: Penguin Books, 2007).

Ousby, Ian, *Occupation: The Ordeal of France, 1940–1944* (London: Pimlico, 1999).

Paldiel, Mordecai, *Diplomat Heroes of the Holocaust* (Jersey City, KTAV Publishing, 2007).

—— *The Righteous Among the Nations: Rescuers of Jews During the Holocaust* (Jerusalem: The Jerusalem Publishing House & Yad Vashem, 2007).

Ramati, Alexander, *The Assisi Underground*, (London: Unwin Paperbacks, 1985).

Rosbottom, Ronald, *When Paris Went Dark* (London: John Murray, 2014).

Rubinstein, William D., *The Myth of Rescue: Why the Democracies Could Not Have Done More to Save Jews from the Nazis* (Abingdon: Routledge, 1997).

Scriverner, Jane (Mother Mary St Luke), *Inside Rome with the Germans* (New York: The Macmillan Company, 1945).

Shirer, William L., *The Rise and Fall of the Third Reich* (London: Arrow Books, 1998).

Silver, Eric, *The Book of the Just: The Silent Heroes Who Saved the Jews* (London: Weidenfeld & Nicholson, 1992).

Simpson, William C., *A Vatican Lifeline '44* (London: Leo Cooper, 1995).

Spotts, Frederic, *The Shameful Peace* (New Haven: Yale University Press, 2010).

Stourton, Edward, *Cruel Crossing: Escaping: Hitler Across the Pyrenees* (London: Black Swan Publishing, 2014).

Tec, Nechama, *When Light Pierced the Darkness* (Oxford: Oxford University Press, 1986).

Tittmann, Harold H. Jr., *Inside the Vatican of Pius XII* (New York: Doubleday, 2004).

Tokayer, Marvin and Swartz, Mary, *The Fugu Plan: The Untold Story of the Japanese and the Jews in WWII* ((Jerusalem, Gefen Publishing, 2004).

Trevelyan, Raleigh, *Rome '44: The Battle for the Eternal City* (London: Pimlico, 2004).

Vinen, Richard, *The Unfree French* (London: Penguin Books, 2007).

Wilmot, Chester, *The Struggle for Europe* (Ware, Herts.: Wordsworth Editions, 1997).

Zuccotti, Susan, *Père Marie-Benoît and Jewish Rescue* (Bloomington: Indiana University Press, 2013).

www.belgiumww2.info A very comprehensive website curated by John Clinch.

www.evasioncomete.org A remarkably detailed record of all the activities of the Comet Line and those whom it rescued, curated by Phillipe Connart, Michel Dricot, Éduard Reniere and Victor Schutters.

www.ww2escapelines.co.uk The website of the WW2 Escape Lines Memorial Society.

www.jewishvirtuallibrary.org The website of the American-Israeli Co-Operative Enterprise.

PICTURE AND TEXT CREDITS

Photograph 21: courtesy of the U.S. National Archives and Records Administration (NARA).

I am grateful to Oxford University Press for permission to quote from *Diary of the Dark Years, 1940–44*, by Jean Guéhenno, translated and annotated by David Bell.

NOTES

Chapter 1

1. Paldiel, Mordecai, *Diplomat Heroes of the Holocaust* (Jersey City: KTAV Publishing, 2007) p.74.

2. Franco, Manuela and Fevereiro, Maria Isabel, *Spared Lives: The Actions of Three Portuguese Diplomats in World War II* (Lisbon: Portuguese Ministry of Foreign Affairs, 2000) pp. 93–9.

3. Ibid.

4. Levine, Hillel, *In Search of Sugihara* (New York: The Free Press, 1996) p. 125.

5. Ibid. p. 165.

6. Ibid. p. 172.

7. Lewin, Isaac *Remember the Days of Old: Historical Essays* (New York: Research Institute of Religious Jewry, 1994) p. 174.

8. Levine, Hillel, *In Search of Sugihara*, p. 257.

9. www.jewishvirtuallibrary.org

10. Sugihara records this as the date he decided to issue visas to everyone irrespective of what papers they had. In fact he may have started doing so earlier and this was an effort to 'cover his tracks'.

11. Levine, Hillel, *In Search of Sugihara*, p. 195.

12. Ho, Feng Shan, *My Forty Years as a Diplomat* (trans. Dr Monto Ho, Pittsburgh: Dorrance Publishing, 2000) p. 2010.

13. Paldiel, Mordecai, *Dipomat Heroes of the Holocaust*, p. 186.
14. Paldiel, Mordecai, *The Righteous Among the Nations* (New York: Harper Collins, 2007) p. 319.
15. Ibid.

Chapter 2

1. Jackson, Julian, *The Fall of France* (Oxford: Oxford University Press, 2003) p. 176.
2. Ousby, Ian, *Occupation: The Ordeal of France, 1940–1944* (London: Pimlico, 1999) pp. 43.
3. Rupert Downing, *If I Laugh: The Chronicles of My Strange Adventures in the Great Paris Exodus – June 1940* (London: Harrap, 1941) pp. 17–8.
4. Ousby, Ian, *Occupation: The Ordeal of France, 1940–1944*, p. 44.
5. Ibid. p. 86.
6. Guéhenno, Jean, *Diary of the Dark Years* (trans. David Ball, Oxford: Oxford University Press, 2014) p. 3.
7. Ibid. p. 5.
8. Ibid. p. 38.
9. Ibid. p. 18.
10. Du Cros, Janet Tessier, *Divided Loyalties* (Canongate Classics, 1992) p. 278.
11. Guéhenno, Jean, *Diary of the Dark Years*, p. 28.
12. Caskie, Donald, *Tartan Pimpernel* (Edinburgh: Birlinn, 1999) p. 53.
13. *Irish Times*, 8 July 2016.
14. Neave, Airey *Saturday at M.I.9* (London: Coronet Books, 1965) p. 35.
15. Nabarro, Derrick, *Wait for the Dawn* (London: Cassell, 1953) p. 204.
16. Spriewald and Blanchain were married in London subsequently.
17. In total sixty-seven personnel were evacuated by sea during this period.

18. Ousby, Ian, *Occupation: The Ordeal of France, 1940–1944*, p.208.

19. Guéhenno, *Diary of the Dark Years*, p. 101.

20. Ibid. p. 95.

21. Guéhenno, Jean, *Diary of the Dark Years*, p. 83.

22. www.HolocaustResearchProject.org accessed 2 March 2018.

Chapter 3

1. Guéhenno, *Diary of the Dark Years*, p. 143.

2. See particularly www.evasioncomete.org and www.evasioncomete.org

Chapter 4

1. Keegan, John, *The Second World War* (London: Pimlico, 1997) p. 288.

2. Kiernan, Thomas J., *Pius XII*, (Dublin: Clonmore and Reynolds, 1958) p.41.

3. De Wyss, M., *Rome Under the Terror: A diary of events in Rome from April, 1943 to June, 1944* (London: Robert Hale, 1945) p.48.

4. Scrivener, Jane (Mother Mary St Luke), *Inside Rome with the Germans*, (New York: The Macmillan Company, 1945) pp. 2–3.

5. Ramati, Alexander, *The Assisi Underground* (London: Unwin Paperbacks, 1985) p.5.

6. Ibid.

7. Ibid. pp. 6–7.

8. Scrivener, Jane, *Inside Rome with the Germans*, p. 173.

9. Ramati, Alexander, *The Assisi Underground*, p. 178.

Chapter 5

1. De Wyss, M., *Rome under the Terror*, p. 131.

2. Ibid. p. 144.

INDEX